# Enduring Bonds

# EDUCATING THE YOUNG CHILD

## VOLUME 1

This academic and scholarly book series focuses on the education and development of young children from infancy through eight years of age. The series provides a synthesis of current theory and research on trends, issues, controversies, and challenges in the early childhood field and examine implications for practice. One hallmark of the series is comprehensive reviews of research on a variety of topics with particular relevance for early childhood educators worldwide. The mission of the series is to enrich and enlarge early childhood educators' knowledge, enhance their professional development, and reassert the importance of early childhood education to the international community. The audience for the series includes college students, teachers of young children, college and university faculty, and professionals from fields other than education who are unified by their commitment to the care and education of young children. In many ways, the proposed series is an outgrowth of the success of *Early Childhood Education Journal* which has grown from a quarterly magazine to a respected and international professional journal that is published six times a year.

*The titles published in this series are listed at the end of this volume.*

Mary Renck Jalongo

Editor

# Enduring Bonds

The Significance of Interpersonal
Relationships in Young Children's Lives

 Springer

Mary Renck Jalongo
Indiana University of Pennsylvania
Indiana, PA 15701
USA
mjalongo@iup.edu

*Series Editors:*

Mary Renck Jalongo
Indiana University of Pennsylvania
Indiana, PA 15701
USA

Beatrice S. Fennimore
Indiana University of Pennsylvania
Indiana, PA 15701
USA

Joan P. Isenberg
George Mason University
Fairfax, VA 22030
USA

*Library of Congress Control Number:* 2007935306

ISBN -13: 978-0-387-74524-4 (hardcover)          e-ISBN-13: 978-0-387-74525-1

ISBN -13: 978-0-387-75937-1 (softcover)

Printed on acid-free paper.

9 8 7 6 5 4 3 2 1

springer.com

# Contents

# Introduction

**Mary Renck Jalongo**

Interpersonal relationships present an interesting paradox to the young child. Although human bonds are a source of love, security and joy, they are, at the same time, the context in which children feel intense and complicated emotions such as jealousy, shame, resentment, sorrow, and rage. To illustrate, consider a series of incidents in the life of a young child named Melissa. All of these events were so memorable that they became oft-repeated family stories. At age 4, after Melissa was reprimanded by her mother, she packed a small plastic suitcase and announced that she was running away. Her mother kept a watchful eye while the preschooler stood at the end of the driveway for several moments. The child's sister—eight years her senior—decided to go out and gently inquire about her younger sibling's plans, to which Melissa responded ruefully, "I can't run away. I remembered that I'm not allowed to cross the street by myself." Months later, Melissa enters kindergarten and she arrives home at the end of her school day, obviously upset. When asked about it, she says, "One of the kids told me I was doing my work wrong and it ruined my whole day." In first grade, Melissa has experience with one of the school child's greatest fears: a mean teacher. So mean, in fact, that the teacher is fired but not in time to prevent the first grader from vomiting each day before school starts. As Melissa's case illustrates, interpersonal relationships at home, with peers, and with educators can be the source of considerable consternation.

Even the process of sorting out the interpersonal network can represent a challenge. A young child may know that he is a son but find it difficult to simultaneously think of himself as somebody's brother or nephew or grandson. Understanding interpersonal roles can become even more mystifying when the roles are applied to others—for instance, young children often are amazed to discover that one of their female teachers is also someone's child, wife, mother, sibling, or grandchild.

The ability to interpret and successfully navigate interpersonal dynamics is further compounded by changes in the larger social contexts in which they exist. As this volume will amply demonstrate, even the taken-for-granted definitions of the terminology that we use to describe human relationships have been modified considerably in modern society. A word such as "primary caregiver," for instance,

Indiana University of Pennsylvania

M.R. Jalongo (ed.), *Enduring Bonds.*
© Springer 2008

can mean the child's mother or father but also a member of the extended family or an employee, such as a nanny. In some instances, the very young spend more of their waking hours in group care with an early childhood educator, a situation that pushes against conventional definitions of primary caregiver. Contemporary young children form ties with a wide range of people—adults and children—from inside and outside their families and they are enrolled in programs at an early age in unprecedented numbers, not only in the United States but in many other countries as well.

## Purpose for the Book

This distinguished group of teacher/scholars from diverse backgrounds and cultures has approached the topic of interpersonal ties during early childhood from multiple perspectives. Our goal in producing the volume was, first and foremost, to be consistent with the purpose for this new edited book series. The series' title, *Educating the Young Child: Advances in Theory and Research, Implications for Practice,* captures its emphasis: to focus on the young child (birth through age 8), to synthesize classic and current theory and research, and to examine implications for practice in the field of early childhood education. The purpose for the Springer series and for this, the first book in that series, is to enrich and enlarge early childhood educators' knowledge, enhance their professional development, and reassert the importance of early childhood education to the international community.

The audience for the series includes college students, teachers of young children, college and university faculty, and professionals from fields other than education, all of whom are unified by their commitment to the care and education of young children. In many ways, the proposed series is an outgrowth of the success of *Early Childhood Education Journal* which has evolved from a quarterly magazine to a respected and international professional journal that is published six times a year. *Enduring Bonds: The Significance of Interpersonal Relationships in Young Children's Lives* has the honor of inaugurating the new series.

## Overview of the Book

In Medieval times the word "child" was not associated with any particular age group and was instead used to describe a biological relationship in much the same way that we now use the word "offspring." Likewise, the concepts such as "family" or "sibling" have undergone considerable change and are no longer applied exclusively to kinship ties; today, our notion of family includes groups of people– in addition to or instead of–blood relatives that reside together and share a relationship. Interpersonal relationships are indeed a perplexing aspect of the young child's experience.

Part One of the book includes three chapters that form a foundation for this discussion of relationships. The book begins with Sue Wortham's observational study of the distinctive types of family relationships in three developing countries that share a history as French colonies: Senegal, Burkina Faso, and Haiti. Using Bronfenbrenner's ecological systems as a theoretical base, she contrasts the three and, in doing so, stimulates readers' thinking about the ways in which children shape and are shaped by their cultures. Chapter 2 is Wanda Boyer's interview study with parents and educators concerning a skill that is fundamental to developing positive bonds with others: self-regulation. Teachers and parents describe, in their own words, the challenges and insights they have acquired from guiding young children's behavior. Early childhood is, without a doubt, prime time for the development of language. In Chapter 3, Marilyn Roseman analyzes the young child's acquisition of language, not merely as a set of skills, but from the perspective of the supportive relationships that under gird the growth in oral language which leads to literacy with print.

Part Two focuses on key relationships in the family: parents, siblings, and grand-parents. In Chapter 4, Olivia Saracho and Bud Spodek challenge harmful stereotypes of Mexican American fathers and present a more comprehensive and accurate view of the assets that Mexican American fathers bring to the parenting role. Eighty percent of us have at least one brother or sister and sibling relationships are among the most enduring interpersonal influences, commencing in childhood and continuing through adult life. In Chapter 5, I collaborate with Denise Dragich to explore the effects of connections with brothers and sisters.

Kevin Swick and Reginald Williams advocate for new perspectives on family support in Chapter 6 as they explore the profound consequences of homelessness and recommend ways of responding to and preventing young families' loss of house, home, and sense of place. In Chapter 7, Natalie Conrad argues that the warmth, closeness, and supportive interactions that characterize book sharing within the home are a key component in motivating children to read.

Grandparents are raising their children's children in unprecedented numbers and, even when they are not identified as the primary caregivers, they often exert a major developmental influence on grandchildren. Chapter 8, written by Laurie Nicholson with Pauline Davey Zeece, delves into the bonds that young children form with their parents' parents.

Part Three of the book extends beyond the immediate family to the ties that children form with early childhood educators. Increasingly, parents/guardians who are employed rely on professional caregivers to care for their infants and toddlers, the focus of Chapters 9 and 10. In Chapter 9, Marjory Ebbeck and Hoi Yin Bonnie Yim investigate infants' bonds with their primary caregivers in Australian group care settings and offer research-based recommendations for programs and infant/toddler child care providers. There are key characteristics that result positive relationships between the youngest children and their caregivers, an important topic that Mary Beth Mann and Russell Carney delve into in Chapter 10.

Many young children have to contend not only with the complexities of interpersonal dynamics in the school setting but also with an entirely new cultural context. In Chapter 11, a trio of former international doctoral students and mothers–all of whom relocated to the United States, and are now university faculty–describe from an insider's view the challenges that young children confront when everything and nearly everyone around them is unfamiliar. The book concludes with a chapter exploring a particular type of interpersonal relationship that is underrepresented in the professional literature: young children's connections with school administrators, written by former principal and teacher educator Sue Rieg. In Chapter 12, the author examines young children's misconceptions about the principal/headmaster role and the strategies that administrators throughout the world use to connect with the young children for whom they are responsible.

Understanding and learning to fulfill multiple social roles is the very essence of human development; it is a primary way in which we become more fully human. As with so many other important types of learning, what occurs early, during childhood, frequently sets the tone for a lifetime.

# Part One
# Foundations of Interpersonal Relationships

# Chapter 1
# The Young Child and Social Relationships in Developing Countries

## A Contrast Among Senegal, Burkina Faso, and Haiti

Sue C. Wortham

**Abstract** This chapter examines the development of young children's interpersonal relationships in three developing countries that share a history as French colonies. The author uses Bronfenbrenner's ecological systems theory as the theoretical base and observations, and interviews gathered across a 4-year period as the data. The result is a comparison of the multi-layered social contexts of Senegal, Burkina Faos, and Haiti and the effects of those contexts on the lives of young children in each.

**Keywords** social relationships, interpersonal relationships, families, developing countries, young children, ecological systems theory, Bronfenbrenner, microsystem, mesosystem, exosystem, macrosystem, Africa, Senegal, Burkina Faso, Haiti

## Introduction

In keeping with the focus of this volume on the significant interpersonal relationships in young children's lives, this chapter focuses on how these relationships evolve in developing countries. Two countries in the African continent, Senegal and Burkina Faso, and Haiti, located in the Antilles and Caribbean Oceans south of Cuba will be included. All three countries have some common features. They were French colonies during the European colonization period, French is the educational language, and the population is of African heritage.

How are the interpersonal relationships experienced by young children significant in these three countries? How do cultural, religious, and economic factors impact the young child's social development? Bronfenbrenner's Ecological Systems Theory will be used to understand how intrafamilial and extrafamilial forces in children's lives form their social and cultural milieu (Puckett & Black, 2005).

Professor Emerita, University of Texas at San Antonio

M.R. Jalongo (ed.), *Enduring Bonds.*
© Springer 2008

## Bronfenbrenner's Ecological Systems Theory

Urie Bronfenbrenner believes that human development must be explained within the influence of the family, school, community, and state and national governments. He proposed that there are multiple ecologies or social settings that form systems around the child (Bronfenbrenner, 1986; 1995). He described these spheres of influence in terms of concentric circles with the child at the center (See Figure 1). The widening circles represent systems of influence titled the microsystem, mesosystem, exosystem, and macrosystem.The young child first interacts with the microsystem which includes the immediate and extended family, playmates, and child care in countries like the United States where the majority of mothers are employed outside the home.

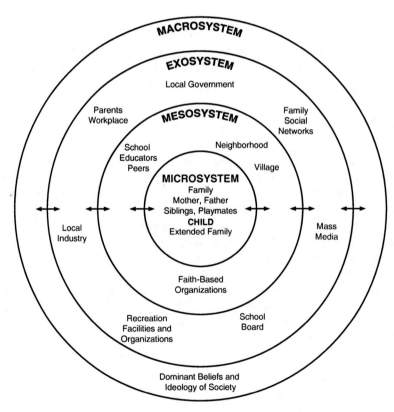

**Figure 1**   Adaptation of Urie Bronfenbrenner's Ecological System Theory

In the next wider sphere of influence, the child interacts within the mesosytem that includes the neighborhood, school, and religious organizations. In the exosystem the child is influenced by the wider community that includes local government, parents' workplaces, local industry, family social networks, mass media, and social welfare services. Finally, at the macrosystem level, the child interacts with the attitudes and ideologies of the culture. The ecological system as described reflects western cultures with advanced economic systems. There are variations depending on the size of the community where the child lives, whether the area is urban, suburban, or rural, and what types of resources are available to the family and child. These variations are significant when describing ecological systems in developing countries. Before applying the ecological model to the three developing countries, background information on each country will establish the context for understanding how the family, community, and culture interact with the child and the child's development.

## The Countries: Senegal, Burkina Faso, and Haiti

### Senegal

Senegal is located on the northwestern part of Africa adjacent to the Atlantic Ocean. Dakar, the capital city, is a major African port as well as the location of Goree Island where Africans were enslaved and then shipped to countries to serve as slave laborers. Goree Island was engaged in slave trade for more than two hundred years. Many African Americans in the United States are descendents of Africans who passed through Goree Island. Others were shipped to the Caribbean Islands that included Haiti. Dakar is a bustling city; however, the majority of its people live in rural areas where agriculture is the mainstay of the national economy. Senegal is predominantly a Muslim country with a minority that are Christians.

The Fatick region, the location for this study, is one of the most remote areas in Senegal. The small city of Fatick in the Fatick region is surrounded by small villages where transportation is mostly by carts pulled by a horse or a donkey. The villages outside of Fatick are made up of family compounds. There are no developed roads other than the main highways and families living out in the savanna are reached by sandy tracks that crisscross to reach the small villages. Although there are some private vehicles, long-distance travel for most of the population of Fatick is by small and large buses with a wide range of ages and state of repair.

### Burkina Faso

Burkina Faso is a land-locked nation to the east of Senegal with the country of Mali in between. It is similar to Senegal in terms of villages composed of compounds of homes in remote rural areas. Ouagadougou, the capital city, is experiencing economic development. Bicycles and motorbikes are the major form of transportation both in cities and rural areas. Donkey and horse carts are also common in the rural areas. Like Senegal, long-distance travel is usually by some type of bus.

The majority of people in Burkina Faso are Christians of various denominations. There is a large Muslim population as well. The economic resource in rural areas is primarily agriculture. Locally grown crops are the main food sources. The area chosen for the study in Burkina Faso is in the rural district of Les Bale. The district consists of small villages made up of housing compounds clustered together. Villages are separated by fields and undeveloped countryside. There is an elephant reserve in the area. Larger villages have small shops and a market. There is no larger community or small city nearby.

Villages in both countries have local market areas and small shops where people can gather for trading and purchases. French bread, a popular food left from French colonization is available fresh daily, even in rural areas. Breakfast consists of French bread with coffee or tea in both countries.

## *Haiti*

Haiti occupies half of an island in the Antilles and Caribbean Oceans that was originally named Hispaniola. The other half of the island is the Dominican Republic. The Dominican Republic is a Spanish-speaking country that was originally part of the Spanish empire. Haiti, established by France with slaves from Africa, is a French–speaking country as was mentioned earlier. However, Creole is the preferred language for communication.

Haiti has been known during recent decades for its unstable governments. This has resulted in a serious decline in the economy, social services, and infrastructure. Agriculture is the rural economy with market days in local areas in the countryside. Families live in individual homes, usually constructed of concrete blocks and tin roofs. Extended families and neighbors live in nearby houses and the community. The Catholic Church was the original religion established by the French. People also Practiced the voodoo religion that is still continued by some today. There are also many Protestant denominations with small community churches in rural areas. Local transportation is by foot, bicycle, motorbikes, cars, and trucks. Long-distance transportation is by bus, the back of a pickup truck, motorbikes, and private cars.

The capital city of Port Au Prince is the most urban area, but is frequently too dangerous to visit. The area used for this study is Les Cayes on the southwest coast of Haiti on the Caribbean Ocean. The city of Les Cayes is made up of many old buildings that have deteriorated significantly in recent years. The neighborhood areas in the study are on the outskirts of Les Cayes into the rural countryside.

AFRICAN FOLKLORE: THE BAOBAB TREE. *For the poet Rene Ferriot, they are trees "frozen in their wandering like a herd of elephants that have taken root" (Les Baobabs, 2007). Photo by Marshal Wortham*

## Applying Bronfenbrenner's Ecological Theory

### *Senegal and Burkina Faso: It Takes a Village*

There is a legend in Senegal about the Baobab tree. These are very large trees with huge trunks. They live for hundreds of years and dominate the landscape where they grow. It is said that when the tree reaches a hundred years it acquires a spirit. The spirit in the tree can reach out and hit people. At night people are forbidden to sit under the Bao Bao tree because the spirit comes out to sit there.

A large Baobab tree sits in the central schoolyard at the Diaoule School in the village of Diaoule. Villagers have great respect for this particular tree that is about three hundred years old. Many villagers in Diaoule believe there is a spirit in the tree.

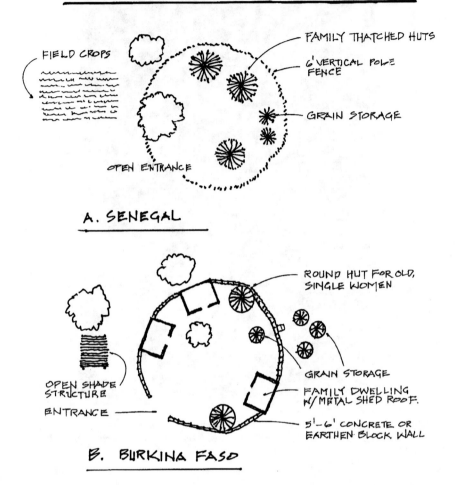

**Figure 2** Typical Organization of Family Compounds in Senegal and Burkina Faso. Drawing by Marshal Wortham

(Interview with Safietou Fall, World Children's Relief Country Director for Senegal, March, 2007).

## The Microsystem

The children and families studied in these two countries live in family compounds. The compound consists of the extended family living within the compound. A man will build a house and surround it with a fence. In Senegal the fence will be made of canes. In Burkina Faso the fence will be made of bricks. Gardens outside the compound will be enclosed in a cane fence. The man might have several wives. With each new wife another house is built. As another generation matures, the sons might build their own houses within the compound or outside with the fence enlarged. The original compounds had round brick houses with thatched roofs, but more recently the younger generations have tended to build rectangular homes with a sloping tin roof. Large, round woven structures with thatched covers are within or outside the compound to store grain. (See Figure 2). The parents and older children work in the fields owned by the family. During school vacation boys as young as six tend cattle, goats, and sheep. The compound will also have chickens and pigs roaming about during the day. Donkeys and horses are part of the family animals (Interview with Emmanuel Sam, Country Director of World Children's Relief for Burkina Faso, 2007).

The children who live in compounds grow up within the extended family. Children play with all their siblings and cousins within the compound when they are very young. The peer group of children is multi-aged and may consist of as many as 30 children of varying ages. When the children are babies they are carried on the mother's back. When they are old enough they join the playgroup in the compound.

Thus there are always adults to tend to the children. The mother is the major caregiver for the infants and toddlers and the family community shares the nurture and supervision of the older children. As children mature, they share in the care of a baby or toddler. When a training workshop was held in Senegal in 2007, two nursing mothers who were teachers participated in the training. An older child would carry the baby on his or her back to the school where the training was held when the baby needed to be fed. The school director and his family lived on the school ground. His toddler son was with an elementary age son throughout the day.

The child growing up in the compound learns how to be a part of a group very early in life. Multi-age playgroups model language and behaviors for the younger children. The very young child is comfortable with many adults, animals, playmates, and the routines of living in an agricultural society.

## The Mesosystem: The Neighborhood, School, and Faith-Based Organizations

A group of family compounds make a village. The concept of a neighborhood only exists in more urban areas. Each family compound has its own fields and animals. If the village is large enough, small shops and a market appear.

The village school is a center of life for children. They will enter school as young as age 3 if there is a preschool class. The preschool class will include 3–4- and 5-year olds. The concept of a preschool is just beginning to become important in the two countries. The school is often located adjacent to a village, but children from several different villages might walk to school each day.

The schools are organized by the national government with local educational officials in each area known as districts. Teachers and school directors are assigned by the government and may live at the school if it is a distance from a larger community. Because the teachers live at the school, they are well acquainted with the local families and the children. The school director also knows all of the families and their children. Unfortunately only a small percentage of children have the opportunity to attend school. Many children live out their lives without achieving literacy. At best the children receive an elementary education. Once they have graduated from the sixth grade, they must be able to travel a distance to a secondary school. Only 40 percent of the children who are able to attend elementary school graduate. Only 1 percent graduates from a secondary school and completes college. A current effort is underway in both countries to improve the quality of education and to increase the percentage of children who can attend school (Personal interviews with Made Faye, Inspector of Education in the Fatick District, Senegal and Koinda Lassane, Inspector of Education for the District of Les Bale, Burkina Faso, 2007).

Every small village is likely to have a faith-based church or mosque. In Senegal, which is predominantly Muslim, the day is organized around the calls to prayer beginning before dawn and continuing into the evening. The child growing up in a small village observes and lives the faith within the family each day. There are Christian churches in Senegal, but they were not present in the very small, rural villages used in this study. Christians and Muslims live together peacefully. They gather during religious feasts. At the end of a fasting period Christians used to give Muslims Nagalax, a dish made of millet flour, peanuts and sugar. During a Muslim sacrifice feast, Muslims give mutton or mutton sauce to Christians.

They mourn together. When a Catholic or Muslim dies, the two communities are both affected and meet to say prayers for the dead. There are also intermarriages between Muslims and Catholics.

In Burkina Faso the village might have a church and/or a mosque. The young children in Burkina Faso learn about both types of religions and the two faiths exist in harmony within the adults in the community. Early in the history of Senegal and Burkina Faso, families were organized into tribes or ethnic groups. When France controlled the two countries, the Catholic religion was the first to build churches and encourage the natives to become members. Later, the Muslim religion attracted a large number of people, and finally, protestant denominations sent missionaries. Today the majority of people in Burkina Faso are Protestant Christians (Interview with Alassane Compaore, Assistant Manager of the Parole d'Espoir orphanage in Ouagadougou, Burkina Faso, 2007).

## The Exosystem

The exosystem is much smaller for young children living in rural villages in Senegal and Burkina Faso. There is no local industry other than agriculture. Most

parents do not have a separate workplace other than the local fields. In larger villages, a parent might be a shopkeeper, but the commercial market area will be close
to the family compound.

The local governments in rural villages in Senegal and Burkina Faso date
back to the original tribes and ethnic groups. Each village is headed by a chief
and village elders. The role of the chief is to settle disputes and other issues
within the village. Meetings are called and moderated by the chief. The position
of chief is inherited. The chief officially represents the village at local functions. Village elders also represent the village and have a voice in decisions that
are made. Young children are aware of the village elders and the village chief.
They may not be aware of the structure of a municipal government in a larger
town or city

Family social networks likewise may be confined to the immediate and surrounding villages. The child becomes familiar with relatives and friends of the
family who are connected by the local school and place of worship. When the
child becomes a part of the family social relationships, more playmates are
encountered and the child acquires a broader understanding of the wider network
of villages.

Villagers are involved with decisions at the school through a committee. The
committee is composed of parents, village members and leaders, and personnel
from the school. School committees may be very active in supporting the school.
In March, 2007 village school committees in Senegal were engaged in constructing apartments for teachers who could not get housing in the remote areas.
Commonly the teachers were younger, unmarried men who were still free of
family obligations and could move to teach at a rural school.

There is very little access to media in rural villages. There are no newspapers or television. Some villagers might be able to access a radio station in a
larger community. Young children will possibly have no exposure to the world
outside their village. Likewise there are no recreational facilities other than
what nature provides. Schools may have a field where children can play soccer, but community centers and other municipal organizations are unlikely to
be present.

## The Macrosystem

The macrosystem, the widest sphere of influence, is based on the dominant beliefs of
the larger society. Young children are immersed into these beliefs and practices from
infancy. A baby carried on its mother's back may extend a hand in greeting when
encountering someone from the community. In Burkina Faso young school children
cross their arms on their chest and bow when meeting adults. Because all children are
an integral part of the compound, village, and school, they are continually exposed to
the ways of the local society and culture.

## Conclusion

The children in rural Senegal and Burkina Faso are raised by the village. The microsystem and mesosystem are the most important spheres in their lives. They have a very strong extended family relationship which expands into the village, places of worship, and the school. Children and adults are not separated in community life, but mutual interaction allows the child to influence and be influenced by a large group of family, relatives, and other villagers. Older siblings teach the younger children how to play and take responsibilities. They can model appropriate behaviors and social practices. The exosystem and macrosystem are experienced in the context of the local and nearby villages until they are older. They mature within a stable and secure family, religion, and social system.

# Haiti

## Haitian Rituals: Voodoo Flags

Flags and banners used in Haiti and countries in South America have their origin in Africa and have long been used to demonstrate religious affiliations and culture. The flags were also influenced by European colonial practices and the Catholic religion.

Vodou (or voodoo) in Haiti is regarded as witchcraft and sorcery by many Americans. In reality it is a practical religion based on the belief that the universe is inhabited by a variety of deities who are intermediaries between humans and God (Polk, 1997). Each Vodou church has two ritual flags that represent deities (Iwa). Made of brightly colored sequins and fabric, the banners are also collected as examples of Haitian art. The photograph that follows shows a mermaid (La Sirene), the enchantress of the deep.

Today many banners are simply colorful designs. Flagmakers also cover purses, bottles, and boxes with sequins for the tourist trade.

## The Microsystem

The young child growing up in Haiti experiences a different type of family and extended family environment. Children in rural areas usually live in a small home within a small community or farming area. There may be more than one generation living in the home with the extended family and neighbors living in homes nearby. Family members who have died are buried in tombs in the yard of the family home, giving children an early experience with death. If the family has lived in one location for several generations, some of the tombs will be very old.

Children have responsibilities by the time they are in elementary school. They might be sent to get water from a community water source or help with family

A Mermaid Flag Owned by the Author. Photo by Marshal Wortham

activities such as baking bread or washing clothes. Caring for a younger sibling is important as well as assisting with all family chores.

   Haitian families are more transient than families in Senegal and Burkina Faso. The death rate for adults and children is high in Haiti, and families are frequently displaced. Because of the lack of means of support, there is a constant migration out of the country, particularly to the United States. Parents frequently go to the United States and leave children in the care of a relative. As their finances improve, they are able to send for the children to join them (Personal communication with Ghislaine Georges, Country Director for World Children's Relief in Haiti, 2005). Parents might leave the children in rural areas and try to find work in Port Au Prince. Displaced or orphaned children might be living with a relative or with older siblings who are raising younger siblings. In one home visited in 2004, a young adult was caring for his three younger sisters. Their parents were living in Port Au Prince. A sister who lives in the United States supported the four siblings. She sent money for the small home where they lived as well as funds for food and clothing. The young man prepared meals, served as a parent to the young girls, and attended school himself.

Young children growing up in Haiti might be fortunate and have an intact family with extended family within traveling distance or in the immediate community. Their playmates might be siblings, cousins, or neighborhood friends. They also might live with a relative in their extended family or a cousin, aunt and uncle, or grandparent. Older children might be offered a home with a more prosperous member of the community. The owner provides the child with food, clothing, and school fees. In turn the teenager helps with household tasks when not in school.

The mainstay of the rural economy is agriculture. Each family has chickens, goats and/or sheep, pigs, perhaps a cow or two, primarily to feed the family, but also to sell or trade at area market days. Root vegetables, rice, and corn are raised for food as well as cash crops. A second source of income is fishing. The Les Cayes region is on the west coast and people have easy access to the sea and local rivers for fishing. Fish are sold along roadways and in local marketplaces. The making of charcoal can be a small industry. All cooking is done outdoors using charcoal. Wood that has been converted into charcoal is placed in very large bags to sell in Les Cayes and in more rural areas. If the community is large enough, there are small shopkeepers or vendors of needed goods.

## *The Mesosytem*

The neighborhood is a very important part of the larger community for young Haitian children. In rural areas houses might be located along an unpaved road or dotted around the countryside where families live near their fields. Initial social relationships are developed as children play with the children living near their home.

There are many small churches in rural areas. They might be within walking distance of the family home or require some type of transportation. A set of parents with up to three young children might be seen on a bicycle or motorbike traveling to church on Sunday morning. Children wear their best clothes on Sunday, even if the family does not attend church. Some men enjoy cockfights on Sunday afternoons.

Schools are a very important part of life. In Haiti, government schools serve a very small percentage of children. Parochial schools, small community schools, schools meeting in churches or other available buildings are numerous as people try to provide an education for the community's children. In areas where there are no schools, local residents frequently build a small school to serve the children living in that location. Other than the government schools, there is no national control of schools. There is a national curriculum, but small, independent schools in rural areas can set their own policies.

Children in all but the poorest schools wear a uniform. Each school has its own colors and style of uniform. Checkered shirts with solid pants or skirts are a popular choice. If the school has a preschool, children begin to attend at the age of three. Girls wear many ribbons in their hair to match the school uniform. In the morning streams of children can be seen walking down the country roads to their respective schools with older children guiding the youngest. Some children walk several miles back and forth to school each day.

Unfortunately, the level of poverty makes it difficult for children to attend school regularly. When the family cannot pay the very small fees, the child has to drop out. As a result of frequent moving and change of schools, children may attend several schools. The impact is that children repeat grades or are behind their age peers when they can attend school again. There is a national policy that a child must attend every grade to be permitted to take the national exam to graduate from elementary school. Children may not skip a grade or receive extra instruction to allow them to move more quickly through the curriculum. As a result there are older teenagers still in elementary school. It is sometimes difficult to determine a child's age because malnutrition is prevalent leading to stunted growth. Regardless of children's age when entering school, they must begin in first grade and pass an exam at the end of the school year to be promoted to the next grade. If they have to leave school, they must repeat the grade where they had been before leaving.

Parent involvement in school decisions varies from school to school. There might be a school committee at an individual school, or the school leaders might make the decisions. Teachers are paid very poorly and turnover is frequent. The level of teacher training varies from person to person. Some teachers have not completed secondary school or received any teacher training prior to beginning as a teacher. Others enter the teaching profession because there is no other work available. The teachers usually are local and live near the school. The majority of them are committed to doing the best they can for the children and are eager to attend any training that might be made available.


## The Exosystem


The rural communities in this study are under the government of the Les Cayes region centered in the small city of Les Cayes. There is a police department, local hospital, and some social services available to the area. Even small children might have experienced traveling to Les Cayes when they are young. The family can buy construction materials, fabrics and other goods, and food at stores in the large market area. They can also bring products from their farms to sell in the main market or other small market areas in the city. Haitian children have more exposure to a large community than children studied in Africa. They are more familiar with motor vehicles of various types because a major highway runs through the countryside moving from Les Cayes to other smaller and larger communities or to Port Au Prince.

In recent years there have been periods of political uprisings and changes in the national government. In an effort to keep control there is a military presence that reaches to Les Cayes. Armed uprisings can occur in some areas in the country that always affect Port Au Prince. As a result of the most recent uprising against then President Aristede, the United Nations has peacekeepers in Haiti, including the Les Cayes region. Children are very aware of the presence of the peacekeepers, although they might not see them on the more remote roads. Even if small children don't understand the nature of the political situation, they grow up with a sense of unease and fear because violence is a real possibility for the Haitian people. Some parents raise their children to be able to defend themselves.

Although there is no newspaper in the area, some children do have access to television and radio broadcasts from Port Au Prince. Young children are aware of what is happening in their area and the country through these media sources. They are also aware of other countries because so many adults have traveled back and forth between Haiti, the United States, and other countries where they have sought work. Because Haiti is close to the United States, particularly Florida, people travel back and forth to visit their families when their economic situation makes it possible.

This ability to travel within and outside Haiti makes the family social network more extended for many children, even if they live in a more remote rural area. Family and neighbors might move and the children are aware of where people live away from Les Cayes. They are particularly familiar with Miami, Florida and New York City, since these are the major ports of entry for Haitian emigrants.

Rural children have little access to recreation facilities and organizations. Even very small communities might have an open space for soccer or there might be a soccer field at a school. Soccer is the most popular sport for young people as well as adults. Children play after school and adults play in the evening and on the weekends, frequently in a cleared field with makeshift goals. Basketball is also popular.

When children enter school they become acquainted with children outside their neighborhood. The transition from home to school can be difficult for very young children who have mostly been in a neighborhood with a small group of children. Entering the institution of school with hundreds of students and teachers they may not know is a major adjustment.

If a parent travels each day to work in Les Cayes, children in those families are more aware of occupations other than farming. In addition, because teachers usually come from the local area, they are familiar with their students' homes and families.

## The Macrosystem

Political positions and conflicts are a very important factor in the lives of young children. Adults in their lives will discuss the political situation frequently and engage in conversations explaining their ideas and positions. Children are aware of events such as kidnappings in Port Au Prince or uprisings and demonstrations. The larger society is not united in a single political ideology, and children experience the effects of uncertainty of national governance and instability in the economy.

Religious beliefs are important to the Haitian people. Prayers are said in secular schools and hymns sung at the beginning and end of the school day. The influence of the church is felt in communities because both the church and school can also serve as community centers. Many small schools are led by a pastor or sponsored by a church. There are religious events and festivals periodically during the year. School and church are one in some areas, so their influence can be integrated for families and children.

## Conclusions

The young rural Haitian child experiences a different type of ecosystem than the rural African child in Senegal or Burkina Faso. The components of the microsystem can be more variable and family structures less defined. Because the child grows up in a rural neighborhood, the influence of the mesosytem is experienced early in life; however, the toddler and preschool child may be more familiar with other families living nearby than the extended family. The school and church are also important elements of the mesosystem.

Haitian children may have more awareness of the bigger world through television, radio and occasional journeys into the City of Les Cayes. Because motor transportation is more accessible, they might have traveled to other rural communities to visit extended family and friends. They are likely to have an awareness of the world beyond the Les Cayes area due to the prominence of political affairs in Haitian life. They also are likely to be exposed to other countries, especially the United States, because family and community members may be living there or return home periodically. Haitian children live in a more informed world than their African peers, but they may not be as secure from constant changes in their life.

Despite the current life conditions of young children in rural Africa and Haiti, the 21$^{st}$ century has arrived. Cell phones are a priority for all but the poorest families. People are able to communicate across the countryside and with those living in major cities and in another country. In Africa a teacher might travel from village to village on a donkey cart, but he will have a cell phone in his pocket. When the current generation of young children become adults in these three countries, their ecological system will reflect a more connected society and culture. For now, they live a rural life with many hardships.

### Author's Note

This chapter is the result of working in three developing countries over the span of four years. Five visits were made in Haiti between 2003 and 2005 to conduct teacher training workshops in the rural area of Les Cayes. Various types of school were visited as well as homes of school children. The two African countries, Senegal and Burkina Faso, were visited in 2005 and 2007. Again, the purpose of the visits was to conduct teacher training in rural areas. In 2007 the training in Africa was conducted for a four-week period. Observations were made and information solicited specifically to acquire the needed background to be able to develop this chapter. The information in this chapter is a result of living and working in the villages and rural areas and interacting with the lives of children, educators, families and chiefs and elders.

## References

Bronfenbrenner, U. (1986). Ecology of the family as a context for human development: Research perspectives. *Developmental Psychology, 22*, 723–742.
Bronfenbrenner, U. (1995). The bioecological perspective from a life course perspective. Reflections of a participant observer. In P. Moen, G.H. Edler, & K. Luscher (Eds.), *Examining lives in context* (pp. 599–618). Washington, DC: American Psychological Association.
Campaore, A. (2007, March). Personal interview.
Fall, S. (2007, March). Personal interviews.
Faye, M. (2007, March). Personal interviews.
Lassane, K. (2007, March). Personal interviews.
"Les Baobabs": Senegal of yesterday and today (2007, March-April). *Teranga: The magazine of Air Senegal International, 17.*
Polk, P. A. (1997). *Haitian vodou flags*. Jackson, MS: University Press of Mississippi.
Puckett, M. B., & Black, J. K. (2005). *The young child. Development from prebirth through age eight.* (4th ed.). Upper Saddle River, NJ: Pearson.
Sam, E. (2007, March). Personal interview.

**Sue C Wortham**
2600 FM 3237
Wimberley, TX 78676
swortham@hughes.net

Sue C. Wortham, Ph.D. is retired from the University of Texas of San Antonio where she was Professor of Early Childhood and Elementary Education. She is the author of 10 textbooks and many articles on various topics in early childhood education. She served as a Fulbright Scholar to Chile in 1992 and President of the Association for Childhood Education International (ACEI) from 1995 to 1997. She has served as a volunteer for World Children's Relief (WCR) in Haiti, Burkina Faso, and Senegal since 2004. She is currently Director of Educational Programs for WCR, a registered NGO with the United Nations.

# Chapter 2
# Parental and Educator Perspectives on Young Children's Acquisition of Self-Regulatory Skills

**Wanda Boyer**

**Abstract** The principal goal of this study was to understand how preschool children of ages four to five years acquire self-regulation. This study aimed to understand the essence of the experience for parents and educators of developmentally guiding children toward autonomous and socially competent self-regulating behaviors. Using a phenomenological research design to analyze multiple data sources including 200 pages of interview and focus group transcriptions from 12 parents and three educators, this study found: (1) there is a developmental trajectory for the acquisition of self-regulatory skills for children as well as their parents and educators, (2) synchronous adult-child affect has significant impact on a child's ability to self-regulate, (3) parents and educators clearly articulated child centered and developmentally appropriate guidelines for nurturing self-regulation in preschool children, but they were surprised by the sophistication, duration, and reciprocity of growth that occurs in the acquisition of self-regulation of four and five year olds. The implications have a resounding influence on the future of education and include examining the development of self-regulatory skills for both the preschoolers, and parents/educators and how more synchronous adult-child affect can promote each child's optimal readiness to learn.

**Keywords** self-regulation, emotion regulation, emotions, social competence, moral reasoning, early childhood, families, parents, teachers, early childhood educators, child development, behaviour, routines, preschool, preservice teachers, qualitative research, interviews

University of Victoria

M.R. Jalongo (ed.), *Enduring Bonds.*
© Springer 2008

# Introduction

*"You don't tell me what to do. I make the rules..."*

*"Don't be mean to my friend. You can't tell my friend what to do. I tell you what to do."*

*– A five year old to his Mother*

The words of this five year old clearly illustrate the new and increasing challenges facing those charged with guiding the development of the next generation of society. The purpose of this study is to generate knowledge on how children between the ages of four and five learn to self-regulate. Self-regulation is defined

> as the ability to comply with a request, to initiate and cease activities according to situational demands, to modulate intensity, frequency, and duration of verbal and motor acts in social and educational settings, to postpone acting upon a desired object or goal, and to generate socially approved behavior in the absence of external monitors (Kopp, 1982, pp. 199–200).

When demonstrated, self-regulation is considered "among the hallmarks of development and socialization during the early years" (Kochanska, Coy, & Murray, 2001, p. 1091).

Current research indicates that misbehavior, aggression, violence and victimization in the learning environment are becoming fundamental concerns (Boyer, 2004). By analyzing the reflective writings of 151 preservice teachers, the study found that these concerns were prevalent and seemed to contribute tangibly to overall misgivings about entering the teaching profession. In a study of caregiver involvement in peer interactions among preschool and kindergarten aged children, caregivers became involved in approximately 5 peer interactions in a 30-minute period, most frequently to state rules and commands or to break up a disruptive peer interaction (Kemple, David, & Hysmith, 1997). Behavior problems that emerge at such an early age often become stabilized (Arnold, McWilliams, & Arnold, 1998). On the other hand, the ability to act in accord with social standards by regulating personal behavior at an early age is predictive of higher social competence in school aged children and adults (Eisenberg, Fabes, Shepard, Murphy, Guthrie, Jones, Friedman, Poulin, & Maszk, 1997). Thus, there is a need to target the early years as a critical time to support and understand the attainment of self-regulation (Bronson, 2000a; Bronson, 2000b; Kemple, et al., 1997; Wolfgang, 2000). However, a recent analysis of over 100 years of self-regulation research has found that studies of self-regulatory practices within families and caregiving relationships lack contextualization by the natural learning and living environments of the children (Post, Boyer, & Brett, 2006). Moreover, particularly at the preschool level, caregivers identify a lack of support and understanding of the life experiences of parents and early childhood educators in addressing the needs of children with behavior problems (Boyer, Blodgett, & Turk, 2006).

In order to explore the experiences of parents and educators in their support of preschoolers' self-regulation, this study posed the following research question: How do *preschool* children acquire self-regulation, which is the ability to initiate, cease or modulate behaviors in accordance with caregiver and parental standards? The purpose of this research was to listen with care to the voices of families and educators as a channel of information about how they help young children become independent and responsible for their own behaviors, problem-solving skills, language, social interactions, emotions, and moral decisions. A specific purpose of this study was to identify how and under what circumstances parents and educators assisted children at ages four and five in acquiring the ability to initiate, cease, and modulate their own responses to their learning and living experiences. The results of this study have the potential to strengthen educational practice by giving parents and educators an opportunity to reflect on themes that can be used to help stimulate preschool children's self-regulation in living and learning environments.

## Method

### *Participants*

Purposeful criterion sampling (Creswell, 2008) was used for a larger scale qualitative study to select 150 families of preschool children ages 4–5 and their 15 early childhood educators from seven locations in the Pacific Northwest. These participants were willing to participate in an individual audio-taped interview, a focus group session for parents, or an educator focus group. This study focused on the 12 families and three educators from a randomly selected site from among the seven locations. Half the parent participants were one career families with either the mother or father as a stay-at-home caregiver. The average age of parents was 36 years. The parent participants represented professions including Architecture, Bartending, Corrections, Engineering, Hotel and Restaurant Service and Management, Law, Sales, Real Estate Marketing, and Nursing. Parent participants defined their ethnic ancestry, which reflected European ancestry (German, French, English, Italian), First Nations (Métis), Hispanic, Bi-racial, and North American. The preschool educators indicated that their ethnic ancestry was European. The average age of the preschool educators was 48.7 years. The preschool educators had an average of 2.7 years of preservice training and an average of 10 years of experience teaching preschool children.

### *Instruments*

Multiple data sources including interviews with participants, focus group sessions with parents, focus group with the educators, official school documents, field notes and journals were used to support inter-subjective validity or "coming to know someone or something … [via] commitment to co-presence and community as a way to verify, accentuate, and extend knowledge and experience" (Moustakas, 1994, p. 57). Thus, inter-subjective validity provided a more complete understanding of the experience of assisting preschoolers in the acquisition of self-regulatory skills. The eighteen open-ended individual interview questions and the twelve open-ended focus group questions were based upon the literature (Boyer, 2004; Bronson 2000b; Kemple, David, & Hysmith, 1997; Kopp, 1982) and the phenomenological research guidelines identified by Moustakas (1994). The eighteen questions regarding acquisition of self-regulatory skills of 3–5 year olds thematically covered child temperament, the process of initiating activities, modulating activities, and ceasing activities, and strategies adults use to support the growth of self-regulation. The twelve focus group questions involved the group in synergistically discussing the definition of self-regulation, the effects of nature and nurture on the acquisition of self-regulatory skills, attitudes contributing to self-regulation, developmental differences in self-regulatory skills across age groups, and the importance of self-regulation to the caregiving process.

## *Design and Procedure*

Using a phenomenological research design (Moustakas, 1994) this study analyzed the interviews and focus groups involving the parents and teachers and included the use of official school documents (e.g., school philosophy statements). According to Moustakas, the phenomenological analysis should involve a seven step process, including:

1. Horizontalizing, or listing every relevant expression. For example, in this study, expressions made by the participants were considered if they related to the topic of acquiring self-regulatory skills for 3–5 year olds.
2. Reduction and elimination of experiences to ensure that the essence of the experiences and the invariant constituents or common representations of the experiences were captured. Overlapping, repetitive or vague expressions were eliminated. For example, in this study, common representations involved experiences in which adults worked with the children in their care and how their efforts changed behaviors.
3. Clustering and thematicizing of the invariant constituents to create core themes.
4. Final identification and validation of the invariant constituents to ensure that the themes were explicit and compatible representations of the experiences compared to the multiple data sources. In this study, the themes were derived from the experiences the parents and educators had while developmentally guiding children toward autonomous and socially competent self-regulating behaviors. These themes were then compared to the interview and focus group transcripts, school documents, field notes and journals to verify accuracy and clear representation in the data sources.

5. Individual Textural Descriptions were constructed from participants in the study (e.g., parents and preschool educators).
6. Construction of the individual structural description were based on the individual textural description and imaginative variation. In this study, grasping the structural essence involved identifying parents, and educators, comparability and consistency of ideation and vision as they helped 3–5 year olds acquire self-regulatory skills.
7. The final step of weaving the texture and structure into a group essence or expression of the experience. In this study, the shared vision of both parents and educators were combined into a unified narrative.

After receiving informed consent from all participants in the study, two research assistants scheduled individual interviews and focus groups at a convenient time at the preschool for each participant. An informal conversational interview or dialogue style (Kvale, 1996) was employed for the 15 individual interviews. The research assistants received 10 hours of training in the interview questions and protocol, the informal conversational interview style, relationship building in the interview process, and taping procedures. The interviews were led by the research assistants and lasted 40–60 minutes. The field notes were taken before and after the interviews while the personal journal entries were completed immediately after each interview. The tape-recorded interviews were typed into transcripts by the graduate assistants. The researcher led the four focus groups with attention to group dynamics, freedom for all members to contribute to the discussion, and support of respectful interaction between all focus group members (Anderson & Arsenault, 2000). Child care was provided to families in order to support their late afternoon or evening participation in the focus groups. The three focus groups for the parents were 60–90 minutes in length and the focus group for the educators was 180 minutes in length. Field notes for the focus groups were recorded before and after each focus group session. Journal entries were recorded by the primary researcher after each of the four focus groups. Using the multiple data sources, the researcher developed a composite structural description derived from the seven steps of the phenomenological analysis (Moustakas, 1994).

# Results

The following five themes were derived as a synthesis and derivation of the rich textural material found in the interview and focus group transcripts, school documents, field notes and journals. This textural material elucidated the "lived experience of parents and educators" as they induced the acquisition of self-regulatory skills in preschool children. The five themes derived from the present set of transcripts were as follows:

1. Deepening adult involvement: Communication, interpretation, encouragement
2. Adults learning how to modulate their own self-regulatory skills

3. Adult and child reciprocal attunement.
4. Burgeoning experiential contexts.
5. Internalizing adult rules.


## *Deepening Adult Involvement: Communication, Interpretation, Encouragement*

All 15 participants admitted that they were humbled by the caregiving process and needed to be vigilant and always ready to learn. With laughter and nodding in agreement, they described their steep learning curve. They recognized the importance of the caregiving task and also the pressure to possess all knowledge about caregiving when they needed it. One participant described the situation in the following terms:

"This is a hard job because not everything is clear and straight forward in caring for children. We don't know it all right now and we seem to need to." (P9)

Over time, study participants realized that they needed to watch and learn about the child slowly and with care. They felt that children were a "mystery to be solved over time." One participant related:

"My four year old girl covered herself in glue and sparkles and I still don't know why she did this. I recognize now that I really needed to watch, listen, and learn from her in order to find out why she does what she does." (P3)

Another part of the discomfort of not having immediate answers came from the need for better communication with the child in order to gain an understanding of the problems faced by the child. The participants felt awed by the volume and variety of learning experiences required for children to develop the capacity to communicate openly, manage their emotions, and find their own voice:

"Children go through so many different experiences at so many different times, so they need to be involved in what is going on and that's a big thing–having a voice. I'm all for my four year old child telling us what is happening or what feelings are behind her emotions instead of just acting on the emotions. It's all about finding out why a behavior is occurring instead of being at the receiving end of the bad behavior and uncontrolled emotions." (P5)

The study participants felt that their ability to guide their children improved when they thought about the impact of past experiences on the child's present behaviors and ability to self-regulate. The following extract illustrates this recognition:

"A brief minute of separation from an adult caused my child to be fearful about elevators and this has made her safety conscious. I got on the elevator and the door started to close and she was on the outside. It was horrible. The door hadn't closed so I brought her in but she cried and cried. To this day my four year old is afraid of elevators but is very cautious in situations. I watch her and see that she is protective of herself. But I've also watched and discovered that this has carried over into so many other things like how she relates protectively towards her sister and other children with lots of hand-holding during play." (P11)

The participants also conveyed that when they took the child's perspective and thoughtfully interpreted a child's questions, they would leave the interaction feeling that they really understood the child:

> "My little girl of four was having trouble with bedtime routines or that's what I thought. She asked me at the end of every day before bed, 'What day is it tomorrow?' Then a couple of hours later she would still be up and would continue to ask me the same question. After many nights, it finally dawned on me that she wasn't struggling with having to go to bed. She struggled with 'Today is what I know; tomorrow's unknown.' The thing that worked was understanding what the missing link was for her. So I finally clued in to her need to understand what tomorrow would bring, and I answered her that 'Tomorrow is preschool and then you will see your best friend.' And so she said 'Oh, okay. Goodnight.'" (P3)

Another participant added that the bedtime routine helped the child learn to self-regulate by providing an opportunity to give a rationale in support of the child's controlled behavior:

> "When my four year old son doesn't want to go to bed I have to tell him that it is getting very late and that he has to have his bath and tomorrow we are going to have another busy and fun day and because I don't want him to get tired tomorrow, he needs to go to sleep so that he can grow and be ready for tomorrow." (P4)

More generally, the participants observed that the use of routines provided children with opportunities for acquiring or refining skills as well as opportunities for adult caregivers to recognize a child's successes, not just areas needing improvement:

> "We tend to focus on when things are *not* happening and the negative side of things. By providing a basic routine and having certain boundaries, we keep our expectations in reason and appropriate for their age. We really could do more of this all of the time so that we are encouraging to them when they are managing to do their best." (P14)

Overall, participants recognized that the effort of interpreting a child's behavior, mannerisms, and words acknowledged the child's need to be understood by their adult caregiver, which in turn made each child feel secure and happy. The participants observed that when a child expressed insecurity, adult caregivers could use their understanding of the child's context as well as knowledge about the child's successful behaviors to help build the confidence it takes to wake up and embrace each day. Participants asserted that "no matter what happens in the geopolitical world, our children need security and a sense of hope." (P10)

## Adults Learning How to Modulate Their Own Self-regulatory Skills

As participants described the skills that their children needed to learn in order to self-regulate, a theme emerged in which adults expressed the necessity of *modulating their own self-regulatory skills*. The first two excerpts below illustrate the surprise participants felt as they discussed the skill set they would need in order to help their children:

"I wonder how much self-regulation they model after how we self-regulate as adults? As adults we all have areas that we're not good at self-regulating. For me it would be sticking to my work schedule. The kids are watching us constantly! So what are they learning? My 4 year old daughter is really good at monitoring the self-regulation of others but not so good with herself. (P3)

"It's embarrassing but I yell a lot. I grew up with parents that yelled. I'm a yeller and my husband is not. If my husband raises his voice my five year old child knows that it is bad. But I yell all of the time. So I guess that's why it doesn't work with them like it does for my husband because I raise my voice all the time. I am patient to a point. Maybe I should self-regulate?" (P6)

In order to support self-regulation in their children, they saw themselves as having to modify and control their behavior because they were role models and "little eyes are watching." One participant described the situation in the following terms:

"A five year old says to me, 'you ask me to use my words and be polite. What you ask me to do, you have to do too.' So then I have to use proper language and speak with respect." (P1)

In these next two extracts the participants identified ways they practiced to consciously modulate their responses,

"I have to walk away, I have to leave him alone. Like I leave the room or busy myself with something. I have to just leave him to calm himself down so he's not feeding off me. I try not to react badly when he is acting badly." (P6)

Other participants recognized the need to see their child's behavior in context so they could show more patience and support. For one mother of a 4 year old girl being potty trained, supporting the self-regulation in her child was an act of willpower on her part:

"I try to remember what it was like when I was four. I try to understand the bigger scheme of things so that I can help her understand the bigger scheme of things. In the case of potty training, it's not just me being the boss and telling her to go. It's a matter of making life easier now for herself and easier for her when she starts school to go to kindergarten. Having a kindergarten friend wet her pants while she is playing with you is not something that a lot of kids understand." (P3)

In summary, participants in this study felt that they were learning how to regulate their own behaviors. The words of Participant 8 aptly summarize the theme:

"I am sort of developing at the same rate that my kid has. I am learning and affirming what is important to me and as a result, my child is learning what their limits are." (P8)

## Adult and Child Reciprocal Attunement

The theme of parity between adult behavior and child behavior continued to manifest itself during the transition to *parent and child reciprocal attunement*. The participants indicated that having adults predict, respond to, and dialogue with the preschool child about his or her need for sleep, food, attention, and affection could help the child learn to label needs and find socially appropriate ways in which to satisfy those needs. The ability to "read" the child also had the effect of creating a stronger relationship between the adult and child, which can increase the child's willingness to comply with the adult's requests:

"I have to read my 4 year old son to see if he is tired, hungry, or sick. Even though he's close to 5 he still gets upset when he is feeling any of these feelings. He gets emotional. He trusts me to know him and help identify what can be done to make himself feel better." (P4)

Two participants further captured the intentionality of the adult response to the child, saying:

"as adults, we really need to understand when to use physical presence and proximity, removal from negative experiences and movement of the child to a quiet space to think." (P2)

"Well, I think that if we listen to their emotions, they feel better about complying because their feelings are acknowledged. In this way there is less of a power struggle, and you can say 'I know that you really don't want to clean up right now because you were having fun with those blocks, but you will be able to play with the blocks tomorrow. Just acknowledging how they're feeling can help them to self-regulate." (P14)

The participants reflected that when they understood the child and communicated with the child, they could predict what the child would do before the child did it, which made them better able to reinforce positive behaviors and circumvent negative behaviors,

"And you have to understand your child, you have to understand what they can take and what they can't or what you can push them into doing and what you can't push them into. They have to learn how to take on hard tasks because they have to do things that they don't want to do, but as we care for the child we have to prepare them for the hard task. For instance my son is taking piano, and he doesn't want to take lessons. I know that he wants to be out playing, but he has to spend time practicing, and I set these boundaries, and if he doesn't practice, there are consequences, but after practice he can go out to play. So he wants to get the practicing done so he can go out and play ball. I really understand why he tries to rush the practice, but I still challenge him to take piano lessons even though he may not become the greatest pianist in the world. I really understand him and why he does what he does." (P12)

In fact, dialogue with and observation of the child in their care allowed the participants to become more attached to the child. The following extracts highlight how participants felt more cognizant of who the child was and why the child behaved as s/he did:

"a child can be like me and also unlike me. She is learning what I expect, what my limits are, and why I have set these expectations and limits. I am learning about their needs and they are learning my expectations and limits." (P15)

Participants in the study identified the value of having known strategies in their 'bag of tricks' to help overcome difficult situations. They felt that it was important that they acknowledged relational challenges between themselves and child in their care, and that they were able to express grievances induced by the choices the child was making:

"You have to acknowledge when it's difficult for you. The expectations have to be clear at the start, and you have to try and give the child certain tools like 'Can I have a turn with that?' or 'I don't like it when you do that.' [Adults need to be] showing them, modeling for them, telling them what the alternatives are... and sometimes you really have to be right there to carry them through when they're not able to do it without that support." (P13)

"Well, I would say, 'Remember when this happened? Do you want to go that route again? And like, last time you did it that way it was taken away from you for a day or a weekend or whatever. Do you want to go that way again?' And sometimes she doesn't remember but a lot of times she does." (P2)

Participants also spoke about the fact that when an adult was able to read and respond to a child's emotional needs, the child began to more easily understand the emotional needs communicated by the adult:

"Mostly, I guess she doesn't recognize the importance of my needs, my time, my agenda. She's just feeling that she should be left to do her own thing and shouldn't have to change what she is doing to suit me so she feels frustration that I'm trying to change her plan or her time schedule. However, if I remind her 'You know the reasons why this needs to happen' well she can usually acknowledge the importance of doing the task to me and that the task has to be done for a reason. She is quite empathic and is pretty good at putting herself in my shoes when I take her though the process." (P7)

Clearly, adult efforts at fostering attunement were dominant since the child's reciprocation was often based on prompting. However, the study participants saw the dialogue ensuing from reciprocal attunement as having the potential to help children self-regulate over time:

"I'm sure that what I say to them and how I respond to what they say to me is only one part of the way that my child will end up learning how to self-regulate but I'm sure that it has an effect. So I believe part of helping my five year old child is for me to be careful with how I word my encouragement and even how I try to change her behavior. I try to involve her in the process of learning how to behave in a proper manner when I am there and when I'm not there. I give her snippets of information about how her behavior affects others so that she sees that it's not just how she affects me but other people in her world. I believe that kids need to think of other people." (P7)

## Burgeoning Experiential Contexts

Despite the adult participants becoming increasingly attuned with the children through their mutual experience of varied learning and living contexts, challenges ultimately arose as each child's world grew to include more experiences with others. The adult participants reflected this when they said,

"I thought it was so great I knew everything she liked and didn't like. Then she came into the preschool context, before and after school programs, week-end programs, the influence of new friends, grandparents and other family members, and now there is more for me to know. I can't know everything." (P3)

Participants also noted the effects of people in their child's expanding experiential context, including siblings or friends and their influence on the acquisition of self-regulation:

"It's one thing to self-regulate when they're on their own, but it is very different when they are with a sibling or friend. I find that they like to 'egg on' the younger child. When they are on their own, they can take that nap or eat that snack or play with one toy, but it's very interesting to see how they play off each other and also try to understand the purpose of their game." (P11)

Participants felt that learning how to self-regulate in varied groups and with varied people was "really hard, but a process that three to five year olds were busy learning" (P13). In order for the children to be able to do what they desired, they were required to perform tasks for other children or adults, such as sharing or cleaning up before the next activity. As a result, they also had to learn to create relationships with others:

"Children are learning how to work in a group and how to carry out things they want to do and things that they need to do in a group in such a way as not to be… well… difficult with different people, how to make friends and how to be the kind of person people want to play with." (P13)

Participants noted that children also had variations of behavior based on their evaluation of the people in a learning environment. For example, if a child perceived any inequity, the child had more difficulty practicing self-regulatory skills. One father encapsulated this thinking:

"My guy has an attitude about the world and the people in it that fair is what is right. Some of the things that make him upset and lose personal control and emotional regulation are when he sees sort of injustice amongst his friends. His behavior can change quite dramatically based on how he perceives the fairness of what is going on around him." (P8)

More generally, as a result of multifarious experiences with other groups and individuals, participants observed that children began to question and test caregiver expectations in different environments:

"They are sort of aware of where your line is and how far they can go. Some of it requires testing on their part like what's going to happen if I do this here, what happens at home, what happens on the week-end with other people." (P14)

## Internalizing Adult Rules

With the expansion of the child's world of people and learning contexts, they eventually began to learn different sets of adult rules. This increases the complexity of compliance for children as varying contexts imply the ability to read subtle subtextural expectations that arise as an activity progresses:

"They have to know what is accepted, knowing what is required at different times by different people and across different activities and be able to read the rules of the activities and what's expected." (P13)

In some cases, the children used this knowledge to retest boundaries from context to context and attempt non-compliance through indirection:

"my five year old child will tell another child to throw a hard boiled egg at the wall saying 'It's okay.' Well it's not okay. The things he wants to do, but *knows* are wrong, he gets others to do for him." (P1)

However, more often the child seemed to be seeking greater attunement with each adult by asking that adult for a rationale for that particular adult's rules:

"Sometimes we just act like we are conveying the gospel. We'll tell them something, and they'll say 'Why?' and we'll say 'Just because!' and my daughter will come back with 'But because isn't an answer.' At three or four you can tell them something and they'll do it, but as they get older they need to know what's behind your answer. They can't go further until they get that." (P5)

Furthermore participants recognized children who understood the underlying rationale for and patterns of various adult rules would still only *internalize* these expectations into self-regulatory behaviors over a long period of time:

"We teach my 5 year old to love and to respect people, to love and respect themselves, and to be respectful of teachers by listening to them. All of those things have helped them with their self-regulation for example understanding why you can't hit people. I mean they didn't listen right away but we kept conveying the same message to them and they kept hearing it and it did sink in." (P9)

One reason for the length of the period of internalization is that it takes time to resolve the conflict between the wish to comply and the desire to be autonomous. Once a child has embraced the adult caregiver's agenda, the child experiences compliance as self-generated and not interfering with autonomy. The participants described their efforts to provide the child with an understanding of the necessary steps to gradually gain autonomy:

"I try to provide my five year old child with adult rules and guidelines, but I also try very much to allow my child to have the freedom of choice in what they do so that rather than feeling like they are robots who are controlled by me that they actually have some say in how they are going to behave and how their life will progress. So I'm hoping that by doing this I'm making it possible for them to behave in a proper way when I'm not there." (P7)

# Discussion

## *Limitations*

This study offers insights into the lived experience of adults in supporting preschool children in their acquisition of self-regulation, especially for parents and educators. Two limitations of the study should be noted. First, the small sample size is not intended to promote generalizability of the results. Second, the generalizability of the findings should be tested in different contexts (e.g., cooperative parent preschools, Christian, non-denominational, subsidized preschool, day care, and rural settings) and varied self-defined ethnic groups (e.g., African American, Arabian, Chinese, Filipino, Japanese, South African, South East Asian). Results from the larger grounded theory study of 150 families will help to confirm the reliability and accuracy of the results and provide insights from the parents and educators as they help their children acquire self-regulatory skills in varied learning and living environments.

## Conclusions

The purpose of this research was to listen with care to the voices of families and educators in order to learn how they help the young children in their care to become independent and responsible for their own behaviors, problem-solving skills, use of language, social interactions, emotions, and moral decisions. Through the individual interviews and four focus groups, the 15 participants shared their thoughtful reflections on *how* preschool children acquire self-regulation, which is the ability to initiate, cease or modulate behaviors in accordance with caregiver and parental standards. This phenomenological research study focused on parents and educators as they actually *lived through the experience* of helping the preschool children in their care to achieve self-regulation.

From the construction of individual and composite textural descriptions, it became clear that acquisition of self-regulatory skills in preschool children followed a developmental trajectory consisting of five themes. This developmental pathway began with adults needing to deepen their involvement with the children in their care through communication, interpretation of children's behaviors, and positive encouragement for compliant behaviors. Adults then moved into a process of self-examination in which they learned more about themselves as role models. This process was necessary for adults to establish consistent patterns of expectations for the children. From self-examination, adults then recognized that both the adult and child needed to be better attuned to one another in order to maximize the efforts of the child to acquire self-regulatory skills. According to the participants, this reciprocal attunement led to an adult appreciation of the child's expanding world and the influence of varied learning and living contexts on the child. Ultimately, the adults pondered the influence of these varied experiential contexts on the child's ability to strike a balance between compliance and autonomy.

The findings from the present study corroborate observed phenomena in a number of prior research studies. However, the present study contributes to a deeper understanding of why these phenomena occur based on their connection within the five developmental themes for young children's acquisition of self-regulation. In this way, the observed phenomena can be seen as special cases of the more general, progressive pattern.

For example, an adult's recounting of events from the child's perspective supported cooperative interactions with the child and set up conditions for compliance and attunement (Dix, 1991; Hastings & Grusec, 1997; Schaffer & Crook, 1980). In the context of the five developmental themes, the taking of the child's perspective can be seen as one strategy an adult can use to improve understanding of the child's behavior and improving communication, which the development progression indicates will be followed by attunement and ultimately autonomous compliance.

The findings from the present study also corroborated the assertion of Kemple and others (1997) that rules and commands need to be stated and re-stated. The present study attributes this phenomenon to the significant impact of varied learning and living contexts on young children. Preschoolers have a great deal to learn. They need time to: 1) learn, re-learn and remember limits; 2) use materials properly; 3) consider safety issues for themselves and others; 3) understand how others self-regulate, and 4) decide when to self-regulate within these many varied learning and living contexts. Therefore, rules and commands need to be stated and re-stated to provide consistent care as well as to promote a feeling in children of security and safety within and across the *varied learning and living environments*. Insecurity due to a perceived injustice of inconsistent expectations is an inhibiting factor in the development of self-regulation.

Kochanska et al. (2001) observed that compliance with the maternal agenda in *Do* contexts, which are affirmative requests to initiate behaviors, are much lower than compliance in *Don't* contexts, which are admonishments to modulate or cease behaviors. Kochanska et al. suggested that strategies for increasing compliance in *Do* contexts should result in a "solution to two contradictory developmental forces: the wish to comply and the desire to be autonomous" (p. 1108). In the findings of the present study, it is clear that the final theme of internalizing adult rules is an iterative process in which the prior themes have a cascading effect. The burgeoning experiential context of a child leads to questioning of rules. The adult response that promotes the acquisition of self-regulation involves communication and dialogue regarding the rationale for rules, which results in heightened attunement between the agendas of the adult and child.

Based on the connections established between prior research and the present study, future research should use experimental analysis to examine the efficacy of strategies and interventions targeted at specific themes of the development progression for self-regulation acquisition identified in the findings. Future research should also more closely examine the correlation between children's acquisition of self-regulatory skills with adult self-mastery. These studies would also provide the opportunity to expand the analysis of both the iterative nature of the progressive themes and the self-regulatory attunement of adult and child in the context of primary and elementary age groups.

**Acknowledgements** Thank you to the families and educators who shared their knowledge and love of children with me. Funding for this research study was made by the generosity of the Human Early Learning Partnership (H.E.L.P.) and the Social Sciences and Human Research Council (S.S.H.R.C.) of Canada.

# References

Anderson, G., & Arsenault, N. (2000). *Fundamentals of educational research* (2nd ed.). Bristol, PA: Falmer Press.

Arnold, D. H., & McWilliams, L., & Arnold E. H. (1998). Teacher discipline and child misbehavior in day care: Untangling causality with correlational data. *Developmental Psychology, 34,* 276–287.

Boyer, W. A. R. (2004). Conflicting views of realistic professionalism: Preservice educators' concerns arising from analysis of themes in their reflective writings. *Early Childhood Education Journal, 32,* 51–56.

Boyer, W., Blodgett, L. J. & Turk, E. (2006, June). *Parents and educators supporting the acquisition of self-regulatory skills in children ages 3–5: A large scale qualitative descriptive study across varied communities.* Paper presented at the meeting of the Society for Research in Child Development and Head Start Research Conference. Washington, D.C.

Bronson, M. B. (2000a). Recognizing and supporting the development of self-regulation in young children. *Young Children, 55,* 32–37.

Bronson, M. B. (2000b). *Self-regulation in early childhood: Nature and nurture.* New York: The Guilford Press.

Creswell, J. W. (2008). *Educational research. Planning, conducting, and evaluating quantitative and qualitative research* (3rd ed.). Upper Saddle River, NJ: Pearson Education.

Dix, T. (1991). The affective organization of parenting: Adaptive and maladaptive processes. *Psychological Bulletin, 110,* 3–25.

Eisenberg, N., Fabes, R. A., Shepard, S. A., Murphy, B. C., Guthrie, I.K., Jones, S., Friedman, J., Poulin, R., & Maszk, P. (1997). Contemporaneous and longitudinal prediction of children's social functioning from regulation and emotionality. *Child Development, 68,* 642–664

Hastings, P. & Grusec, J. E. (1997). Conflict outcomes as a function of parental accuracy in perceiving child cognitions and affect. *Social Development, 6,* 76–90.

Kemple, K. M., David, G. M., & Hysmith, C. (1997). Teachers' interventions in preschool and kindergarten children's peer interactions. *Journal of Research in Childhood Education, 12,* 34–47.

Kochanska, G., Coy, K. C., & Murray, K. T. (2001). The development of self-regulation in the first four years of life. *Child Development, 72,* 1091–1111.

Kopp, C. (1982). Antecedents of self-regulation: A developmental perspective. *Developmental Psychology, 18,* 199–214.

Kvale, S. (1996). *Interview: An introduction to qualitative research interviewing.* Thousand Oaks, CA: Sage Publications.

Moustakas, C. (1994). *Phenomenological research methods.* Thousand Oaks, CA: Sage.

Post, Y., Boyer, W., & Brett, L. (2006). A historical examination of self-regulation: Helping children now and in the future. *Early Childhood Education Journal, 34*(1*),* 5–14.

Schaffer, H. R., & Crook, C. K. (1980). Child compliance and maternal control techniques. *Developmental Psychology, 21,* 1090–1096.

Wolfgang, C. H. (2000). Another view on "Reinforcement in developmentally appropriate early childhood classrooms." *Childhood Education, 77,* 64–67.

**Wanda Boyer**
wboyer@uvic.ca

Wanda Boyer is Associate Professor in the Department of Educational Psychology and Leadership Studies in the Faculty of Education at the University of Victoria. Her research interests are in the development of self-regulation and emotion regulation in young and elementary school children in all areas of their experience and areas of exploration.

# Chapter 3
# Early Language Development and Adult/Child Relationships

## An Intricate Connection

**Marilyn Roseman**

**Abstract** The conversations that adults have with babies provide them with much more than language models for acquiring speech. Perhaps more importantly, they are giving the baby a sense of who he is, what his place is in the world, and the ways that other people can be expected to behave. While adult conversations with infants are rooted in the desire to share meanings together, they are the basic ways that infants acquire models for entering into future relationships. Luckily, the strategies for encouraging a child to engage with adults in conversation also foster strong and secure relationships. Adults who are sensitive to the infant's interests and needs, who recognize a baby's role in a conversation, and who allow the child's interests to dictate the nature of the exchange are using effective strategies for both conversation and for helping the baby learn how to develop satisfying relationships.

**Keywords** infants, infancy, toddlers, babies, language acquisition, attachment, oral language, verbal/linguistic intelligence, language development, relationships, verbal interaction, joint attentional focus, pre-linguistic communication, motherese, child-directed speech, Vygotsky, Bowlby

## Introduction

What milestone in a child's development is more anticipated than the child's first word? It heralds the child's admittance into human culture, for nothing separates humans from other primates more than the ability to talk. For many parents, the first word the infant utters represents the first solid indication of the child's budding intelligence and social abilities. Because language is the first glimpse into what has been going on in the child's mind since birth, no other milestone carries such profound interest and delight. Genetics and environmental forces interact to allow most children to speak their first word at the close of the first year. For although a child's genes provide the hardware for speech, it cannot develop without the models, reinforce-

Mount Aloysius College

M.R. Jalongo (ed.), *Enduring Bonds.*
© Springer 2008

ment, and engagement offered by those people who surround the child in the first years. As much as these interactions influence language and literacy development, they will also determine to a large extent the nature of the relationships the child will form. So related are social relationships, communication, and language that the concepts sometimes overlap with one another (Astington, 2004). This is not surprising given the common goals they share. In this chapter the common bonds that lead to language acquisition and relationships will be explored.

Because of the connection parents make between language and general intelligence, early or late arrival of the first word and sentence can be the cause of great celebration or concern. Katie speaks her first word at 11 months, "moo," and living on a farm with lots of cattle, no one questions how that word arrives. But her brother Jeffrey, despite having a chatty older sister as a model, struggles with speech, perhaps the result of the numerous ear infections that seemed to plague his formative years. Evidence from the same family demonstrates how critical the environment is in its influence on language acquisition—influences that can change the trajectory of a child's literacy development for life (Fowler, 1995). Although genetics plays a hefty role in language development, environmental influences are of profound significance, and can often be ameliorated by parents and teachers, if they are knowledgeable of effective strategies.

Language growth in young children is a phenomenal marriage of innate predispositions that propel the child to sociability and a welcoming, encouraging, expectant social group. In many ways it seems as though both parties are preprogrammed to behave in ways that ensure language will develop. Babies are "cute" and their physical appearance draws adults to them. Adults in most cultures alter their voices to be appropriate to the needs of a baby, such as using a higher pitched voice, repetition and describing the events occurring at the present time. On the infant's part, Selby and Bradley (2003) suggest that inter-dependence is built into the brain at birth and that babies have an innate faculty for the capacity to read and convey mental states, a point that will be elaborated on later. Trevarthen (cited in Selby & Bradley, 2003) asserts that babies are born with a capacity to share states of mind and communicate with sympathetic others. He continues, "Communication with persons is possible from birth, and we should not be surprised at this. It is the nature of human consciousness to experience being experienced" (p.1).

The remarkable journey from pre-linguistic communication to verbal speech is rooted in relationships, as is most of the infant's development. The interrelatedness may be the result of the organization of the brain, because, as Siegel (1999) suggests, the same circuits in the brain necessary for social perception are also used in regulating body states and emotions, for organizing memory, and for interpersonal communication. Seeking interdependence, the brain drives the infant to active interactions with the caregiver, interactions that are critical in establishing relationships. Furthermore, it is within the relationship that the infant's memory, communication, and self-regulation will evolve (Selby & Bradley, 2003). An infant molds to his mother when held, gazes and smiles at her, and begins to anticipate the mother's response. Remarkably, the infant's rhythms quickly begin to match the timing of his mother's interventions (Bowlby, 1988). Through this early nonverbal communication, the dyad learns from each other, as the baby also learns about himself. Although all developmental domains are closely related in early childhood, it is clear that an infant's competency in communication is closely related to cognitive, social and emotional competence (Kubicek, 1996). Of particular note is the way that competence in communication fosters attachment and is fostered by attachment. Attachment is of particular concern because it is from attachment that the infant will learn to self-regulate, develop cognitively, and develop a sense of efficacy. Attachment does not necessarily predict the strength of later relationships, but it does appear to equip a child with a mental representation of what a relationship should be (Fonagy, 2001).

## An Analogy

When considering language and literacy development, Martini (1995) used the metaphor of an apprentice to compare the edge that middle class children have in school over their less fortunate peers. In other words, because they have been steeped in a communication style that is comparable to that of the teachers, subsequent school experiences are more successful. Mindful of a deficit model, this analogy can nevertheless be used to think about the ways that most parents and their infants use collaborative strategies to bring the infant into the culture of the family and the society.

When an apprentice and his master initiate their relationship, each has particular roles to play. So it is with the young language learner. Both master and mother must begin with high expectations that the novice will achieve particular goals through encouragement, modeling, and by setting ever higher standards. Both the novice and infant have to be primed for the huge undertaking that is before him and must be cognitively ready to assume the challenge. Both parties have a stake in the relationship, and it is through the relationship that a positive outcome is realized.

Although a master tradesman can conduct an interview to ensure that the understudy has what it takes to work under him, the mother takes it as a given that the infant just delivered will be not only a suitable understudy of language, but an exceptional one. The two are biologically primed to bond, a process that began in the womb and takes off after birth. The hormone oxytocin, sometimes defined as a bonding hormone, is released, easing the pain of child birth, allowing the "letdown" reflex for nursing, and causing an intense emotional feeling in the mother that promotes bonding. The baby is often in an alert state immediately after being born, and gazes intently at mother. He molds to his mother's body, cries vigorously and may suck greedily (Chamblin, 2007). The mother is a willing participant, for if babies are somewhat misshapen after birth, shortly thereafter they develop facial characteristics such as large eyes and round, cute faces that attract adults to them (Zebrowitz, 1992). As far as the infant is concerned, he has been listening to the sounds of his mother while in the womb, and within a few days after birth, he is able to differentiate between his mother's voice and others', and prefers hers. Similarly, he can differentiate the smell of the mother from other mothers. All these biologically determined, evolutionary characteristics ensure that bonding can begin, and the apprenticeship is off to a good start.

# Attachment: Roles and Requirements

One of the first tasks of the infant is to develop an attachment with the primary caregiver, as the infant needs the proximity of the caregiver that is gained through this attachment. Behaviors such as smiling and cooing, or crying and fussing, are tools infants have available to them to elicit parental attention (Cassidy, 1999). Because humans are born as helpless beings, infants must demand and gain the attention of caring adults. Unlike other animals, humans are born relatively immature; consequently, they need adults who are devoted to them to help them on the journey to adulthood. Through this proximity the dyad is learning about each other and laying the foundation not only for a good relationship, but also for learning and language development.

However, it is the parent who has the control over the proximity and protection offered to the infant (Marvin & Britner, 1999). A sensitive parent who is responsive to the infant's needs, enables the infant to make predictions about his small world, which translates into a particular pattern of attachment (Siegel, 1999). Interactions between the mother and infant are collaborative and are negotiated, requiring that each member of the dyad continually adjust their actions and reactions in order to achieve a desired outcome, such as relieving the baby's hunger (Marvin & Britner). If the mother's part of the dialogue—her reactions—appropriately connects the baby's internal states to external experiences, the sensitive and attuned mother will provide her baby with a way to coherently organize the memories of these experiences (Appelman, 2000). Studies completed by Koren-Karie, Oppenheim, Dolev, Sher, & Etzion-Carasso (2002) have shown that it is the insightful parent that fosters secure attachment. They describe insightfulness as a mother's ability to take the infant's point of view; insightful parents in this study were those parents who were sensitive and responded contingently to the child's needs. This insightful ability is considered a precursor to secure attachment.

Not only must the responses be in tune to the infant's needs, but also they must be regular, because the regularity of the responses the infant evokes from the caregiver enables the baby to construct a working model of how things will occur (Bowlby, 1988). Working models can be thought of as the child's internalization of those regularly occurring events from which the baby frames his expectancies about the mother, about the manner in which other people can be expected to respond to him, and how he should respond in return. And from this earliest of relationships, babies are already establishing a working model of themselves as either efficacious and worthy, or ineffective and helpless, setting the stage for how a child will approach future relationships (Weinfield, Sroufe, Egeland, & Carlson, 1999).

Working models permit the formation of internal representations of experiences and potential experiences that the individual uses to make mental predictions (Bretherton & Munholland, 1999). These predictions include, as suggested above, whether or not caregivers will respond to him, how they will respond, and how reliably. Bretherton and Munholland explain that within this working model the infant develops complementary models of himself and his parents; therefore, he internalizes and constructs a schema about how both sides of the relationship will operate under usual conditions. This working model of relationships will be extended to the schemes he forms about the world and the people in it.

Contingency, characterized as a collaborative give-and-take between mother and child in which they are mutually sharing and influencing one another, is also considered as essential in contributing to a secure attachment and sound emotional development (Siegel, 1999). A contingent response is one that immediately follows an action of the child. Brazelton and Cramer (1990) explain that contingency is about the mother's cognitive and emotional availability, particularly during the baby's alert state when the child is actively sending messages to the mother. The baby signals to the parent through smiling, verbalizing, reaching or leaning, and will respond back to the mother's overtures based on his state of attention, the nature of his needs, and his ability to self-regulate. During an attentive state, if the mother appropriately reads the response, she evokes smiling, cooing, and more eye contact with the infant, whereas non-contingent responses can result in the baby fussing, crying and looking away. Through trial and error, the mother and child learn about each other and the infant learns to expect a particular pattern of behavior that relates to his understanding of himself as an active agent. Even an adult smile in response to an infant smile provides the infant with information that he is positively influencing his environment and fosters a working model that he is efficacious. Absent responses or those that are confusing will cause the baby to develop an attachment that may be anxious or avoidant.

Contingent interactions are enhanced by interactions that are considered synchronous. Synchrony, according to Zeedyk (2006) can also be thought of as attunement, affective sharing, emotional matching, or, as she prefers to consider the harmony that is exhibited by parent-infant interaction, intimacy. While such harmonious interactions are often related to a dance, a more recent analogy is one of a jazz jam session in which the duo feeds off one another's contribution making the resulting performance harmonious and unique (Schogler, cited in Zeedyk, 2006). The mother may take the lead at first, and with questions, imitations, and reinforcement, motivate the infant to engage with her, while also providing time for the baby to become steeped in the regularity of the exchange. It isn't long before the apprentice is assuming his part of the exchange. According to Brazelton and Cramer (1990), parents initiate synchrony, an essential component in the early interactions between mothers and babies, as a way to encourage the baby to pay attention. For example, the mother mirrors her baby's rhythms, which prolongs his interest and focus on her. Both mother and child are working toward symmetry, although the parent must understand and respect the infant's thresholds and needs. A study by Reissland and Stephenson (1999) demonstrated how mothers of premature infants over-imposed their interactions due to their concern for the development of their premature infants. This understandable reaction led to a lack of synchrony that resulted in actions that were in direct opposition to what the parents desired, as the babies were less attentive in their behavior and averted their eyes more frequently than their full-term peers. The authors concluded that by over-imposing their structures on their infants, these mothers were preventing the infants from participating in the interactions. Unfortunately, this led to significantly fewer infant vocalizations. While the study did not analyze the effects this had on subsequent language development, it does reveal the importance of synchrony, sensitivity, and contingency for child development.

Zeedyk's (2006) research on imitation suggests that it is critical to the development of a relationship in that it leads to intimacy. She claims that imitation provides the closest correspondence between the infant and the mother. However, she also adds that exact mirroring is not the goal, for it is the unanticipated response that ensures attention will be maintained. The exchange begins with the mother gazing at the child and offering her full attention, providing the child with information about himself. The baby anticipates that the mother will match his response and learns to expect the unexpected, while he simultaneously learns about his mother or caregiver. This reciprocal and cyclical routine enhances the relationship, as both members of the dyad take a turn, monitor each other, and trust that the other will fulfill his or her role. It is essential that the adult imitate the infant, rather than expect the infant to imitate the adult, because receiving an imitative response from his mother provides the infant with more information about his ability to garner another's attention than does his imitation of his mother.

Auerbach and Blatt (2003) explain that a certain tension surrounds the level of response offered by the parents and the needs of the child. Apparently, there can be too much of a good thing, and the dissonance the baby feels when he has to negotiate a mismatch enables him to differentiate self from other–which sets him on the road to self-regulation. This was suggested by Winnicott (as cited in Fonagy, 2001) who explains that a chief motivator of growth is the mother's imperfection in responding to the infant's needs, and suggests that moderate involvement is preferable to "perfect matching". In other words, the anxious parent needs to have faith that the child can cope with a certain amount of frustration. Defined as interactional synchrony, Isabella and Belsky (1999) suggested that babies need to own part of an interaction in order to develop a sense of self will and autonomy. On the other hand, the authors caution that this should not occur too soon or the child's construction of his identity will suffer. The careful balance that the mother is obligated to assume would seem overwhelming if it were not the case that both partners are striving toward synchrony, both partners reinforce each other, and that the child has few needs that cannot be easily assessed by the sensitive parent.

## Becoming a Subjective Self

Zeedyk contended that imitation and intimacy leads to the development of the subjective self, which Auerbach and Blatt (2001) suggest is well established during the child's second year. Intersubjectivity has been growing since birth, and as suggested earlier, it is thought that the capability for intersubjectivity is inherent. Trevarthen (2001) emphasizes the evolutionary aspect of intersubjectivity, and claims that infants are endowed at birth with a biological system that is in tune with the rhythms of intersubjectivity. That they look for and anticipate responses from others is based on biological and neurophysiological expectations. According to Stern (1985), intersubjectivity has its roots in the earliest stages of parent-child interactions; for example, Fogel (2001) charted the interactions of a mother pulling a young infant from a supine to a sitting position, documenting that when the infant exerts more effort, the mother correspondingly uses less force. During such co-regulation the infant learns about himself when exerting more force, and learns about his mother when the mother's force dominates. Nevertheless, Auerbach and Blatt emphasize that parents must recognize the child as an individual with his own mind and will. Of special importance is the period between 2 and 6 months, described as the most social period an infant experiences, and a time which Stern claims the core self is developing. The broad smiles and vocalizations generate exaggerated responses from the parent, and typical in these verbal interactions are invariants that allow the child to detect differences between self and mother. For example, a mother watching her two-month old playing with a mobile may say, *"Cade, you like your gym, don't you. You do! You are smiling such a big smile. You are happy with your gym."* Babies detect the invariant *"you"*, hear words that are stressed, and map that onto what is occurring at the time. Repetitive games such as *"I'm going to get you"* also play into this understanding of self while the baby also learns to self-regulate from the ways that the game is structured by the parent. These conversations and games are repetitive, but vary enough so that the baby does not habituate and become bored. Because each participant in the dyad does something different from the other, occupies a unique space, and performs separate motion at different times, the sense of self and other is reinforced. Although Auerbach and Blatt suggest that mirroring leads to intersubjectivity, Stern rejected this, suggesting instead that the slight variations of each interaction is vital to the development of a sense of the core self, and asserts that exact imitation would not lead to the subjective and later the objective self. As aforementioned, Zeedyk also noted that it is the unexpected that keeps the baby interested and engaged.

Around 10–12 months, babies being to demonstrate behaviors associated with the subjective self which include pointing, social referencing and requesting items from parents. Fogel (2001) identifies two stages of the subjective self, the participatory in which they demonstrate a need to deliberately communicate what is on their minds, and the conceptual stage in which they can use words such as *I* that show they have the concept of self. Stern describes three aspects of subjectivity: joint attention, sharing intention, and sharing affective states. Joint attention is exemplified when the infant not only follows a point but also that he looks back to his mother to ensure that he has indeed arrived at the correct target. Sharing intention refers to the teasing, flirting, and requesting that can be so appealing in a nine-month old. This characteristic demonstrates that the baby is using communication intentionally and has an expectation of a particular outcome. When a baby checks with a parent to see how they should be feeling, such as looking at the mother when a stranger arrives, they are sharing affectivity or using social referencing. These examples are evidence that the baby not only knows that others have minds of their own, it also demonstrates the appreciation the infant has for being with the adult, and his desire to be in touch with the feelings and thoughts of the other (Bloom, 1993). Autistic children struggle with many of the functions of intersubjectivity described above, such as imitation or initiation of social interactions. Consequently they also struggle with subjective behaviors of social referencing or coordinated joint attention, and pointing (Fogel, 2001). Many autistic children also experience language and speech deficits, highlighting the interconnections between the development of intersubjectivity, the subjective self, and language. Language is critical in the child's development of self because it permits the child to further define himself as an individual, contributes to individuation, and draws mother and child closer through verbal dialogue (Stern, 1985).

## Linking Relationships to Language Acquisition

Like two pieces of a puzzle that fit together, both members of the dyad have certain predispositions that are the building blocks for developing an intimate relationship. All of the practices the mother or caregiver has used to cement a relationship with her baby have also laid down the foundation for the most human of all qualities, the ability to talk and carry on a conversation with others.

Bowlby's theory of attachment highlights the important role that language assumes at the beginning of the infant's experiences, claiming that the working model is "rooted in and organized around the mental representation of early infant-caregiver communication" (Appelman, 2000, p. 193). This reiterates the common early bonds that attachment and language share. In writing about the developing mind, Siegel (1999) claims that secure attachments include both parties sharing verbal and nonverbal communication. When it is collaborative, largely because of the parent's sensitivity and contingency in responses, the baby will more likely experience secure attachment. Siegel suggests that reflection on mental states of self and others emerges from the attachment and that these patterns of communication "literally shape the structure of the child's developing brain" (p. 21). Early reciprocal communication, the root of the attachment relationship, shapes the brain's capacity for regulating emotions, feeling connected to others, and constructing an autobiographical story. The caregiver's role, according to Appelman (1999) is to use language as a way to interpret the child's feelings, and should link internal feelings with the external world, thus enabling the infant to organize experiences.

The theory that language was a necessary component of social development was advanced by Vygotsky. In Williams' (1985) analysis of his theory, she explains that because a child does not have the resources to perform higher cognitive functioning, he must rely on the adults around him to provide the cognitive structures. In essence, Vygotsky claims that only through sustained social interactions can the child create hypotheses about the nature of the world. Unlike Piaget's theory, in which cognitive structures are awaiting social interactions for them to be formed, Vygotsky proposed that cognitive structures are formed because of social interactions. Rather than hidden structures becoming public, he hypothesized that it occurs the opposite way—they have a social origin and then they become private. When the adult reads the child's nonverbal experience correctly and uses referential language to describe it to the child, she transforms the infant's nonverbal experience into a verbal experience, mimicking the ways that sophisticated language users transform nonverbal experiences into verbal expressions of them (Appelman, 1999). A classic example used by Vygotsky depicts this transformation. Pointing develops as a child reaches for a desired object that is out of his reach. The adult interprets this as pointing and attaches language to the experience by naming the point as "light." The infant learns that such a gesture can direct others, and that this point of interest has a name. What has begun as a natural, external activity on the part of the child has become transformed by the adults surrounding the child, provided that the adult is operating within the child's zone of proximal development (Vygotsky, 1978).

Despite the responsibility that the caregiver assumes in translating a baby's internal experiences into external verbal messages, early communication is not as one sided as it may appear at first glance. The infant is predisposed to read nonverbal signals quite well. At birth, the right hemisphere of the brain is more fully developed than the left side of the brain and therefore dominates during the first year. Because the right hemisphere is more related to emotional development and the left side to language, it follows that initially the infant can read emotional cues more easily than verbal clues and is more intuitive. For example, an infant can read his mother's mood and imitate it, demonstrating not only the ability to communicate but also to differentiate between emotions (Eliot, 1999). When language does arrive, the couple can begin to relate verbally, which of course will significantly increase the linking of thoughts and feelings. Nevertheless, this linkage builds on the connections previously established through non-verbal interactions (Bowlby, 1988).

The year before the infant actually speaks a word, he has been busy listening to the people around him, and those sounds have produced efficient neural pathways so that he begins to detect the similarities present in his own language. Speech, according to Eliot (1999) is a powerful stimulator, activating social, emotional, cognitive, hearing, and linguistic centers of the brain simultaneously. She claims that babies are born to listen, and can hear select sounds much better than adults. So, as he is immersed in a stream of sounds and words, the baby begins to become more selective in what he hears, and his babbling begins to contain more of the sounds needed in his own community and fewer of those that are unnecessary. Eliot explains that as human society evolved, individuals benefited from having the protection of the social group, and communication was essential for belonging to the group and receiving that protection. Therefore, language evolved so that it is intimately dependent on the precise linguistic environment into which the child is born. Only those sounds and forms of language to which the brain has been exposed will begin to be hardwired onto it. Other sounds and forms of language, even though they were once within the child's capabilities, will not become part of the child's repertoire.

## Entering the Verbal Stage

Although the infant apprentice has a long way to go before he can be considered a journeyman, think of how far he has come in one year. He has communicated thoughts and feelings to his caregivers by gestures, facial expressions and prelinguistic babble. By the end of the first year, his babbling has begun to sound like speech, and may contain sounds that resemble words. Gestures have progressed from a spontaneous display of interest to an intentional way to communicate his wants and needs. He reads his parents and caregivers reasonably well and intuits their moods and dispositions. He has the fundamental principles of a conversation ingrained in his interactions, and he has the capacity to organize his experiences in a rudimentary way. He appreciates the unique sounds of his own language, and while he once could replicate all human sounds, he now selectively reproduces only those of his own culture. Additionally, certain physical changes have occurred so that he will be able to produce the first word. The oral cavity and vocal tract have widened and lengthened, permitting him to take in more air and push it out for language use (Fogel, 2001). He is physically ready to talk, has things to talk about, and people to talk to.

Is the child who is securely attached also going to be the one who utters the earliest word and is more successful with literacy? Sensitivity is important for a secure attachment and for language learning, while intrusiveness is a risk factor of insecure attachment (Fish, Jacquet, & Hadassah, 2002). Both attachment and language, as has been suggested, are vital to the infant's survival and his acceptance into his culture. Consequently, similar strategies work on both aspects of development because at the onset, they are not separate. However, as development continues, language development begins to benefit from additional strategies that are more pertinent to this higher mental function.

Contingency has been explained as necessary in attachment and is an immediate response to a child's needs. Temporal contingency in language acquisition theory is defined as an adult response that follows within seconds after the dyad engages in a coordinated gaze (Bloom, Margulis, Tinker, & Fujita, 1996). The literature also defines topic contingency as a parent response to the infant's vocalizations while he is focusing on a particular point of interest. Contingency in language development, as in attachment, requires an attuned and sensitive parent, aware of what the baby finds interesting and knowledgeable about his vocalizations and gestures.

Coordinated eye gaze is the basis for joint attentional focus. Slaughter and McConnell (2003) found that an infant's ability to follow the gaze of the parent positively influenced his later ability to learn names for specific objects for infants 8–14 months old. However it is most effective in language acquisition if the mother shifts her attention to that of the child rather than the other way around. When the adult attaches language to the child's point of interest, it is thought to enhance language development because it reduces mapping errors for the child (Marcus, Mundy, Morales, Delgaldo, & Yale, 2000) and provides clear pragmatic cues for word learning (Tamis-LeMonda, Bornstein, & Baumwell, 2001). Like imitation, allowing the infant to be the agent and following his agenda is beneficial to his development of self and language acquisition.

Joint attention according to Carpendale and Lewis allows an "epistemic triangle" to form, defined as the active child, the knowledgeable adult, and an object of knowledge. Through the adult's mediation, the child is led to higher and more complete understandings of objects of knowledge, contexts, and social understandings. It is from the interactions of this epistemic triangle that language and all else follows, according to Ross' (2006) interpretation of Carpendale and Lewis.

Not surprisingly, Marcus, et al. (2000) found joint attention to be associated with larger vocabularies in those children whose mothers employed it. As suggested above, the adult needs to be sensitive to the amount of stimulation a child requires, while maintaining a focus and providing structure to the interactions. The adult who makes joint episodes interesting and elaborative will increase the infant's ability to benefit from them. Joint attentional focus is not only focusing on the same referent point, it is also awareness that the partner shares that focus, ensured through attempts to direct the other's attention. The research by Markus, et al., leaves no doubt about the relationship between joint attentional focus and language development. It is associated with how children become proficient in their attempts to learn new words. On the infant's part, those who are successful in following their mothers' gazes are able to engage in relatively complex social-communicative interactions by the end of their first year (Slaughter & McConnell, 2003).

One way that parents successfully manage appropriate coordination is to develop frames in which joint focus is a natural outcome. Frames are often used during routine transactions that bring the mother and baby close together, using familiar recurring scripts while they ensue. This allows the parent to emphasize features of the child's life to which she can attach language, such as the feeding and changing. During these settings, the sensitive parent notices what interests the child and then uses language to maintain and continue the coordinated focus until the child indicates he is no longer interested. She will use animated speech and motions to increase the baby's attention, enabling him not only to learn language more easily, but also the mental perspectives of others (Morales, Mundy & Rojas, 1998). In contrast, when the parent continually expects the child to shift his focus to meet her point of interest, she interferes with mapping opportunities and is negatively influencing word learning (Dunham, Dunham & Curwin, 1993). By nine or ten months, infants can initiate or continue the coordination by banging and grinning at the parent, demonstrating that they see the connections between the adult, the object and their own actions (Fogel, 2001).

Motherese, or child-directed speech (CDS), has also been related to language learning. Trevarthen (2003) has summarized various studies that show infants have a preference for friendly or singing voices and appreciate natural melodies. Therefore, when mothers use the higher pitch associated with child-directed speech, they are matching, however unknowingly, the very tone preferred by infants. In almost all cultures including sign languages, mothers and other adults habitually use a slower tempo, more exaggeration, more repetition, and more simplicity when talking to infants. Nelson (2007) describes child-directed speech as a particular register of the language used by adults in which prosody is exaggerated, sentences are short, and words are simple and repetitive. Fernald (cited in

Nelson, 2007) claims that the use of exaggeration aids in the child's ability to parse words and phrases. Similarly, Gogate, Babrick, & Watson (2000), contend that it elicits and sustains the infant's interest in language while highlighting through exaggeration and repetition, the most important parts of speech. Child-directed speech helps to objectify the child's thinking; initially attached to the baby's activities or attentions, it slowly shifts to references that do not involve the child. It offers a backdrop to the infant's interactions with others, becoming a significant part of the infant's experiential history (Nelson, 2007).

The apprenticeship that started at birth has been fostered through the prototype of a conversation. As Snow (1977) demonstrated, even newborns are immersed in the routines of conversation. When the mother jiggles the nipple to get the child to feed, she is expressing her nonverbal desire to her baby. As the baby responds, he is receptive to her requests. He also takes a turn by stopping his sucking and waits expectantly for another response. This is the beginning of the give-and-take associated with conversation that is repeated in many other forms as the baby progresses to verbal conversations. Most mothers take the child's turn in conversations, either by asking questions and answering them, using facial expressions that indicate they are waiting and expecting the child to take a turn, or by attaching language as is fitting for the circumstance. A salient point that Snow makes is that the mother continually acts as if the child were a willing and competent participant in the conversation, and expects that he will take up his part as soon as he is physically ready. As suggested earlier, this mindset on the parent's part plays into the child's developing intersubjectivity. Conversations allow parents and caregivers to fine tune their understanding of the child's abilities and proceed in a sensitive and appropriate way to help the child progress (Bruner, 1983). Although they continually raise the acceptable standards to ensure success, what most mothers want at this point is to foster relationships with their infants. Conversations are the tools to do so (Snow, 1977), and parents will use all available strategies to enable the conversation to continue and satisfy their need for engaging interactions and sharing meanings with their children. Bruner suggested that during conversations, mothers appear to be remarkably sensitive to the child's abilities and needs, and when appropriate, they remove unnecessary support and allow the baby to assume the skill they were previously providing.

Careful attention to the nature of the discourse directed to the child can make a difference in language growth. For example, longer maternal utterances are beneficial for the language apprentice because they are more complex, have a variety of words, and offer more variance in syntax, all positively related to language growth. On the other hand, the use of prohibitions and directives has been shown to inhibit a child's vocabulary (Dodici, Draper, & Peterson, 2003). Directives and prohibitions are not meant to engage the child, and consequently overuse of these language forms stifles language and the occasional use does not enhance it. Furthermore, the simplicity of directives and prohibitions cannot offer the apprentice a model of varying syntax and words. Parents and caregivers can use other strategies to enhance language growth. For example, when parents elaborate on the words offered by the child, either by extending or expanding them, the parent is offering more opportunities to hear varying syntax and word usage. Labeling is also helpful for the young child, as well as particular kinds of questions, such as *wh* questions (Girolametto & Weitzman, 2002). The literature on language acquisition invariably stresses the need to follow the child's agenda in language learning, noting the child's interest and gaze, and letting him lead playful exchanges.

It appears that sheer volume of input is helpful in learning language. According to researchers (Monastersky, 2001), babies use what is considered a subconscious form of statistics that enable them to record the number of times they hear a sound. This helps to explain how babies learn to segment sounds and decode words. The example provided by Monastersky is particularly good at describing this phenomenon. He explains that upon hearing "funny puppy" infants will segment the "ny" with "fun" rather than with pup, having never heard "ny-pup" previously as a discrete sound. Additionally, it appears that infants can detect minute differences in speech that occur at ends of words. A language environment that is filled with opportunities to detect similarities and differences will move the infant along to becoming a competent language user. High frequency words in a toddler's vocabulary may be related to parent use, the ubiquity of the words in the child's environment, or their utility or interest value (Rescorla, Alley, & Christine, 2001). Obviously, high frequency words must be used contextually.

For the above strategies to work, the infant must be able to pay attention and participate in the mother's prompting. Research by Bloom et al. (1996) suggests that the infant is far more implicated in the process than most approaches to language learning assume. Rather than the parent providing the impetus for language learning, this position holds that it is the child's inner resources that determine the language learning and the conversational exchanges rather than the intent of the parent. The premise is advanced by the claim that mothers are more likely to respond to than initiate an exchange with their infants. The child speaks about what he already knows and the adult follows the initiation, indicating to the child that she has understood and shares his meaning. Trevarthen (2003) also noted infants' affinity for conversing with others, and found that this desire included siblings and peers. Perhaps as vital as being sensitive to the infant's needs and interest, parents and caregivers need to recognize that the infant's drive to be an active participant in relationships is vital to his emotional and cognitive development.

# Conclusion

When Bowlby wrote about the benefit of speech to attachment, he aptly described the emergence of speech as the "powerful and extraordinary gift of language" (Bowlby, 1982, p. 354). Considering the infant's innate qualities and the proclivity of adults to provide custom-designed stimulation to suit the child's particular needs, the incredible acquisition of language does indeed seem to be a gift. Fowler (1995) suggests two points regarding putting this gift to its best use. First, he suggests that many infants say words long before adults realize it, making it important that parents do not underestimate the developing capabilities of the child and that they be very attentive to the sounds being produced before the first birthday, for within those sounds might be the child's first words. Secondly, he also relates that with fastidious attention, adults can do quite a bit to enhance language development, and this will have major implications for future intellectual development. For the busy parent or caregiver, perhaps it is more important to value the gift of a strong and solid relationship with the infant. Its affect can be very far reaching, not only providing the basis of a sense of self, the sensitivity to enhance language, and the opportunity to foster a secure attachment, but also establishing a positive approach to the world and to people, an approach that lasts a life time.

# References

Appelman, E. (2000). Attachment experiences transformed into language. *American Journal of Orthopsychiatry 70*(2), 192–202.

Astington, J. W. (2004). What's new about social construction? Distinct roles needed for language and communication. *Behavioral and Brain Sciences, 2*(1), 96–98.

Auerbach, J. S., & Blatt, S. J. (2003). Self-reflexivity, intersubjectivity, and therapeutic change. *Psychoanalytic Psychology, 18*(3), 427–450.

Bloom, L. (1993). The *transition from infancy to language: Acquiring the power of expression.* New York: Cambridge University Press.

Bloom, L., Margulis, C., Tinker, E., & Fujita, N. (1996). Early conversations and word learning: Contributions from child and adult. *Child Development, 67,* 3154–3175.

Brazelton, T. B., & Cramer, B. G. (1990). The *earliest relationship: Parents, infants, and the drama of early attachments.* Reading, MA: Addison-Wesley.

Bretherton, I., & Munholland, K. A. (1999). Internal working models in attachment relationships: A construct revisited. In J. Cassidy and P. R. Shaver (Eds.), *Handbook of attachment: Theory, research, and clinical applications.* (pp. 89–11). New York: Guildford Press.

Bruner, J. (1983). *Child's talk: Learning to use language.* New York: Norton.

Bowlby, J. (1969/1982). *Attachment and loss: Vol. 1. Attachment.* New York: Basic Books.

Bowlby, J. (1988). *A secure base: Parent-child attachment and healthy human development.* New York: Basic Books.

Carpendale, J. I. M., & Lewis, C. (2004). Constructing an understanding of mind: The development of children's social understanding within social interaction. *Behavioral and Brain Sciences, 27,* 79–151.

Cassidy, J. (1999). The nature of the child's ties. In J. Cassidy and P. R. Shaver, (Eds.), *Handbook of attachment: Theory, research, and clinical application,* pp. 3–20. New York: Guildford Press.

Chamblin, C. (January 25, 2007). Infant feeding cues during the early days of life. Retrieved February 15, 2007 from http://www.breastbabyproducts.com/firstdays.html

Dodici, B. J., Draper, D. C., & Peterson, C. A. (2003). Early parent-child interactions and early literacy development. *Topics in Early Childhood Special Education.73*(3), 124–136.

Dunham, P. J., Dunham, F., & Curwin, A. (1993). Joint-attentional states and lexical acquisition at 18 months. *Developmental Psychology, 29*(5), 827–831.

Eliot, L. (2000). What's *going on in there? How the brain and mind develop in the first five years of life.* New York: Bantam Books.

Fish, M., Jacquet, E., & Frye, H. (2002). Early development of low-income rural Appalachian children. *Rural Health Monograph, 2*(1).

Fogel, A. (2001). Infancy: *Infant, family, and society, (4th ed.).* Belmont, CA: Wadsworth.

Fonagy, P. (2001). *Attachment theory and psychoanalysis*. New York: Other Press.

Fowler, W. (1995). Language interaction techniques for stimulating the development of at risk children in infants and preschool day care. *Early Child Development and Care, 135*, 41–77

Girolametto, L., & Weitzman, E. (2002). Responsiveness of child care workers in interactions with toddlers and preschoolers. *Language, Speech and Hearing Services in Schools, 33*, 268–281.

Gogate, L. J., Babrick, L. E., & Watson, J. D. (2000). A study of multimodal motherese: The role of temporal synchrony between verbal labels and gestures. *Child Development, 71*, 878–894.

Koren-Karie, N., Oppenheim, D., Dolev, S., Sher, E., & Etzion-Carasso, A. (2002). Mothers' insightfulness regarding their infants' internal experience: Relations with maternal sensitivity and infant attachment. *Developmental Psychology, 38*(4), 534–542.

Marcus, J., Mundy, P., Morales, M., Delgaldo, C. E. F., & Yale, M. (2000). Individual differences in infant skills as predictors of child-caregiver joint attention and language. *Social Development, 9*(3), 302–315.

Marvin, R. S., & Britner, P. A. (1999). Normative development. In J. Cassidy and P. R. Shaver (Eds.), *Handbook of attachment: Theory, research and clinical applications*. (pp. 44–67). New York: Guilford Press.

Monastersky, R. (2001). Look who's listening. *Chronicle of Higher Education, 47*(3), 14–17.

Morales, M., Mundy, P., & Rojas, J. (1998). Following the direction of gaze and language development in 6-month-olds. *Infant Behavior and Development, 21*(2), 373–377.

Nelson, K. (2007). *Young minds in social worlds: Experience, meaning, and memory*. Cambridge, MA: Harvard University Press.

Reissland, N., & Stephenson, T. (1999). Turn-taking in early vocal interactions: A comparison of premature and term infants' vocal interaction with their mothers. *Child: Care, Health, and Development, 25*(6), 447–456.

Rescorla, L., Alley, A., & Christine, J. B. (2001). Word frequencies in toddlers' lexicons. *Journal of Speech. Language, and Hearing Research, 44*(3), 598–609.

Ross, H. (2006). Theory of mind goes social: Essay review of *How children develop social understanding by Jeremy Carpendale and Charlie Lewis. Human Development, 49*, 375–379.

Selby, J. M., & Bradley, B. S. (2003). Infants in social groups: A paradigm for the study of early social experience. *Human Development, 46*, 197–221.

Siegel, D. J. (1999). *The developing mind: How relationships and the brain interact to shape who we are*. New York: Guilford Press.

Simpson, J. A. (1999). Attachment theory in modern evolutionary perspective. In J. Cassidy and P. R. Shaver (Eds.), *Handbook of attachment: Theory, research, and clinical applications*. (pp. 115–140). New York: Guilford Press.

Slaughter, V., & McConnell, D. (2003). Emergence of joint attention: Relationships between gaze following, social referencing, imitation, and naming in infancy. *Journal of Genetic Psychology, 164*(1), 54–72.

Snow, C. E. (1977). The development of conversation between mothers and babies. *Journal of Child Language, 4*, 1–22.

Stern, D. N. (1985). *The interpersonal world of the infant: A view from psychoanalysis and developmental psychology*. New York: Basic Books.

Tamis-LeMonda, C. S., Bornstein, M. H., Baumwell, L. (2001). Maternal responsiveness and children's achievement of language milestones. *Child Development, 72*(3), 746–767.

Trevarthen, C. (2001). Intrinsic motives for companionship in understanding: Their origin, development and significance for infant mental health. *Infant Mental Health Journal, 22*, 95–131.

Trevarthen, C. (2003). Infant psychology is an evolving culture. *Human Development, 46*(4), 233–246.

Weinfield, N. S., Sroufe, L. A., Egeland, B. & Carlson, E. A. (1999). The nature of individual differences in infant-caregiver attachment. In J. Cassidy and P. R.

Shaver (Eds.), *Handbook of attachment: Theory, research, and clinical applications* (pp.68–88). New York: Guilford Press.

Vygotsky, L. (1978). Mind *in society*. Cambridge, MA: Harvard University Press.

Zebrowitz, L. A., & Montepare, J. M. (1992). Impressions of babyfaced individuals across the lifespan. *Developmental Psychology, 28,* 1143–1152.

Zeedyk, M. S. (2006). From intersubjectivity to subjectivity: The transformative roles of emotional intimacy and imitation. *Infant and Child Development, 15,* 321–344.

**Marilyn Roseman**
School–Mount Aloysius College
7373 Admiral Peary Highway
Cresson, PA 16630
Home Address—384 Park Hill Drive
Johnstown, PA 15909

Marilyn Roseman is the chairperson for the Education and Sign Language/ Interpreter Education Department at Mount Aloysius College and is an Associate Professor in Early Childhood Education. She received her doctoral degree from Indiana University of Pennsylvania in Elementary Education and her research interests include development during infancy and early childhood, especially the development of language in infants and toddlers.

# Part Two
# Family Ties

# Chapter 4
# Challenging the Stereotypes of Mexican American Fathers

**Olivia N. Saracho and Bernard Spodek**

**Abstract** This critical review presents studies of Mexican American fathers in the United Sates to provide researchers with an understanding of contemporary fatherhood. It describes the myths that caused methodological and conceptual problems in interpreting the results of studies on Mexican American fathers. Several common challenges and limitations in those studies are identified and discussed, such as conflicting cultural perceptions, traditional and contemporary perceptions, and social stereotyping of the Mexican American fathers' family roles. This review also provides guidelines for future research and practical applications for Mexican American fathers' involvement in their children's education. In doing this, it contributes to an emerging understanding of the complexity of Mexican American fathering.

**Keywords** parents, parent involvement, fathers, fatherhood, Mexican American fathers, Hispanic, social stereotypes, interviews, qualitative research

> We need to be conscious of our responsibility to our children. I generally believe that we are the basis of society, and if we, as fathers of young children, don't instill the best habits that we can, in general, then we will see the decline of children, family, community, and our country. If we want Mexico [or the U.S.] to be great, we have to start with our children. (father in the study by Taylor & Behnke, 2005, p. 116)

## Mexican American Fathers

The Mexican American population is the largest and most rapidly developing ethnic group in the United States today (U. S. Bureau of the Census, 2001). It is estimated that by 2050, the Hispanic population will be more than 30% of the United States

---

University of Maryland

University of Illinois

M.R. Jalongo (ed.), *Enduring Bonds*.
© Springer 2008

population. The United States has a heterogeneous Hispanic population of over 35 million (Pinal & Singer, 1997; Zinn & Wells, 2000); approximately two-thirds of this group is of Mexican descent, a population which includes two-parent, working-poor families with distinctive needs, and families with limited cultural resources (Coltrane, Park & Adams, 2004). Mexican Americans have a distinctive cultural heritage and a unique pattern of immigration (Parke, Coltrane, Borthwick-Duffy, Powers, Adams, Fabricius, Brever & Saenz, 2004).

Researchers have developed an interest in Mexican American fathers because of their increasing numbers, their economic marginality, and their disproportionate exposure to various risk factors, including school dropout, crime victimization, and teenage pregnancy. However, Mexican American families have traditionally dis-played strengths, such as positive approaches to child rearing and enduring primary and extended family bonds (Coltrane, et al., 2004). For example, Mexican American children cooperate more than European American children (Knight & Kagan, 1977; Rotherman-Borus & Phinney, 1990), are provided with interdependence in their socialization patterns, practice family rituals (Delgado-Gaitan, 1994), show respect and honor toward parents and other elders, and maintain family cohesion as a cen-tral value (Coltrane, et al., 2004).

Mexican American fathers are of specific interest to researchers because of their longstanding focus on child rearing practices and extended family bonds. In assessing father involvement in Mexican American families, it is important to consider the children's direct care, shared activities, monitoring, housework, and other sustained efforts on behalf of children. For Mexican American fathers, it is critical that researchers understand more fully the norms, expectations, and beliefs that govern father involvement and the types of father-child activities that are considered culturally appropriate. Researchers with different expectations across ethnic groups may develop erroneous measurements and fallacies which interfere with their results. To guard against such assumptions and errors, meth-odological and conceptual challenges need to be considered in gaining the Mexican American fathers' perspectives on the other family members and their contribution and the general expectations of what constitutes good fathering (Parke, et al., 2004).

Researchers have joined forces to reconstruct a view of fatherhood, especially with respect to Mexican American fathers. There have been many attempts to resolve the issues that are raised in researching Mexican American fathers. The purpose of this paper is to review studies on the roles of Mexican American fathers in the United Sates, to provide researchers with an understanding of contemporary fatherhood for this population. It describes the myths that have created methodo-logical and conceptual problems in conducting research studies that characterize Mexican American fathers. Several common stereotypes that researchers have used in their studies are presented and discussed. In addition, the challenges and limita-tions of studies are identified, including conflicting cultural perceptions, traditional and contemporary perceptions, and social stereotyping of the Mexican American fathers' roles.

## Research Challenges and Debates

All approaches to research have challenges and limitations (Christie, Ross, & Klein, 2004). Researchers have contended that studies on the fathers' roles have often been taken for granted, held negative connotations, or had been inadequately conceptualized. This reconstruction has changed the way researchers have conceptualized, collected, and measured data on fathers. Studies of father involvement have increased over the past three decades (Cabrera, Ryan, Shannon, Brooks-Gunn, Vogel, Rakies, & Tamis-LeMonda, 2004; Lamb, 2004, Tamis-LeMonda, Shannon, Cabrera, & Lamb, 2004). Initial research in this area compared the absence or presence of fathers, their financial contributions, and time they spent with their children. Researchers considered the outcomes of fatherhood studies and the methodological and conceptual problems in these studies. The traditional perception that fathers' contributions did not affect the children's development or learning has been challenged. New research studies have been formulated to accurately conceptualize and measure father involvement and to assess the consequences of the fathers' involvement in their children's well being and development. The results in these studies indicated challenges and limitations in conducting research with Mexican American fathers, including the following:

- *Incompatible cultural perceptions.* Studies on Mexican American fathers have too often used the Euro-American family as a guide to measure the Mexican American fathers' behavior.
- *Contemporary vs. traditional perceptions.* Studies were based on traditional rather than contemporary views of Mexican American fathers; the researchers used old descriptions instead of the current ones of the Mexican American fathers.
- *Social stereotyping of the Mexican American fathers' roles.* Studies have used the traditional views of men, often providing a distorted portrait of Mexican American fathers.
- *Consensus use of the expression Mexican Americans.* Researchers have combined studies of Spanish speaking fathers, studying them as if they were all the same, and generalizing to the entire Hispanic population.

According to La Rossa (1997), the concept of fathers as their children's competent caretakers and socializing agents has been altered twice during the 20th century. The current concept that fathers are "involved and nurturant," surfaced during the 1930's and early 1940's. During this era, several socio-historical factors emerged, including similarities in birth rates, mothers' participation in the labor force, and increase advocacy of egalitarianism. Mexican American fathers have modified their family roles within their changing society, but researchers continue to stereotype them and provide negative descriptions. These issues are further discussed in the following sections.

## *Incompatible Cultural Perceptions*

Research on Mexican American fathers is generally based on the researcher's frame of reference. Most researchers have depended on an Anglo American perception and used the Euro-American family as a frame of reference. These studies have overlooked the Mexican American fathers' language, culture, beliefs, and level of acculturation. Modern researchers needed to consider the Mexican American fathers unique cultural characteristics (See Table 1.).

Contemporary researchers have challenged the traditional perception of the Mexican American family as patriarchal and authoritarian. Traditionally, researchers disregarded father-child interactions and fathers' contributions in a family environment. Studies of roles within the family have either examined the mothers' roles or the process of the married couple's decision-making, disregarding the Mexican American fathers' roles. Researchers assumed that the fathers' involvement did not contribute to their children's cognitive development. They generally focused on mother-child interactions, family systems, or on the family process in general without

**Table 1** Description of Mexican American Fathers by Contemporary and Traditional Researchers

| Contemporary Research | Traditional Research |
| --- | --- |
| Redefine *machismo* and acknowledge its positive elements in understandings of Mexican American culture (Ramirez, 1979). | *Machismo* is a stereotyped term with negative characteristics that has become synonymous with Mexican American males and with male chauvinism (Ramírez, 1979). |
| *Machismo's* new definition provides positive cultural qualities such as respect, honesty, loyalty, fairness, responsibility, trustworthiness (Coltrane, et al., 2004), egalitarian, warm, caring (Mirandé, 1991, 1997), "true bravery or valor, courage, generosity, stoicism, heroism, and ferocity" (Mirandé, 1997, pp. 78–79). | *Machismo* refers to the Mexican American men's role with negative associations, including "exaggerated masculinity, physical prowess, and male chauvinism" (Baca-Zinn, 1994, p. 74). |
| Roles related to *machismo* have been replaced with more ground-breaking and progressive roles including loving husband, the committed father, and the family man (Coltrane, 2001; Gutmann, 2003; Mirandé, 1997). | Mexican American fathers possessed characteristics such as "fighting roosters," "macho," "borracho" (drunk), and "buen gallo" (good fighter) (Madsen, 1973; Rubel, 1966). |
| *Machismo* in fathers has been related to being a family provider (Taylor & Behnke, 2005). | The macho (i.e., male) is considered to be the "lord and master" of the household. |
| Mexican American fathers spend time at home. They spend most of their non-working hours and their days off at home or in recreational pursuits with their families (Bronstein, 1984). | Mexican American fathers have been considered to be dominant, withdrawn, aggressive, and tyrannical rulers of the household (Mirandé, 1991, Mayo, 1997, Powell, 1995). |
| When Mexican American fathers are with their children, they are genuinely involved with them, in friendly, nonauthoritarian interactions (Bronstein, 1984). | A *macho* gets into fights or abuses drugs and alcohol. A *macho* is a drunkard, a troublemaker, or fails to assume responsibility for his family. |

acknowledging the roles of fathers. Studies of families only reported the absence or presence of fathers in the family environment. Fathers who were considered family members were reported to be too busy to participate in their children's learning. For example, Blankenhorn (1995) described how fathers were absent from family life because of changes in family structures (e.g., high divorce rates, high numbers of out-of-wedlock births, neglect). Fathers who were considered family members were reported to be too busy to participate in their children's learning.

Researchers took fathers' contributions for granted, attributing negative connotations, or conceptualizing them inappropriately. Research problems emerge when the roles of the fathers were ignored in family studies (Marks and Palkovitz, 2004). The design of many of these studies had methodological and practical challenges that created gaps in the researchers' understanding of the nature and meaning of fathering in economically challenged and ethnically diverse groups (Cabrera, et al., 2004). In addition, the results of these studies can be methodologically and conceptually disputed concerning the way fatherhood was examined in diverse settings (Coltrane, et al., 2004), especially in Mexican American families which represent 60% of the Hispanic population (Parke, et al., 2004).

Modern society has influenced the fathers' transformation of their family roles to include those of nurturing caregivers and active teachers (Lamb, 2004). Researchers need to be aware of the Mexican American fathers' contemporary roles. Traditional researchers have theorized that Mexican American families would modify their roles through an acculturation or assimilation process as families shifted from a traditional structure to the more egalitarian structure found in American families (Ortiz, 1995). Although Mexican American fathers have assumed contemporary roles and many contemporary researchers are reexamining the fathers' roles, some researchers continue to base their studies on the traditional perspective that Mexican American fathers are cold and distant.

Lately, researchers have distinguished between traditional and contemporary perspectives of Mexican American fathers. Traditionally, Mexican American fathers were characterized as cold, distant, and authoritarian while the traditional Mexican American family was described as an authoritarian and patriarchal body with women portrayed as quiet, submissive, and subservient in the home. On the other hand, the macho (i.e., male) was considered to be the lord and master of the household. Traditional researchers (e.g., Madsen, 1973; Rubel, 1966) attributed characteristics to Mexican American fathers such as "fighting roosters," "macho," "borracho" (drunk), and "buen gallo" (good fighter). The role of the fathers was misunderstood with the attitude that Mexican American fathers are dominant, withdrawn, aggressive, and tyrannical rulers of the household (Mirandé, 1991, Mayo, 1997, Powell, 1995).

## Gender Roles

This neglect has caused a lack of knowledge about the role of fathers in the family, the relationship between fathers and children, and the shifting perceptions of masculinity. In addition, this oversight provided little information about the way Mexican American men responded to transformations in the conventional gender roles and perceptions of masculinity. In examining the impact of cultural values in relation to gender roles on the fathers' role identity, Taylor and Behnke (2005) found that Mexican American fathers assumed two gender roles within their families' lives: *gender essentialism* and *gender progressive* attitudes. *Gender essentialism* attitudes are when both males and females performed their exclusive roles, such as in the traditional Mexican American father role as head of the household. For example, the essential character of their conventional gender role is provided in the following statements:

> *I think that the father's role is very important. I'm not saying it's more important than the mother's, but because of my experience, if the father is absent, a void is felt. Although sometimes the mother fills the role of father, it's not the same.* (p. 107)

> *the mother is the complement [but not a replacement] to what one does as a [father].* (p. 107).

These statements support the importance of the fathers in their children's lives. On the other hand, *gender progressive* attitudes are acknowledged when both fathers and mothers perform the same domestic and occupational labors. For example, the fundamental disposition of their traditional gender role is portrayed in the following statements:

> *Well, when the father and mother are mutual about things, it's easier to raise a family. It should also be a role of collaboration and guidance, not only of provider.* (p. 107)

Researchers (e.g., Daly, 1995, Taylor & Behnke, 2005) found that in the United States most fathers had *gender progressive* attitudes. In Daly's (1995) study, the majority of the Mexican American men maintained a *gender progressive* ideology. Both fathers and mothers were believed to be equal and established the same goals for both their sons and daughters. Apparently, in the United States contemporary North American social values have reshaped those social values of the Mexican American fathers, including those from both rural and urban areas. The fathers' roles and behaviors were the same regardless of their children's gender. Taylor and Behnke (2005) investigated the difference in the fathers' expectations between their sons and daughters. They found that sex differences were not important to the fathers. Fathers treated both their sons and daughters the same, but they differed in their relationships with their children based on the age of their children. Fathers had a closer relationship with their younger children than with their older children. In addition, both fathers and mothers had the same roles as parents. Luzod and Arce (1979) assessed these roles using three parenting scales and showed no significant sex differences. Their results disputed the long-established conviction of the Mexican American family and proposed a more egalitarian concept of the Mexican American father and mother roles. Luzod and Arce (1979) concluded that fathers of Mexican ancestry have a much more important role in the family than has been generally believed. They affirmed that "…it therefore appears erroneous to focus only on maternal influence in the Chicano family since Chicano fathers are seen as being important to their children, and moreover, may provide significant positive influences on the development of their children" (p. 19).

*Fathers' vs. Mothers' Roles.* Further studies support the contemporary view of the Mexican American father. Bronstein (1984) found that Mexican fathers were more playful and sociable with their children, and engaged in playful, companionable interaction with their children more than mothers. Bronstein (1984) arrived at the conclusion that Mexican fathers

> ... *played a distinct and salient role of their own, different from mothers, and very different from the traditional view of the aloof Mexican patriarch. Although there is no measure of the hours per day each father in the present sample spent at home, most did seem to spend most of their non-working hours and their days off there or in recreational pursuits with their families. Furthermore, when they were with their children, many of the fathers seemed genuinely involved with them, in friendly, nonauthoritarian interaction* (p. 1800).

Rubel's (1966) study supported these results. He observed how young Mexican American men from "across the tracks" in a Texas city were believed to be distant and aloof, particularly by other young men. He found these fathers to be very warm and affectionate with both their young sons and daughters, who were less than ten years of age. Sometimes the fathers were observed to be gentler with their children than were the mothers.

Researchers need to understand and accept the Mexican American families' current realities instead of continuing to rely on traditional inappropriate stereotypes. Mirandé (1997) interviewed Mexican American fathers who were living at home. The Mexican American fathers in his study were a diverse sample who had children whose ages ranged between four and eighteen, lived in four geographic areas, and represented a wide cross-section of Mexican American fathers (e.g., middle class, foreign-born, native-born men). His results challenged the preponderant views on Mexican American men, masculinity, and gender, which ignored their well-defined cultural beliefs. Zapata and Jaramillo (1981) also disputed the predominant literature that describes families to be strictly limited in reference to gender. Their study of Mexican American families from a large Southwestern city challenged the concepts that (a) Mexican American fathers are dominant and distant, (b) mothers are passive and dependent, or (c) children are socialized into rigid gender roles. They found that children perceived females to be somehow "socially more cooperative" and their relationships within the family were sex-biased. On the other hand, both fathers and mothers made choices regardless of the family member's gender. Children were able to clearly distinguish between their sibling roles and alliances, although "neither parents nor children identify either parent to have the responsibility for managing" the household.

*Employment Circumstances.* Mexican American fathers are frequently employed in high-risk industries (e.g., meat-packing plants, construction, and agriculture), performing low paying tasks that are dangerous and physically demanding (Guzman & McConnell, 2002, Taylor & Behnke, 2005). In these jobs, Mexican American fathers usually have to work long hours and odd shifts (Guzman & McConnell, 2002). This type of employment is usually on the edge of the economy and can easily vanish. These employment predicaments may persuade Mexican American fathers to transform their traditional role of provider (Gutmann, 2003) to nurturing caregivers. The women in the workforce movement prompted an adjustment in the long-established Mexican American family and its strict gender roles (e.g., Hondagneu-Sotelo, 1992; Zavella, 1987). Furthermore, job markets that neglected to maintain full employment had a harmful effect on the Mexican American family (Coltrane, et al., 2004). Fathers who suffered the loss of their jobs often assumed the role of regular child caregiver within the family, even though several studies showed that employed fathers showed more supportive behaviors than did the unemployed fathers (Harold-Goldsmith, Radin, & Eccles, 1988). Coltrane and Associates (2004) reported that the fathers' egalitarian gender attitudes and mothers' education had an impact on the higher levels of father involvement. They found that (a) the fathers supervised their children frequently when mothers were employed more hours and (b) they carried out more housework when mothers earned more and when the family experienced economic strain.

## "Machismo" Stereotype Labels

Contemporary researchers characterize Mexican American men as individuals with a range of attitudes that disputed the stereotypical roles concerning machismo (Coltrane, et al., 2004; Fuller, 2001; Gutmann, 1996; Mirandé, 1988). (See Table 2.).

*Machismo* is a popular stereotyped term with negative characteristics that has become synonymous with Mexican American males and with male chauvinism (Ramírez, 1979). It describes the Mexican American men's role with negative associations, including "exaggerated masculinity, physical prowess, and male chauvinism" (Baca-Zinn, 1994, p.74). Patriarchy, machismo, and excessive masculine demonstrations have been attributed to endure among Mexican American families. Actually, there are insufficient research data to support the macho masculinity myth of Mexican American men.

Contemporary researchers have demonstrated that this image is bogus. Fuller (2001) and Mirandé (1997) challenged and cast doubt on the accuracy of countless widespread myths and misconceptions about Mexican American men. Ramírez (1979) argued that researchers need to redefine the term *machismo* and acknowledge its positive elements to understand the Mexican American culture. *Machismo's* new definition provides positive cultural qualities, such as respect, honesty, loyalty, fairness, responsibility, trustworthiness (Coltrane, et al., 2004), egalitarian, warm, caring (Mirandé, 1991, 1997), "true bravery or valor, courage, generosity, stoicism, heroism, and ferocity" (Mirandé, 1997, pp. 78–79). *Machismo* in fathers has been related to being a provider for the family (Taylor & Behnke, 2005). Unfortunately, its positive characteristics have been overlooked; while the negative stereotypes have endured. Society's lack of valid knowledge, social stereotyping, and negative beliefs have victimized the Mexican American males (Mayo, 1997).

Stereotypes like "macho" are antipodes. Mexican American fathers have been observed to supervise children and participate in conventionally feminine activities (Coltrane, et al., 2004). Traditional roles associated with *machismo* have been

**Table 2** Description of Gender Roles in Mexican American Fathers by Contemporary and Traditional Researchers

| Contemporary Research | Traditional Research |
| --- | --- |
| The Mexican American fathers' egalitarian gender attitudes and mothers' education have an impact on the higher levels of father involvement: (a) fathers supervise their children with more frequency when mothers are employed more hours and (b) fathers carry out more housework when mothers earn more and when families experience economic strain (Coltrane, et al., 2004). | Mexican American fathers are dominant and distant, mothers are passive and dependent; children are socialized into rigid gender roles (Zapata & Jaramillo, 1981). Mexican American fathers are restricted in reference to gender. |
| Both fathers and mothers are believed to be equal and establish the same goals for both their sons and daughters. The fathers' roles and behaviors are the same regardless of their children's gender (Daly, 1995). Both fathers and mothers have the same roles as parents. (Luzod & Arce, 1979). | Patriarchy, machismo, and excessive masculine demonstrations have been attributed to Mexican American families (Baca-Zinn, 1994). |
| The fathers' expectations for their sons and daughters are the same. Gender differences are not important to the fathers. Fathers treat both their sons and daughters the same (Taylor & Behnke, 2005). | Mexican American families modify their roles through an acculturation or assimilation process through which families shifted from a traditional structure to a more egalitarian structure found in American families (Ortiz, 1995). |
| Mexican American fathers supervise children and participate in traditional feminine activities (Coltrane, et al., 2004). | Mexican American fathers are cold, distant, and authoritarian; while the traditional Mexican American family is an authoritarian and patriarchal body with the woman portrayed as quiet, submissive, and subservient in the home. |

replaced with more ground-breaking and progressive roles including loving husband, consummate father, and family man (Coltrane, 2001; Gutmann, 2003; Mirandé, 1997).

## Consensus Use of the Expression Mexican Americans

Several researchers seem not to be aware of the variation among Hispanic groups and the Mexican American community. They tend to generalize results from their studies to all Mexican Americans without considering that the studies were conducted with a small-group, one sub-population, or Mexican Americans with particular backgrounds and might be taken out of context. Researchers have studied a broad and diverse population and arbitrarily labeled their subjects Mexican American for convenience.

Although Mexican Americans are a diverse group of people, they are only one of many Hispanic groups. The results of these studies can only be generalized to the Mexican American population which the sample represents; the results cannot be generalized to the entire Hispanic population or even to the entire Mexican American population. Mexican Americans share the same language – Spanish - with other Hispanic groups. Since Spanish explorers, traders, and colonists founded several geographical areas of North, Central, and South America, Mexican Americans and Hispanics share several elements of their cultural heritage. Nevertheless, circumstances and experiences of the different groups and individuals in their countries of origin and in the United States have personalized both their language and culture (Bernal, Gilmore, Milgren, Melandez, Selome-McDermott, & Vasquez, 2000), which has led them to be unique and different individuals. For example, Hispanic members differ in their language competence. Some Hispanics are bilinguals who have the ability to speak, read, and write in both Spanish and English. Other Hispanics can speak both Spanish and English, but they are only able to read and write in one language, either English or Spanish. Several Hispanics, like new immigrants, are able to speak Spanish, have a limited formal education, and are not able to read or write well in either Spanish or English. Furthermore, Hispanics differ in idiomatic language usage across geographic areas. For that reason, it is important that researchers know the Spanish and English language fluency and the language-use predilection of the particular population in their study before making any generalizations about Hispanics or Mexican Americans (Bernal, et al., 2000).

Researchers also need to know about the Mexican American's culture before generalizing about their behaviors. Mexican American immigrants may have the same country of origin; however, they may differ in their beliefs, customs, and values. These differences are influenced by family background, recentness of immigration, degree of acculturation, regional concentration, level of educational attainment, income, and English language proficiency. The Mexican origin immigrant is the group that is currently most represented in the United States immigration. Immigrant groups are created based on their historical experiences and reasons for leaving their homelands; the legal and political environment; and the reception they experience when they arrive to the host country (Feagin, 1989, Rogler, 1994), even though the young Mexican origin cluster has become acculturated (Sands & Plunkett, 2005). Researchers need to learn and respond properly to the intricacies of the cultural groups that they are investigating (Powell, 1995).

Research, policy, and practice must understand and respect the Mexican Americans' language and cultural diversity. Hunnicutt and Castro (2005) assessed the attempts to help improve the education, language, and legal policy for Mexican Americans. They determined that existing legal, language, and education initiatives (such as efforts to force an official English language and to impede the use of native languages in schools) have been at odds with the Mexican Americans' problems, and has built up hostility toward those individuals of Mexican-origin (Hunnicutt & Castro, 2005), who are Spanish speakers. Traditionally, educational reforms failed to acknowledge the needs of Mexican American English language learners (Wright, 2005). Concurrently, the number of school-age non English speaking children increased from 9% in 1979 to 19% in 2003, going from 3.8 million to 9.9 million. Most of these children usually speak Spanish at home (National Center for Educational Statistics, 2005). It is crucial that the school experiences of Mexican American children be extended to the home. The family's reinforcement positively influences the children's school achievement (Prelow & Loukas, 2003).

# Recommendations

Studies of Mexican American fatherhood need to consider and address the issues discussed here to better understand and study Mexican American fathers. This will also provide a basis on which to offer high-quality services to them. Methodological and conceptual challenges affect the way the Mexican Americans are educated and studied. Educators and researchers need to have an accurate understanding of Mexican American fathers, because their knowledge influences the educational applications they provide to this linguistic and cultural group.

## *Educational Applications*

Since parent programs have primarily focused on mothers, an essential goal is to encourage fathers to become involved in parenting programs. The supposition that fathers are indifferent to participating in the care and encouragement of their children frequently dissuades attempts to integrate fathers into parenting programs (Powell, 1995). Gender neutrality in parenting needs to be altered and to acknowledge the fathers' current gender and roles. These programs also need to consider the interests of fathers and build on their interests.

Parent programs also need to concentrate on the Mexican American community's strengths and needs (e.g., family's low-income, absence of extended family in the area, language barriers, immigration issues) and help them to resolve their needs. In these programs, fathers can learn to model appropriate behaviors to promote their children's development. When working with fathers, Ortiz (1998) provides the following suggestions:

- Begin with informal and simple activities where only one parent and the child are involved.
- Teach fathers ways to take advantage of spontaneous and incidental learning (e.g., reading mail, letters).
- Encourage fathers to be patient to help children be comfortable. Children frequently find that adults engage in activities (e.g., reading, writing) about which they have limited understanding. As a result, fathers may raise questions. Teachers need to respond with language terms fathers can understand.

Mexican American fathers living in Los Angeles participated in a combination of parent group meetings and home visiting. Fathers reported that they valued sharing this experience with their spouse/partner, friendliness with the other parents in the group, and interacting with professional males in the staff (Powell, 1995). Parent programs can help fathers feel welcome and motivate them to participate in their children's educational program. Parent programs need to be responsive to Mexican American fathers' cultural and linguistic needs as well as to the Mexican American fathers' complexities and preferences (Bernal, et al., 2000).

When Mexican American fathers assume the role of teachers of young children, school-based programs need to provide strategies that fathers can use to teach their young children. In addition, teachers need to help fathers identify activities that can be used at home to provide their children with learning experiences. Mexican American fathers can be encouraged to attend and participate in Parent Teachers Association (PTA) meetings, open house, and other school-related functions when these activities reflect fathers' interests. They can also engage in home activities such as reading with their children about upcoming events through letters, flyers, and memoranda sent home by the school. Mexican American fathers who are active participants can be "meaning makers" for their environment. Parents assume a critical role in their young children's education. Teachers need to encourage and support the Mexican American fathers' attempts to assist their children in learning, which is a worthwhile goal (Ortiz, 1998).

## Research Applications

Researchers who are investigating Mexican American fatherhood need to consider and address these issues to be able to generalize appropriately about the Mexican American fathers. According to Lamb (1987), the modifications in the conceptualization of paternal roles that have occurred need to be investigated to obtain an understanding of the contemporary concern with fatherhood and its effects on their children. In colonial times, the prevalent concept of father was considered to be a "moral teacher," proceeded by "breadwinner," "sex-role model," while the present concept is "nurturant" father. These stages are of critical importance, because in our pluralistic society, "various conceptions of the father's role coexist" (Lamb, 1987, p. 6). Becoming aware that fathers assume various roles assists in positioning "fathering" in multicontext circumstances, which recognizes the fathers' different roles and responsibilities for their children (e.g., bread-winning, sex-role modeling, moral guidance, emotional support).

Researchers need to know and use the contemporary term for *machismo* in their studies. A *macho* Mexican American father matches the description of affectionate, hard working, and amiable. Male dominance, aggressiveness, and a tendency toward violence are traditional characteristics that conflict with the contemporary definition of *machismo* (Mirandé, 1997). Delgado (1974–1975) also disputes such a definition and states that a real *macho* does not pick fights or abuse drugs and alcohol. A *macho* in the Mexican American culture is not described as a drunkard, a troublemaker, or irresponsible toward his family. Conversely, he takes care of his wife and children for whom he acquires a sense of accomplishment and self-worth. Additionally, a Mexican American *macho* is reliable, responsible, honest, and honorable within the family and in the community. Unfortunately, researchers have concentrated on the negative components of *machismo* and overlooked its positive qualities like "responsibility, being a good husband and father, providing for one's family, strength in adversity" (Sánchez, 1979, p. 55). His most pervading attribute may be his noncompromising or intransigent disposition. "This does not mean that a macho does not change his mind or that he doesn't bargain on a trade or issue, but he does this before arriving at a non compromising level from which he is immovable even if it costs him his life" (Delgado, 1974–1975, p. 6).

Researchers and educators confront the challenge of improving their techniques for engaging the fathers in their children's education. Powell (1995) observed a model program where the Mexican American fathers' involvement was given low priority, propagating a self-fulfilling prophesy. Fathers will notice if the teachers use their participation as a bonus instead of a necessary requirement for their children's well-being. Professionals need to dispute and challenge the belief that fathers are indifferent about participating in their children's development. When fathers know how to contribute to their children's lives (Bernal, et al., 2000), they become involved in their children's education.

More studies are needed to be able to understand culturally and linguistically distinct Mexican American fathers of all ages and their families. These studies can provide information to help families, educators, social services, and health providers to successfully work with Mexican American fathers. Future generations of Mexican American fathers and families can be better served with these changes (Bernal, et al., 2000).

# References

Baca-Zinn, M. (1994). Adaptation and continuity in Mexican-origin families. In R.L. Taylor (Ed.), *Minority families in the United States: Comparative perspectives* (pp. 64–81). Englewood Cliffs, NJ: Prentice Hall.

Blankenhorn, D. (1995). *Fathers in America.* New York: Basic Books.

Bernal, V., Gilmore, L. A., Mellgren, L., Melandez, J., Seleme-McDermott, C., & Vázquez, V. (2000). *Hispanic fathers and family literacy: Strengthening achievement in Hispanic communities.* A report on a dialogue with community providers of services for Hispanic fathers, national Hispanic organizations, literacy programs, and advocates for fatherhood held on January 13, 2000.Washington, DC: U. S. Department of Health and Human Services, Hispanic Association of Colleges and Universities, and National Practitioners Network for Fathers and Families. Retrieved on September 3, 2005, from http://purl.access.gpo.gov/GPO/LPS20410 and http://fatherhood.hhs.gov/hispanic01/

Bronstein, P. (1984). Differences in mothers' and fathers behaviors toward children: A cross-cultural comparison. *Developmental Psychology, 20,* 995–1003

Cabrera, N., Ryan, R., Shannon, J., Brooks-Gunn, J., Vogel, C., Rakies, H., & Tamis-LeMonda, C. (2004). Low income biological fathers' involvement in their toddlers' lives: The Early Head

Start National Research and Evaluation Study. *Fathering: A Journal of Theory, Research, and Practice about Men as Fathers, 2*(1), 5–30.

Christie, C. A., Ross, R. M., & Klein, B. M. (2004). Moving toward collaboration by creating a participatory internal-external evaluation team: A case study. *Studies in Educational Evaluation, 30*, 125–134.

Coltrane, S. (2001). Stability and change in Chicano men's family lives. In M. Kimmel & M. Messner (Eds.), *Men's lives* (5th ed., pp. 451–466). New York: Macmillan.

Coltrane, S., Parke, R. D., & Adams, M. (2004). Complexity of father involvement in low-income Mexican American families. *Family Relations, 53*, 179–189.

Daly, K. (1995). Reshaping fatherhood: Finding the models. In W. Marsiglio (Ed.), *Fatherhood: Contemporary theory, research and social policy* (pp. 21–40). Thousand Oaks, CA: Sage.

Delgado, A. (1974–75). Machismo, La *Luz, 3, 6.*

Delgado-Gaitan, C. (1994). Sociocultural change through literacy: Toward the empowerment of families. In B.M. Ferdman, R.M. Weber, & A.G. Ramirez (Eds.), *Literacy across languages and cultures* (pp. 143–169). Albany, NY: The State University of New York Press.

Feagin, J. (1989). *Racial and ethnic relations* (3rd ed.). Englewood Cliffs, NJ: Prentice Hall.

Fuller, N. (2001). The social constitution of gender identify among Peruvian men. *Men and Masculinities, 3*, 316–331.

Gutmann, M. (1996). *The meanings of macho: Being a man in Mexico City.* Berkeley: University of California Press.

Gutmann, M. (2003). *Changing men and masculinities in Latin America.* Durham, NC: Duke University Press.

Guzman, B., & McConnell, E. D. (2002). The Hispanic population: 1990–2000 growth and change. *Population Research and Policy Review, 21*, 109–128.

Harold-Goldsmith, R., Radin, N., & Eccles, J. (1988). Objective and subjective reality: The effects of job loss and financial stress on fathering behaviors. *Family Perspective, 22*, 309–325.

Hondagneu-Sotelo, P. (1992). Overcoming patriarchal constraints: The reconstruction of gender relations among Mexican immigrant women and men. *Gender and Society, 6*, 393–415.

Hunnicutt, K., & Castro, M. (2005). How Census 2000 data suggest hostility toward Mexican-origin Arizonians. *Bilingual Research Journal, 29*(1), 109–125.

Knight, G. P., & Kagan, S. (1977). Acculturation of prosocial and competitive behaviors among second- and third-generation Mexican-American children. *Journal of Cross-Cultural Psychology, 8*, 273–284.

LaRossa, R. (1997). *The modernization of fatherhood: A social and political history.* Chicago: University of Chicago Press.

Lamb, M. E. (1987). Introduction: The emergent American father. In M. E. Lamb (Ed.) *The father's role: Cross cultural perspectives* (pp. 3–25). Hillsdale, NJ: Lawrence Erlbaum.

Lamb, M. E. (2004). *The role of the father in child development.* New York: Wiley.

Luzod, J.A., & Arce, C.H. (1979). An exploration of the father role in the Chicano family. Paper presented at the National Symposium on the Mexican American child, Santa Barbara.

Madsen, W. (1973). *The Mexican-American of south Texas.* New York: Holt, Rinehart & Winston.

Marks, L., & Palkovitz, R. (2004). American fatherhood types: The good, the bad, and the uninterested. *Fathering, 2*(2), 113–129.

Mayo, Y. (1997). Machismo, fatherhood and the Latino family: Understanding the concept. *Journal of Multicultural Social Work, 5*(1/2), 46–91.

Mirandé, A. (1988). Chicano fathers: Traditional perceptions and current realities. In P. Bronstein & C. P. Cowan (Eds.), *Fatherhood today: Men's changing role in the family* (pp. 93–106). New York: Wiley.

Mirandé, A. (1991). Ethnicity and fatherhood. In F. W. Bozett & S.M.H. Hanson (Eds.), *Fatherhood and families in cultural context* (pp. 53–81). New York: Springer.

Mirandé, A. (1997). *Hombres y machos: Masculinity and Latino culture.* Boulder, CO: Westview Press.

National Center for Education Statistics. (2005). *The condition of education*. Washington, DC: U. S. Department of Education, U. S. Government Printing Office. Also online. Retrieved on June 18, 2005, from http://nces.ed.gov/pubs2004/2004077.pdf http://nces.ed.gov http://nces.ed.gov/pubsearch http://nces.ed.gov/programs/coe/

Ortiz, V. (1995). The diversity of Latino families. In R.E. Zambrana (Ed.), *Understanding Latino families: Scholarship, policy, and practice* (pp. 18–39). Thousand Oaks, CA: Sage.

Ortiz, R. W. (1998). Chipping away at the monolith: Dispelling the myth of father noninvolvement in children's early literacy development. *Family Preservation Journal, 3*(2), 73–94.

Parke, R. D., Coltrane, S., Borthwick-Duffy, S., Powers, J., Adams, M., Fabricius, W., Braver, S., & Saenz, D. (2004). Assessing father involvement in Mexican-American families. In R. D. Day & M. E. Lamb (Eds.), *Conceptualizing and measuring father involvement.* (pp. 17–38). Hillsdale, NJ: Erlbaum.

Pinal, J., & Singer, A. (1997). Generations of diversity: Latinos in the United States. *Population Bulletin, 52*. Washington, DC: Population Reference Bureau.

Powell, D.R. (1995). Including Latino fathers in parent education and support programs: Development of a program model. In R.E. Zambrana (Ed.), *Understanding Latino families: Scholarship, policy, and practice* (pp. 85–106). Thousand Oaks, CA: Sage.

Prelow, H., & Loukas, A. (2003). The role of resource, protective, and risk factors on academic achievement-related outcomes of economically disadvantaged Latino youth. *Journal of Community Psychology, 31*, 513–521.

Ramírez, R. (1979). Machismo: A bridge rather than a barrier to family and marital counseling. In P. Preciado Martin (Ed). La *frontera perspective (pp.* 61–62). Tucson, AZ: La Frontera Center.

Rogler, L. (1994). International migrations: A framework for directing research. *American Psychologist, 49*, 701–708.

Rotherman-Borus, M. J., & Phinney, J. S. (1990). Patterns of social expectations among Black and Mexican-American Children. *Child Development, 61*, 542–556.

Rubel, A. J. (1966). *Across the tracks: Mexican-Americans in a Texas city*. Austin, TX: University of Texas Press.

Sánchez, A. F. (1979). History and culture of the tecato (Chicano "junkie"): Implications for prevention and treatment. In P. Preciado Martin (Ed), *La frontera perspective* (pp. 51–57), Tucson, AZ: La Frontera Center.

Sands, T., & Plunkett, S. W. (2005). A new scale to measure adolescent reports of academic support by mothers, fathers, teachers, and friends in Latino immigrant families. *Hispanic Journal of Behavioral Sciences, 27*(2), 244–253.

Tamis-LeMonda, C. S., Shannon, J. D., Cabrera, N. J., & Lamb, M. E. (2004). Fathers and mothers at play with their 2- and 3-year-olds: Contributions to language and cognitive development. *Child Development, 75*(6), 1806–1820.

Taylor, B. A., & Behnke, A. (2005). Fathering across the border: Latino fathers in Mexico and the U.S. *Fathering: A Journal of Theory, Research, & Practice about Men as Fathers, 3*(2), 99–120. Also on line from http://www.findarticles.com/p/articles/mi_m0PAV/is_2_3/ai_n14738211

United States Census Bureau. (2001). Census 2000. Retrieved September 3, 2005, from http://www.census.gov/

Wright, W. E. (2005). English language learners left behind in Arizona: The nullification of accommodations in the interjection of federal and state policies. *Bilingual Research Journal, 29*(1), 1–30.

Zapata, J. T., & Jaramillo, P.T. (1981), The Mexican American family: An Adlerian perspective. *Hispanic Journal of Behavioral Sciences, 3*, 275–290.

Zavella, P. (1987). *Women's work and Chicano families: Cannery workers of the Santa Clara Valley*. Ithaca, NY: Cornell University Press.

Zinn, M. B., & Wells, B. (2000). Diversity within Latino families: New lessons for family social science. In D. H. Demo, K. R. Allen, & M. A. Fine (Eds.), *Handbook of family diversity* (pp. 252–273). New York: Oxford University Press.

**Olivia N. Saracho**
University of Maryland
Department of Curriculum & Instruction
College Park, Maryland 20742
Telephone: (301) 405-3155
FAX: (301) 314-9055
E-mail: ons@umd.edu

Olivia N. Saracho is Professor Department of Curriculum and Instruction at the University of Maryland. Dr. Saracho began her career in education by teaching Head Start, preschool, kindergarten, and elementary classes. Her current research and writing is in the field of early childhood education. She has written several works on early literacy such as *Language and Literacy in Early Childhood Education, Literacy Development: The Whole Language Approach, Language and Literacy Programs in Early Childhood Education, Literacy Activities in a Play Environment, The Roots of Reading and Writing,* and many others.

**Bernard Spodek**
Emeritus, University of Illinois
Department of Curriculum & Instruction
Champaign, Illinois 61820
E-mail: b-spodek@uiuc.edu
b-spodek@uiuc.edu
217-352-1682
http://www.ed.uiuc.edu/faculty/b-spodek/

Bernard Spodek is Professor Emeritus of Early Childhood Education at University of Illinois at Urbana-Champaign. He taught preschool, kindergarten and elementary grades before completing his doctorate at Teachers College, Columbia University. He has published extensively in the area of early childhood Education. Bernard Spodek was President of the National Association for the Education of Young Children (1976–78) He is currently president of the Pacific Early Childhood Education Research Association

# Chapter 5
# Brothers and Sisters

## The Influence of Sibling Relationships on Young Children's Development

**Mary Renck Jalongo and Denise Dragich**

**Abstract** Influences in contemporary society such as blended families created by remarriage, international adoptions, and reproductive technology have expanded the definition of sibling relationships. Bonds with brothers and sisters occur early and exert a profound effect on young children's overall development. This chapter synthesizes the research on sibling relationships in early childhood, identifies four recurring themes, and offers research-based recommendations to early childhood educators and families.

**Keywords** siblings, brothers, sisters, families, family relationships, early childhood development, adoption, blended families, sibling rivalry, death of a sibling, siblings with disabilities.

During a recent holiday, three adult siblings and their families expended significant time and money to travel and spend time together. They happily reminisced and discussed family memories. "Remember," said the middle child, "when Mom and Dad would let one of us have a turn sitting in the front seat? I loved sitting up there! I would always pretend that the back seat was empty and that I was an only child!" Now, many years later, the three are committed to each other, and even though their homes are on opposite U.S. coasts, they make a concerted effort to provide ongoing support to one another through frequent telephone conversations and periodic reunions.

As this anecdote illustrates, sibling relationships can be among the most influential, lasting, and emotionally-shaping experiences we have (Fritz, 2006). In the fifteenth anniversary edition of a classic book in the field, *The Sibling Bond,* Stephen Bank and Michael Kahn (2003) refer to more than twenty years of research to support their assertion that bonds with siblings are unique, enduring, intense, and

Indiana University of Pennsylvania

Indiana Area School District

M.R. Jalongo (ed.), *Enduring Bonds.*
© Springer 2008

sometimes hidden relationships that affect who we are and who we become. The connections between brothers and sisters exist long before a child forms lasting friendships, outlast parent-child relationships most of the time, and are established well before one chooses a spouse (Deater-Deckard, Dunn & Lussier. 2002; Volling & Blandon, 2005). A leading child development textbook contends that the sibling bond has an intensity and uniqueness that seldom is duplicated because children from the same family typically share the same roots, values, and daily life (Papalia, Olds & Feldman, 2005).

Sibling relationships represent some of the best and worst among human interpersonal ties, ranging from lifelong support and a pool of shared memories to destructive influences that persist across the lifespan (Todd, 2001). Of particular importance is the way that these relationships are defined, understood, and handled by adults. The seemingly small steps that educators and parents/families take to support the formation of healthy, positive sibling relationships during early childhood have lifelong consequences. This chapter synthesizes quantitative and qualitative research as well as theory and practice in psychology to 1) provide a contemporary definition of the sibling bond, 2) examine four recurrent themes in the literature on siblings, and 3) offer research-based recommendations to early childhood practitioners.

## Understanding the Sibling Bond

The Oberlands had been married for three years and were deeply disappointed by four pregnancies that resulted in miscarriages. After weighing their choices, they made the decision to pursue the international adoption of a biracial child. Much to their surprise and delight, when their adoptive son was three, Mrs. Oberland carried a child to term and Brianne was born. When their children were age three and age five respectively, Mrs. Oberland's sister and brother-in-law tragically were killed in an auto accident. Long ago, the two couples had drawn up legal documents that made the Oberlands the legal guardians of her sister's only child, Tony, in the event of his parents' death. Today, siblings in the family now consist of eight-year-old Tony, six-year-old Hong, and four-year-old Brianne. From a biological perspective, none of these children are siblings; however, from a practical point of view and family perspective they truly are brothers and sister.

This scenario underscores the first important understanding about siblingship; namely, that residing together and being part of the same family often defines brotherhood or sisterhood. As increasing numbers of children are conceived through artificial reproductive means, born to surrogates, adopted from throughout the world, become a family by remarriage, or are brought together following a crisis, the classification of the sibling bond has expanded beyond the criterion of shared heredity.

Interestingly, in comparison to the research on other interpersonal relationships, the sibling bond has received relatively little attention. The study of relationships between parents and children has been the focus of critical inquiry while bonds between and among siblings have received far less attention (Miller & Yavnek, 2006). Historically, even within the study of siblings, the effects of the birth order of children has overshadowed research on the nature of the relationship between and among siblings.

One consistent finding is that the tie between siblings is constructed over time such that the nature and intensity of the relationship may differ dramatically from one period of life to another (Edwards & Hadfield, 2006). Sherrie and her younger sister Candy, for example, are three years apart in age and had an intense sibling rivalry during their early childhood years. Their father left the family while the girls were still preschoolers and their mother was an alcoholic—not violent, but neglectful. Sherrie attempted to mother Candy but her baby sister thought it was bossy and conflict was the result. As adults residing in the same community, both young women married and divorced young, both had a child, and each was in desperate financial circumstances. They decided to "throw in together," rent a trailer, enroll their preschool children in the same Head Start program, and participate in a training program that would improve the quality of their lives. The sisters have talked about their particular recollections of childhood and sources of resentment. They have come to realize that so many points of friction in the past were attributable to the fact that "we were just kids." Each now considers the other to be a best friend as well as a sister.

As this situation illustrates, there is a developmental interplay between the sibling context and children's adjustment that changes over time, sometimes quite dramatically (Richmond, Stocker & Rienks, 2005). For example, in a review of 17 studies from several countries, Hegar (2005) examined the outcomes of sibling placements in foster care and adoptive homes. Siblings that were kept together fared as well—and often better—than those who were separated. Siblings know one another's strengths and weaknesses in ways that affect the course of a brother's or sister's life forever. They also recall both major and minor events, albeit from their own vantage point which can be clouded by a young child's immature reasoning and the inevitable misconceptions that result. There are some predictable consequences—both positive and negative—of first-hand knowledge of personal triumphs, disappointments, and traumatic experiences. The next section examines four strands in the research on sibling relationships.

## Four Recurrent Themes in Sibling Relationships

Siblings can be rivals who vie for attention, culture brokers who orient brothers and sisters to the beliefs and norms of society, supporters of cognitive and social skill development, and family members who adapt to special needs or cope with sibling loss.

## *Theme 1: Sibling Rivalry*

Sibling rivalry is not unique to human beings; it exists across species and is intensified by a struggle for survival (Mock, 2004). Within each family, cooperation and
competition are powerful, competing forces. In many ways, home is the context in
which the evolutionary limits of selfishness are tested (Mock, 2004). Ever since
Alfred Adler described the concept of sibling rivalry in 1927, conflict between and
among siblings has been a dominant theme. This theory had tremendous intuitive
appeal, was well received by professionals, and has dominated thinking about sibling relationships for over half a century. Sibling rivalry is characterized by the
"dethroning" of a firstborn child when the next child arrives. When parents bring
home a new baby or blend existing families, they are saying, in effect, "I'm bringing someone new into the family, but don't worry, (he or she) is great. You have to
be nice and share. You're going to get along well, I'm sure." Feelings of jealousy,
diminished family status and, at times, aggressive words or actions often result.
Recognition of the effects of sibling rivalry as a developmental theme persists to
this day (Rondon, 2007a; 2007b).

Lamb's (1978) research on sibling relationships identified two variables that
promote an older sibling's acceptance of the new baby's presence: 1) an extra time
commitment from fathers to firstborns and 2) the sociability of the younger sibling.
Some babies were more receptive to siblings, and infant reinforcement of the role
as big brother or big sister tended to reduce discord among siblings. Siblings' com-
petitiveness does not necessarily disappear, however, when a younger brother or
sister is no longer a baby. Today's blended families often merge together and create
"new" brothers and sisters who engender all the same rivalry as a newborn and a
child or children of the same biological parents. The most intense feelings of competition often are associated with siblings of the same gender. In his study of sibling
effects on socialization, Cicirelli (1976) concluded that the greatest rivalry occurred
between same-sex siblings and that two brothers were the most quarrelsome combination. A study of 651 young adults concluded that conflict and abuse between
parents was associated with negative parent-child interactions, which in turn was
associated with problems in siblings' relationships with each other; males with
brothers were the type of sibling pair associated with the highest levels of rivalry
and violence (Hoffman, Kiecolt, & Edwards, 2005).

Some siblings may feel a need to retaliate against the younger sibling who is
perceived as receiving preferential treatment. Another less advisable but effective
way of asserting superiority is for older siblings to engage in various forms of
exclusionary behavior such refusing to let younger brothers or sisters participate
in play activities, or teasing until a frustrated or frightened sibling starts to cry.
This stratagem used by older siblings to try and recover what they regard as diminished family status tends to underscore age differences. In the United States, it is
common for children and adults of the same age group to be clustered together—
so toddlers are kept in the company of other toddlers at child care, first graders
interact mostly with other first graders, and elderly adults often reside in the same

facility. Some researchers believe that the age segregation of American culture may partially explain why children from the same family fail to form close relationships as well as explain the diminished intensity of relationships that may exist among adult siblings (Rubin, 1980; Schaneveldt & Ihinger, 1979). Studies suggest that avoidance/denial—rather than outright conflict—is the most frequently reported form of jealousy expression among adults (Bevan & Stetzenbach, 2007).

More recently, the focus of research has been on how parents influence the way children in a family relate to one another. Not surprisingly, parental warmth and affection are associated with positive sibling interactions; the converse also pertains. Distant and harsh parental styles can result in sibling interactions that are antagonistic and unreceptive (Berk, 2001). Current research suggests that family type (e.g. intact, blended, single-parent families) is inconclusive in terms of effects on siblings, their relationships, and future social and emotional adjustment issues (Deater-Deckard, Dunn & Lussier, 2002). There was little or no significant difference in sibling negativity and positivity when intact families were compared with blended families. There is some evidence that single mothers tend to be higher in maternal negativity than mothers who live with partners and this may result in less positive sibling interactions (Deater-Deckard et al., 2002). Frequent partner transitions or the absence of other adults to share daily living responsibilities and economic stressors were some possible explanations for the increase in negativity. Any increase in family disharmony, such as marital strife or economic hardship, may exert an adverse effect on the quality of sibling relationships (Berk, 2001; Deater-Deckard, et al., 2002; Kramer & Koval, 2005).

## Theme 2: Siblings as "Culture Brokers"

When Marjorie, a third-grader enrolled in a gifted and talented program, was given the assignment of writing a journal, her idea was to produce one on George Washington by "reading a lot about him and imagining the rest." Her teacher was not enthused about the idea but Marjorie was determined to pursue it anyway. Marjorie's older sister, Laura, was wise in the ways of the school and had been a student in this teacher's class. Laura's advice was "Just give the teacher what she wants or you're not going to get an A."

Throughout the history of families, older siblings have been a source of information to younger ones. As recent veterans of each grade level in school and still children themselves, they have insider knowledge about the culture of childhood that adults do not. The areas of expertise most often communicated from older to younger siblings are an understanding of school rules and procedures, strategies for meeting academic challenges, dealing with difficult teachers, managing conflicts with peers, and explanation of forbidden subjects such as sex or drugs (Cicirelli, 1976). Older siblings frequently use their advanced experience to protect a younger brother or sister from various unpleasant situations. As Rubin (1980) observed "Throughout the childhood years, older siblings often take a special interest in the well being of their little brothers and sisters. ... The experience of assisting a younger sibling may help the older child to become a more caring and sympathetic person outside the family as well" (p. 122).

Family structures and sibling roles can differ dramatically worldwide, greatly affecting sibling relationships. "Similar to parent-child interaction, siblings teach and model behavior and function as culture brokers in the transmission of cultural values across generations" (Tarakeshwar, Lobato, Kao & Plante, 2006, p. 1). In the dominant culture of the United States, children's relationships are primarily with parents and sibling relationships are secondary. In some African, Polynesian and Hispanic cultures, siblings frequently play a significant caregiving and instructional role with infants and toddlers that commences during their own early childhood years. In Kenya, for example, families may average eight children and siblings as young as five years of age assume responsibility for the care of their younger brothers and sisters (Rogoff, 2003). The availability of siblings varies greatly between cultures, too. In China, with a mandated one child per family rule, siblings and related issues are essentially non-existent. Conversely, in a study of children enrolled in Head Start with mothers of Mexican descent, the researchers concluded that warm relationships with a child closest in age to the preschool-aged child made a significant and unique contribution to the child's adjustment as reported both by the child's mother and teacher (Modry-Mandel, Gamble & Taylor, 2007). Cultures that keep their children in mixed-age groups, rather than segregating them by age, expect older siblings to teach younger ones language, cultural roles and expectations, and forms of conflict resolution and compromise. European-American families seldom use sitters younger than twelve, and with mandatory school attendance in same age groups, siblings have limited experience in the caregiving of younger family members (Rogoff, 2003).

Even when siblings do not have major responsibility for child care, they often are a source of nurturing for their younger siblings. In an observational research project that involved mothers, preschoolers and infants (Stewart, 1983), 52 percent of older siblings reassured and comforted their younger siblings in the absence of the mother. The dyads which were responsible for producing the most care and attention were older brother-younger sister and older sister-younger brother. Stewart's (1983) study further concluded that while the assistance of older brothers was commensurate with the infant's apparent distress, older sisters tended to impose more assistance than actually warranted by the child's level of distress. Whatever help is offered by older siblings to younger siblings, family functioning is directly affected by the relationships among children from the same family (Lerner & Spanier, 1978).

Evidently, there is reciprocity when older siblings lend support and guidance to later-born children (Staub, 1975). Both parties appear to develop a slightly different set of social skills, with older children emerging as more nurturant and younger children becoming slightly more popular with peers (Miller & Maruyama, 1976). In fact, cross-cultural studies of prosocial behavior suggest that firstborns tend to offer assistance more often than children without younger siblings (Whiting & Whiting, 1975). The later-born child's tendency to be more successful in peer interaction is often attributed to experience with managing, in a diplomatic way, the well-intentioned but sometimes domineering personality of older siblings.

These first emotional and social contacts with brothers and sisters may set the tone for styles of interactions with people throughout life (Howe, et al., 2002). If siblings learn to interact in a positive and constructive manner with siblings, they presumably acquire skills that will benefit later relationships (Volling & Blandon, 2005). Sibling relationships in the preschool years, for instance, may lay the groundwork for learning many social behaviors that impact children's future interpersonal relationships and success in social and school adjustment. Researchers who studied children's social adjustment capabilities found that relationships to parents, siblings, and other relatives are important indicators of children's abilities to develop effective social skills (Moore, Evans, Brooks-Gunn & Roth, 2001). Even before kindergarten, differences in social skills and success in social relationships have been observed. Children who display positive social characteristics in their early years are more frequently chosen as friends, are more socially well-adjusted, and experience greater school success. Therefore, the early interactions between and among siblings can be indicators of future success in social and other domains (Moore, et al., 2001).

Children who are able to make friends and who are chosen as friends during early childhood tend to be more successful in later life, not only in social areas, but also in personal adjustment and school achievement (Moore, Evans, et. al. 2004; Thornton, 2001). Berk (2001) looked specifically at sibling factors that affected social development. Play between siblings seemed to help children develop more insight and empathy for another's feelings than did playing with their mothers. Mothers tended to acknowledge and clarify the children's own feelings whereas the siblings would state how they themselves felt. Thus, when siblings engage in sustained play episodes—particularly pretend and imaginary play—the dialogue between them plays a strong role in helping children to understand others' feelings (Berk, 2001; Volling & Blandon, 2005). To summarize, children's relationships with their siblings appear to affect the development of social competence with peers, conflict resolution abilities, and social-emotional development (Volling & Blandon, 2005). There is a direct connection between sibling interactions and how children manage and maintain their friendships with peers in other settings.

Although it may come as a surprise to parents/families, children benefit from moderate degrees of conflict with their siblings. Learning to resolve conflicts with brothers and sisters at home resulted in more social competence, better emotional control, and increased ability to pay attention in school. The quality of sibling interactions relates directly to children's development of prosocial behaviors and understanding. When children learn to positively resolve conflicts with siblings they transfer this learning to their interactions with peers. The reverse also pertains: siblings, use of aggressive and hostile behaviors is associated with a higher incidence of these behaviors during peer interaction as well. When siblings resolve conflicts through aggressive and hostile means, it appears to weaken the bond between them. Sibling interactions may establish patterns for future adult relationships (Deater-Deckard, et al., 2002; Moore et al., 2001; Volling & Blandon, 2005). Longitudinal study suggests that, if positive relationships with siblings are established in early childhood, they tend to persist into adolescence (Kramer & Kowal, 2005; Pike, Coldwell & Dunn, 2005).

Nevertheless, sibling and peer relationships are distinctive. The way children act in one relationship is not necessarily related to the behavior displayed in other relationships (McElwain & Volling, 2005). Parents' observations suggest that specific problem behaviors manifested in interactions with siblings do not necessarily occur when the same children interact with agemates and friends. The age differential between siblings and the perceived balance of power between them may result in a different sort of dynamic than that observed with peers. Siblings of different ages may also have different interests and abilities, resulting in more conflict in play situations. For example, a school-age sibling who is enthralled by a board game with rules such as *Monopoly* often finds a preschool brother or sister without a concept of rules who insists upon joining in to be an annoyance. Play with friends of a closer age may result in more participatory, collaborative play episodes (McElwain & Volling, 2005).

Gender and ideas about femininity and masculinity are affected by siblings as well (Edwards, Mauthner, & Hadfield, 2005). The experience of growing up, caring for siblings, leaving home, and becoming a mother are affected by sistering and ultimately contribute to the social construction of femininity (Mauthner & Weeks, 2005). Interestingly, studies show that gay men and lesbian women often disclose their sexuality to a sibling before anyone else in their families, placing siblings in the position of bridging the two generations (Gottlieb, 2005).

## *Theme 3: Sibling Effects on Cognitive and Social Skills*

Stephanie, a third-grader, said to her sister in first grade, "If you think addition and subtraction are hard, just wait until you have to do multiplication, division, and fractions. But don't worry, I can help you." As this exchange illustrates, cognitive development is influenced by sibling interactions as well. Barr and Hayne (2003) found that infants with older brothers and sisters imitated more behaviors without specific prompting than did infants without siblings. Infants with siblings appeared to be so interested in the older children's activities that they would imitate the behaviors even if not directly instructed to do so. Usually, the infants' imitations were focused on physical and pretend play actions. Pretend play is believed to foster cognitive development by helping children to engage in problem-solving, creativity, planning and negotiation with others (Barr & Hayne, 2003; Berk, 2001). When older siblings prompt and encourage a less competent sibling to practice a particular behavior, they provide the scaffolding that is necessary to learn new processes. Sibling relationships appear to be important in fostering young children's reasoning and growing theory-of-mind skills, particularly during play (Hughes, Fujisawa, Ensor, Lecce & Marfleet, 2006). Conversely, older siblings also can be a source of misinformation during play when the older sibling's conceptual understanding is limited or when, during conflict, they deliberately perpetuate a false belief, such as telling a younger sibling something that would frighten him or her (Foote & Holmes-Lonergan, 2003).

Sibling relationships affect social adjustment in positive and negative ways. A special issue of the *Journal of Family Psychology* included eight articles that explored the potential of sibling relationships to support healthy development and ten articles that focused on sibling relationships as contexts for deviant behaviors and relational difficulties (Kramer & Bank, 2005). When studying children's social adjustment capabilities, Moore, Evans, Brooks-Gunn and Roth (2004) found that relationships to parents, siblings, and other relatives are important indicators for children's ability to develop effective social skills. The early interactions between siblings are indicators of future success in other social domains as well (Moore, Evans, Brooks-Gunn & Roth, 2001). The ability to negotiate conflict is one type of important sibling interaction. In a study by Howe, Rinaldi, Jennings and Petrakos (2002) three patterns in conflict were identified. The first conflict issue observed concerned siblings' plans for play and related tasks. The researchers speculated that children are highly invested in their play ideas which might cause them to hold strong to their own individual positions. Another variable that might intensify conflict is young children's inability to verbally articulate their perspective, making it difficult to come to a mutual understanding. A second source of conflict occurred over concrete items (objects and space). These conflicts seemed to be resolved through negotiations that led to sharing and turn-taking. The third source of conflict studied was procedural in nature, focusing on how to do something. Interestingly, birth order was a variable in resolving these conflicts. First-born and older siblings seemed to attempt to resolve conflicts by taking a more dominant role, while younger siblings relied on a third party, usually a parent. Gender came into play with conflict resolution between siblings, too. This study's results were comparable to other studies that saw girls behave more submissively than boys, suggesting that girls are socialized to be more passive (Edwards, Mauthner, Hadfield, 2005; Howe, et al., 2003; Martin & Ross, 2005).

## *Theme 4: Siblings with Special Needs and Loss of a Sibling*

Ira's six-year-old sister has Down syndrome and when she gets frustrated, she often shows her temper. Although Ira is just seven years old, he has acquired a very mature perspective on all of this. He says, "I used to get mad because Bernice would do things that I'm not allowed to do but she wouldn't even get in trouble. But my Mom explained that she is more like a little kid in her thinking and now I try to remember that." As this brother and sister pair illustrate, a child with special needs can place additional demands on the prosocial skills of brothers or sisters in the same family (Giallo & Gavidia-Payne, 2006). A child with a disability can contribute to stress in the family and the typically developing child needs to learn how to cope. The sibling without the disability often experiences feelings of isolation, grief, anger, and anxiety. These and other emotional issues can have lifelong effects (Strohm, 2005). Psychotherapist Jeanne Safer (2003) conducted 20 in-depth interviews of siblings of individuals with a various mental, physical, and social disabilities. The parents of these children often reacted with anger, sadness, or anxiety toward the afflicted child and sometimes responded in dramatically different ways, ranging from excessive attention to detachment. Themes that emerged for the nondisabled sibling often included fear of contagion as they struggled to understand the disability, premature maturity as they assumed responsibility for sibling's care, compulsion to achieve as they tried to compensate for their sibling's abnormality, and guilt about their own health and success. Siblings frequently experienced the mixed emotions that are associated with strong feelings of attachment for a sibling with a disability and simultaneous resentment over the many ways in which life is made more difficult by his/her presence (McKeever, 1983). Typically developing brothers and sisters often feel a special responsibility to protect brothers and sisters with special needs (Gass, Jenkins & Dunn, 2007; Simeonsson & McHale, 1981)—even siblings with a "hidden" disability, such as diabetes (Loos & Kelly, 2006). Children who have a brother or sister with disabilities are more often involved in disputes at school (Breslau, Weitzman & Messenger, 1981). Overall family functioning was found to be a determinant of the nature of the bond between typically developing child and a sibling with a disability. Whether that disability was a hearing impairment (Verte, Hebbrecht, & Roeyers, 2006) or Down syndrome (Cuskelly & Gunn, 2006), families that functioned well also had siblings that adapted well to a brother or sister with a disability.

If, however, the sibling had a serious social-emotional issue, such as anxiety disorder, more than half of their siblings had elevated scores on anxiety measures that would identify them as needing further assessment or treatment for anxiety disorder (Dia, 2006). Along similar lines, there appears to be a link between negative sibling relationships, sibling conflict, and peer antisocial behavior (Criss & Shaw, 2005).

One traumatic situation that can result in lifelong guilt and anxiety for children is the death of a sibling. The impact of a sister's or brother's death on remaining siblings is enormous. Young children frequently feel a sense of personal responsibility for the sibling's death. Three musical legends—Ray Charles, Elvis Presley, Johnny Cash—lost a brother at an early age and each one of these talented individuals was deeply troubled for a lifetime by the abrupt severing of that bond. In every case, these young boys initially regarded themselves as the culprit: Ray Charles attributed his brother's death to his failure to rescue him from drowning; Elvis Presley was a twin and was haunted by the notion that he was the stronger one and had caused his brother's death; and Johnny Cash believed that his failure to help at the sawmill was responsible for his brother's fatal injury. Consistent with DeVita-Raeburn's (2004) interviews with more than two hundred siblings who experienced the death of a brother or sister, emotions cam range from withdrawal to guilt to rage and self-destructive behaviors may be manifested by the brother or sister left behind following a sibling's death.

## Research-based Recommendations
## of the Sibling Relationship in Early Childhood

As early childhood educators work with young children, colleagues, and professionals in other fields, it is important to consider that understanding the sibling bond is crucial to a fuller understanding of children and families and family-centered practice (Sanders, 2004). Preservice and inservice early childhood educators need to take into account the ties that young children form with brother and sisters in order to know the children with whom they work.

### *Recognize that Issues with Siblings Often Surface at School*

After 3-year-old Tamika's baby brother was born, her play behavior changed in marked ways. Previously she had sought the role of mother, but now she wanted to be the baby—and a very demanding one, at that. She cried incessantly, refused to be comforted, and would toss aside bottle, blanket, and rattle. After exhausting herself with this troublesome behavior, it was not unusual for Tamika to crawl into the wooden cradle, curl up in a fetal position, pull the quilt over herself, and drift off to sleep while sucking her thumb. The teacher wondered if what she was noticing at school was linked to what was happening at home. A conversation with Tamika's parents suggested that she was resentful of the attention given to her new brother and, more than once, she had to be cautioned about her rough ways of interacting with him. Adults often attempt to assuage older children by telling them that they will "have a new baby brother or sister to play with" but this can set entirely inaccurate expectations for preschoolers who may anticipate a "super baby" with physical or cognitive abilities likened to their own. Operating under these misconceptions, preschoolers may disgustedly remark, as 4-year-old Emily did, "That baby can't do anything—all it ever does is sleep and eat and cry" and later, "Why does she stay in her pajamas all day? Why doesn't she have to get dressed like me?" It is better to teach children what to expect from a baby and highlight the older sibling's superior knowledge, maturity, and capacity for nurturing.

There is evidence to suggest that sibling relationships can exert both positive and negative influences on children's behavior in the school setting (Wolkoff, Schwartzber & Meckwood-Yazdpour, 2006). Thus it is particularly important for early childhood educators to communicate with families that a concerted effort can be made to support the child through these important life transitions.

## *Avoid Comparing One Sibling to Another*

When the kindergarten teacher remarked to Amy, "Is Margaret your sister? She was in my kindergarten class last year and was *such* a good student. I expect that you will be too." it only served to strengthen Amy's resolve to be less like her sister. Since the "good girl" role was "taken," Amy embraced a "bad girl" role at school. One consistent finding in the research is that teachers and parents should avoid comparing the capabilities of children from the same family. Comments such as "Why can't you be more like your brother?" or statements overheard, such as "She was such a good baby but her sister was something else!" are divisive. It is important to recognize and highlight each child's unique abilities and interests without overstating them. Siblings often pursue different interests to avoid competing directly with an older, more experienced brother or sister. A boy might have an older brother who is a talented football player and decide instead to pursue a career in music, for instance. Apparently, the best coping strategy is for children to explore their own individuality and identify tasks at which they can become masterful.

## *Provide Undivided Attention and Special Recognition*

In collaboration with a graduate student in early childhood education, the regional medical center offered a "Sibling Class," an educational program designed to dispel the firstborn preschooler's misconceptions about babies, to enhance the older child's self-esteem as a big brother or sister, and to promote prosocial behavior between firstborns and newborns. Children who participated got to put a diaper on a life-size baby doll, taste formula to find out that it isn't that good, and look at the new babies in the nursery through the glass window. After the baby was born, the older sibling received a card inviting him or her to come and visit. One preschooler took the social situation quite seriously and made formal introductions saying, "Baby Joey, this is my mother" and then, "Mommy, this is Baby Joey." Naturally, it was no mistake that the possessive pronoun "my," rather than "your" or "our," was used. This child's reaction is still preferable, however, to the negative responses often elicited when older siblings are totally excluded from the important family event of welcoming a new baby. Experts also advise giving each child a time of undivided attention (Brodkin, 2006). Spending time with each child individually, facilitating one-on-one conversation, and asking lots of questions allow each child in a growing family to feel important and special.

## *Encourage Cooperation and Helpfulness*

A mother of new twin girls had a t-shirt especially printed for her 3-year-old son which read "I'm the big brother." In this way, Darryl received attention for his new role and was included in the family's excitement over the birth of the twins. With sensitive adult intervention like this, older siblings may be encouraged to use a more constructive approach and take pride in being the big brother or sister with superior strength and competence. With the arrival of a new baby, young children may be pressured to grow up a bit faster to make the constant care of a baby more manageable for the parents/families. Dunn and Kendrick (1980) concluded that mothers give firstborns less playful attention, more direct orders, and resort to more disciplinary action after the arrival of a younger sibling. Adults need to acknowledge and appreciate the child's often imperfect efforts to be helpful to a sibling (Goldenthal, 2000). When the children are together, such as during a family outing, it is important to emphasize family togetherness and cooperation. At the center or school, the teacher can reinforce these efforts by being alert for opportunities to praise the cooperation and helpfulness of an older sibling.

## *Allow Children to Express Emotions*

When 3-year-old Scott walked into the living room and saw his mother cuddling the new baby, he directed her to "Put that girl down!" Even though Scott's resentment of the new baby is quite transparent, parents and early childhood educators can take positive action in promoting an older brother's or sister's self-esteem. Children need to be able to confide their fears, worries, and resentments about the new baby at home and at school (Brodkin, 2003; Greenberg, 2007). Particularly when a sibling has a disability, brothers and sisters need to have their questions answered and to share their feelings and concerns with caring adults (Strohm, 2005). The concept here is to allow children to be assertive so that they will not need to resort to aggression (Goldenthal, 2000). The depth and breadth of feelings elicited by and directed toward siblings is well represented in children's literature, and rightly so. These books can help the siblings created by remarriage to realize that they are not alone in apprehensions about their family's reorganization, encourage an older child to see the humor in the annoying antics of a younger sibling, or even aid an only child in vicariously experiencing the pleasures and chalenges associated with of being someone's sister or brother.

## *Help Parents/Families Cope with Sibling Conflict*

Families often fear that the arguments they see in early childhood will escalate and result in lifelong animosity between and among siblings (Jalongo, 1985). They need to be reassured that a certain amount of bickering is to be expected and that squabbles are not predictive of strained relationships in later life. Based on the advice of psychologists and family therapists, parents/families need to avoid making a ruling on every incident and allow children to work out at least some of their differences together. Otherwise, it often sets in motion face-saving efforts on the part of the child who was reprimanded, such as trying to provoke a sibling or catch him or her misbehaving to even the score. If, for example, one sibling tries to distract another from what he or she is supposed to do, parents are advised to use a diversionary tactic and direct the attention of the child who is being difficult to other activities (Greenberg, 2006). Parents/families are advised to try to avoid becoming the referees and to encourage siblings to arrive at peaceable solutions so that they make an investment in the decision and its successful outcome (Price, 2006; Sparrow, 2006). The behavior of caregivers exerts a major influence on a child's coping strategies. Some web sites that can be searched for a variety of resources on siblings include:

American Psychological Association (www.apa.org/)
Tufts University (http://www.cfw.tufts.edu/topic/2/38.htm)
KidSource (www.kidsource.com)
The National Network for Child Care (www.nncc.org)
Foster Care (www.fostercare.org)
KidsPeace (www.kidspeace.org)

## Conclusion

Bank and Kahn (2003), a team of clinical psychologists who gathered longitudinal data on the interrelationships between and among brothers and sisters, have concluded that some of the grandest and meanest of human emotions are evident in sibling interactions. Everyone who is a brother or sister can remember a time when hot-blooded rage, whispered secrets, uncontrollable silliness, or unwavering support were shared with siblings. Developmental research provides a glimpse of the interpersonal relationships that enable children from the same family to better understand their own responses to the resentments and responsibilities associated with the sibling role; this research also offers guidance to adults. Approximately 80% of us grow up in the company of one or more siblings and research suggests that much of our social, cognitive and emotional learning takes place through our interactions with family members. Sibling relationships are among our earliest social relationships, so studying them more extensively would make an important contribution to the field of human development (Thornton, 2001). Enriching and enlarging our understanding of the bond, exploring the major themes in theory and research, and considering the implications for practice can support not only more effective teaching but also more effective parenting of the young child who is or will become a brother or sister.

## References

Adler, A. (1927). *Understanding human nature.* New York: Fawcett.
Bank, S.P., & Kahn, M. (2003). *The sibling bond.* New York: Basic Books.

Barr, R., & Hayne, H. (2003). It's not what you know, it's who you know: Older siblings facilitate imitation during infancy. *International Journal of Early Years Education, 11*(1) 7–21.

Berk, L. (2001). *Awakening children's minds: How parents and teachers can make a difference.* New York: Oxford University Press.

Bevan, J.L., & Stetzenbach, K.A. (2007). Jealousy expression and communication satisfaction in adult sibling relationships. *Communication Research Reports, 24(1),* 71–77.

Breslau, N., Weitzman, M., & Messenger, K. (1981). Psychological functioning of siblings of disabled children. *Pediatrics 67,* 344–353.

Brodkin, A.M. (2006). "That's not fair!" *Early Childhood Today, 20(4),* 18–19.

Brodkin, A.M. (2003). Sibling jealousy. *Scholastic Parent & Child, 10(6),* 30–31.

Cicirelli, V.G. (1976). Family structure and interaction. In M. F. McMillan & S. Henao (Eds.). *Child Psychiatry: Treatment and Research.* New York: Brunner/Mazel.

Criss, M.M., & Shaw, D.S. (2005). Sibling relationships as contexts for delinquency training in low-income families. *Journal of Family Psychology, 19(4),* 592–600.

Cuskelly, M., & Gunn, P. (2006). Adjustment of children who have a sibling with Down syndrome: Perspectives of mothers, fathers and children. *Journal of Intellectual Disability Research, 50(12),* 917–925.

Deater-Deckard, K. Dunn, J., & Lussier, G. (2002). Sibling relationships and social-emotional adjustment in different family contexts. *Social Development, 11*(4), 571–590.

DeVita-Raeburn, E. (2004). *The empty room: Surviving the loss of a brother or sister at any age.* New York: Simon & Schuster.

Dia, D.A. (2006). What about me? Siblings of children with an anxiety disorder. *Social Work Research, 30(3),* 183–188.

Dunn, J., & Kendrick, C. (1980). The arrival of a sibling: Changes in patterns of interaction between mother and first-born child. *Journal of Child Psychology and Psychiatry and Allied Disciplines, 21,* 119–132.

Edwards, R., & Hadfield, L. (2006). *Sibling identity and relationships: Sisters and brothers.* New York: Taylor & Francis.

Edwards, R., Mauthner, M., & Hadfield, L. (2005). Children's sibling relationships and gendered practices: Talk, activity and dealing with change. *Gender & Education, 17(5),* 499–513.

Foote, R.C., & Holmes-Lonergan, H.A. (2003). Sibling conflict and theory of mind. *British Journal of Developmental Psychology, 21(1),* 45–58.

Fritz, G.K. (2006). The importance of sibling relationships. *Brown University Child & Adolescent Behavior Letter, 22(9),* 8.

Gass, K., Jenkins, J., & Dunn, J. (2007). Are sibling relationships protective? A longitudinal study. *Journal of Child Psychology & Psychiatry, 48(2),* 167–175.

Giallo, R., & Gavidia-Payne, S. (2006). Child, parent, and family factors as predictors of adjustment for siblings of children with a disability. *Journal of Intellectual Disability Research, 50*(12), 937–949.

Goldenthal, P. (2000). *Beyond sibling rivalry: How to help your children become cooperative, caring, and compassionate.* New York: Henry Holt.

Gottlieb, A.R. (2005). *Side by side: On having a gay or lesbian sibling.* Binghamton, NY: Haworth Press.

Greenberg, P. (2007). When a child is unkind to others. *Early Childhood Today, 21(5),* 10.

Greenberg, P. (2006). "Quit distracting me!" *Scholastic Parent & Child, 14(3),* 28–29.

Hegar, R.L. (2005). Sibling placement in foster care and adoption: An overview of international research. *Children & Youth Services Review, 27(7),* 717–739.

Hoffman, K.L., Kiecolt, K.J., & Edwards, J.N. (2005). Physical violence between siblings: A theoretical and empirical analysis. *Journal of Family Issues, 26(8),* 1103–1130.

Howe, N., Rinaldi, C. M., Jennings, M., & Petrakos, H., (2002). "No! The lambs can stay out because they got cozies": Constructive and destructive sibling conflict, pretend play, and social understanding. *Child Development, 73*(5), 1460–1473.

Hughes, C., Fujisawa, K., Ensor, R., Lecce, S., & Marfleet, R. (2006). Cooperation and conversations about the mind: A study of individual differences in 2-year-olds and their siblings. *British Journal of Developmental Psychology, 24(1)*, 53–72.

Jalongo, M. R. (1985). Siblings: Can they, will they, ever get along? *PTA Today*, April, 16–18.

Kramer, L., & Bank, L. (Eds.). (2005). Special Issue: Sibling relationship contributions to individual and family well-being. *Journal of Family Psychology, 19(4)*, 483–657.

Kramer, L., & Kowal, A. K. (2005). Sibling relationship quality from birth to adolescence: The enduring contributions of friends. *Journal of Family Psychology, 19(4)*, 503–511.

Lamb, M. (1978). The development of sibling relationships in infancy: A short term longitudinal study. *Child Development, 49*, 1189–1196.

Lerner, R., & Spanier, G. (1978). *Child influences on marital and family interaction.* New York: Academic.

Loos, M., & Kelly S. (2006). Social well-being of siblings living with a child with diabetes: A qualitative study. *Social Work in Health Care, 43(4)*, 53–69.

Martin, J.L., & Ross, H. S. (2005). Sibling aggression: Sex differences and parents' reactions. *International Journal of Behavioral Development, 29(2)*, 129–138.

Mauthner, M.L., & Weeks, J. (2005). *Sistering: Power and change in female relationships.* New York: Palgrave Macmillian.

McElwain, N. L., & Volling, B.L. (2005). Preschool children's interactions with friends and older siblings: relationship specificity and joint contributions to problem behavior. *Journal of Family Psychology, 19(4)*, 486–496.

McKeever, P. (1983). Siblings of chronically ill children: A literature review with implications for research and practice. *American Journal of Orthopsychiatry, 53*, 203–218.

Miller, J.N., & Yavnek, N. Eds. (2006). *Sibling relations and gender in the early modern world: Thicker than water.* London: Ashgate Publishing, Limited.

Miller, N., & Maruyama, G. (1976). Ordinal position and peer popularity. *Journal of Personality and Social Psychology 33*, 123–131.

Mock, D.W. (2004). *More than kin and less than kind: The evolution of family conflict.* Cambridge, MA: Harvard University Press.

Modry-Mandell, K.L., Gamble, W.C., & Taylor, A.R. (2007). Family emotional climate and sibling relationship quality: Influences on behavioral problems and adaptation in preschool-aged children. *Journal of Child & Family Studies, 16(1)*, 59–71.

Moore, K. A., Evans, J. V., Brooks-Gunn, J., & Roth, J. (2001). What are good child outcomes? In A. Thornton (Ed.), *The well-being of children and families: Research and data needs* (pp. 59–84). Ann Arbor, MI: University of Michigan Press.

Papalia, D., Olds, S.W., & Feldman, R.D. (2005). *A child's world: infancy through adolescence* (10th ed.). New York: McGraw-Hill.

Pike, A., Coldwell, J., & Dunn, J. (2005). Sibling relationships in early/middle childhood: Links with individual adjustment. *Journal of Family Psychology, 19(4)*, 523–532.

Price, S. (2006). The sibling saga. *Scholastic Choices, 21(5)*, 14–17.

Rogoff, B. (2003). *The cultural nature of human development,* New York: Oxford University Press.

Rondon, N. (2007a). Sibling competition. *Current Health 2, 33(7)*, 12–14.

Rondon, N. (2007b). Sibling rivals. *Current Health 1, 30(7)*, 22–25.

Richmond, M.K., Stocker, C.M., & Rienks, S.L. (2005). Longitudinal associations between sibling relationship quality, parental differential treatment, and children's adjustment. *Journal of Family Psychology, 19(4)*, 550–559.

Rubin, Z. (1980). *Children's friendships.* Cambridge, MA: Harvard University Press.

Safer, J. (2003). *The normal one: Life with a difficult or damaged sibling.* New York: Dell.

Sanders, R. (2004). *Sibling relationships: Theory and issues for practice.* New York: Palgrave/Macmillan.

Schaneveldt, J., & Ihinger, M. (1979). Sibling relationships in the family. In W. Burr, R. Hill, I. Nye & I. Reiss (Eds.)., *Contemporary theories about the family Vol. I.* New York: Free Press.

Simeonsson, R., & McHale, S. (1981). Review: Research on handicapped children: Sibling relationships. *Child Care, Health and Development 1*, 153–171.

Sparrow, J.D. (2006). Coping with sibling rivalry. *Scholastic Parent & Child, 14*(1), 48–51.

Staub, E. (1975). *The development of prosocial behavior in children*. Morristown, NJ: General Learning Press.

Strohm, K. (2005). *Being the other one: Growing up with a brother or sister who has special needs*. Boston: Shambhala Publications.

Stewart, R. B. (1983). Sibling attachment relationships: Child-infant interaction in a strange situation. *Developmental Psychology 19*, 192–199.

Tarakeshwar, N., Lobato, D., Kao, B., & Plante, W. (2006). Sibling relationships in cultural context. *Brown University Child & Adolescent Behavior Letter, 22*(7), 1–7.

Thornton, A. (2001). Recommendations: Family and child well-being research network. In A. Thornton (Ed.), *The well-being of children and families: Research and data needs* (pp. 437–448). Ann Arbor: University of Michigan Press.

Todd, M.D. (2001). *Linked for life: How our siblings affect our lives*. New York: Kensington.

Verte, S., Hebbrecht, L., & Roeyers, H. (2006). Psychological adjustment of siblings of children who are deaf or hard of hearing. *Volta Review, 106*(1), 89–110.

Volling, B. L., & Blandon, A.Y. (2005). Positive indicators of sibling relationship quality: The sibling inventory of behavior. In K. A. Moore & L. H. Lippman (Eds.) *What do children need to flourish? Conceptualizing indicators of positive development* (pp. 203–213). New York: Springer Science and Business Media

Whiting, B. B., & Whiting, J.M. (1975). *Children of six cultures*. Cambridge, MA: Harvard University Press.

Wolkoff, S.R., Schwartzber, N.S., & Meckwood-Yazdpour, J.E., Eds. (2006). *Raising young children well: Insights and ideas for parents and teachers*. New York: Other Press.

**Mary Renck Jalongo**
Professor
122 Davis Hall
560 North 11th Street
Indiana University of Pennsylvania
Indiana, PA 15705
724-357-2417
mjalongo@iup.edu
654 College Lodge Road
Indiana, PA 15701
724-349-5423

Mary Renck Jalongo, Ph.D. is the editor-in-chief of *Early Childhood Education Journal* and co-editor of the Series. She is the coordinator of the Doctoral Program in Curriculum and Instruction and a professor of education at Indiana University of Pennsylvania. She has published numerous books in the field, including *Exploring Your Role: An Introduction to Early Childhood Education. Creative Thinking and Arts-Based Learning, K-4th Grade,* and *Early Childhood Language Arts.*

**Denise Dragich**
227 North 9th Street
Indiana, PA 15701
724-349-0445

Denise Dragich is a doctoral candidate and principal of Eisenhower Elementary School in Indiana Area School District.

# Chapter 6
# How Attention to Family Stress Dynamics can Prevent Homelessness Among Very Young Families

**Kevin James Swick and Reginald Harrison Williams**

**Abstract** Despite the pervasiveness of homelessness among young families, few early childhood professionals realize the exacerbated stresses that push them into their circumstances. This chapter seeks to explore the etiology of risk factors (especially substances abuse and illiteracy), elaborate on how they affect the lives of young families, highlight ways that they respond to these factors, and detail possible avenues that early childhood professionals can take in empowering these young families to pull themselves out of their homelessness.

**Keywords** families, stressors, stress, chronic stress, family dynamics, homelessness, family support, violence, abuse, illiteracy, poverty, unemployment, chemical dependency, risk factors, family support, social services, Bronfenbrenner, ecological systems theory

A great deal of homelessness among families is preventable (Nuñez, 1996). This is especially the case if we help very young families resolve stress factors before they become chronic and debilitating. Multiple stressors can interact to promote the conditions that create homelessness in very young families (Swick, 2004). Indeed factors that put very young families at high-risk for homelessness are noted in Table 1 (Bassuk, 1991; Dail, 1990; Swick, 2005a). In examining these stress factors we must be careful to avoid seeing each one as an isolated event. Each stress is inter-connected with others that can indeed exacerbate the overall stress of the family (Dunst, Trivette, & Deal, 1988).

Often these stressors appear in patterns of risk factors in families. For example, violence and abuse often appear as a stress factor in a family that is also experiencing chemical dependence (Swick & Williams, 2006). Combined, these stressors can degrade the family's systems for living. Another example is the close relationship between chronic poverty and homelessness (Bassuk, Browne, & Buckner, 1996). Families with little education and few job skills are more susceptible to homelessness (Bassuk, 1991). Also noteworthy is the role of "support resources" in helping

University of South Carolina

M.R. Jalongo (ed.), *Enduring Bonds.*
© Springer 2008

**Table 1**  Stress Factors that Place Young Families At Risk for Homelessness

- Severe trauma
- Violence/abuse
- Chronic severe poverty
- Chemical dependency
- Never married, single parents
- Teen parenthood
- Persistent health issues
- Illiteracy
- Lack of high school graduation
- Unemployed/under-employed
- Below poverty level wages
- Poor or no support
- Isolation from helpful others
- Chronic foster care placement

families respond to stress. Families with few resources are at higher risk for home-lessness (Lewit & Baker, 1996). The combination of chronic stressors in the lives of families and very low support resources does indeed create conditions associated with homelessness (Bassuk, Dawson, & Perloff, 2001).

Various patterns of stressors impact families, with particular emphasis on the interaction of these factors as they happen in specific families. For example, in one case the determining factor may be a serious chemical dependency in a family member that pulls all of the family energy and resources into maintaining that habit and life style. In this way regular family needs are never met, negatively impacting how other family members function in their daily lives (Fals-Stewart, Fincham, & Kelley, 2004). Left unchecked this syndrome can foster conditions for promoting it as an intergenerational situation. In another case it may be the press of external events such as chronic unemployment that acts as the instigator of heavy stress in the family. While we can identify patterns of events and behaviors in families that become homeless we do not have exact insights in this regard. The dynamics of each family influence their resilience or susceptibility to various stressors (Hanson & Lynch, 2004; Swick & Williams, 2006).

## The Etiology of High-risk Stress Factors

Stress factors that create high-risk conditions are the result of bio-ecological trans-actions (Bronfenbrenner, 1979; 2005). In our usage, bio-ecological refers to the fact that both individual and environmental factors interact to create stressors. A stressor is typically the result of environmental interactions that foster the disruption of one's life context. The individual's reactions to an event as well as the substance of the event and the interactions with related events create the stress factor(s). There may also be biological factors that play a role in these stressors.

Thus, some stressors combined with a fragile individual context create high-risk situations (Bronfenbrenner, 2005). For example, a single parent may have access to strong support resources and not be compromised by her status. Strong, supportive parents and family seem to buffer single teen parents from many stressors, making their lives much more manageable (Rosier, 2000). Likewise, supportive school programs that help teen parents stay in school add power to the young person's development. Yet a single teen parent who is abandoned by her supportive adults may be seriously harmed and traumatized by particular stressors (Rosier, 2000). In effect, this parent may find their situation to be over-whelming. It is important to recognize that heavy stress often is interrelated with the family or the parent being isolated from needed supports and resources, a situation which increases the stress on the family (Bronfenbrenner, 2005).

In the case of very young families the sources of "risks" that often lead to homelessness are dynamic – interrelated with each other and often damaging the "systems" of the family to the degree of dysfunction (Swick, 2004). While each case is unique we see some stress factors recur that create high-risk conditions for homelessness or the occurrence of similar situations like doubling up with a relative after being evicted (Wasson & Hill, 1998). Thus, factors like illiteracy, chemical dependency, low-wage jobs, domestic abuse, and poor supports can precipitate homelessness in very young families (Shane, 1996). The impact of these stressors is particularly damaging in the early years because many young families have not had time to develop patterns of social problem solving (Hanson & Lynch, 2004; Wasson & Hill, 1998).

The meaning of "risk factors" and the "degree of risk" fostered offer additional insight into how families are impacted by chronic stressors.

A "risk factor" is any event or situation that *may* signal potential harm to the person. Swick (1993) notes that the "term *risk* implies possible danger or harm is likely unless some preventive or corrective action is taken." (p.75) Risk factors may include individual, environmental, or more likely combinations of these factors. Risks vary in the degree of impact they may have on people. Swick and Graves (1993) delineate low, moderate, and high levels of risk. *Low-risk* is indicative of a situation in which just one or two risks exist and have little long-term impact if attended to effectively. The key is being attended to in an effective way. *Moderate-risk* implies that two or more serious risk conditions are present, pervasive, and do represent a distinct threat to the family. In this situation, it is critical to have family support in responding to the stressors impacting them. *High-risk* indicates that the family is indeed experiencing very high stress from events that place the total family functioning in danger. Usually, there are multiple interacting stressors that combine to create the need for very high support and intervention with the family.

Very young families are especially at risk when their integrity is jeopardized by chronic violence, serious economic problems, lack of needed supports, and other stressors (Nuñez, 1996). Homelessness itself further exacerbates the family's situation. Swick (2004) notes that:

> Family dynamics are impacted in several serious ways due to homelessness: loss of privacy, lack of control over daily routines, isolation from needed support people, loss of social and economic resources, loss of self-esteem, disruption of communication systems, high stress, and constant mobility. (p. 5)

Supports like helpful family and friends and resources like quality child care and job training seem to protect families and provide them with tools to respond to stressors effectively (Garbarino, 1992). When such supports fail, a family may be left without any meaningful alternative. This is especially true of the role extended families play. As a huge source of economic and social dependency, it leaves a gaping hole in a family's reservoir of resources if it is not strong. Without it, the family loses an outlet for networking that will aid them as they face stressors.

## How Risk Factors Interact in the Lives of Families

Stress happens within a socio-cultural context that helps us give meaning to the events and relations we experience (Swick & Williams, 2006). Human perception plays a significant role in the way we interpret and respond to stressors. What happens to us helps to shape our way of seeing the world in which we live. For example, if we are so immune to the dangers of violence because violence is our way of life we fail to see it as a risk factor and thus we relate to it as routine living. If this perception is further reinforced then we see violence not as a risk factor but as a way of life (Swick, 2005). The brain is a patterning organ and if violence is the prevailing imprint on the brain, it is seen as the norm (Goleman, 1995; Goleman, 2006; Restack, 2003). It is important to keep this perceptual issue in mind as we examine how risk factors impact families because the early relations in families often set the tone for how people perceive and then respond to stress (Rogoff, 2003).

For example, Karr-Morse and Wiley (1997) document the life-long negative impact of violence on children and their families. A "pattern of abusive behavior" is often inter-related with a myriad of other "risky" behaviors such as chemical dependency, low self-esteem, and anti-social acts (Peled, Jaffe, & Edleson, 1995). In effect, risk factors tend to nurture other risks in our lives unless we take action to change our lives. If we do not see a stressor as potentially harmful to us we may allow that event or behavior to denigrate our lives (Bronfenbrenner, 2005). The reverse is also true where families develop and refine caring ways of helping each other, thus promoting a pattern of empathy and nurturance in family relations. As Oliner and Oliner (1995) note: "When empathy becomes real through the actions of family, children internalize a more useful concept of caring. They come to see empathy as a part of their daily lives" (p. 16).

A prevailing attribute of very young families experiencing high-risk situations is the "feedback cycle" that degrading risks promote (Bronfenbrenner, 2005). For example, Bassuk (1991) noted that several elements of healthy family life are disrupted by homelessness such as parent-child intimacy, identity development, and rituals like playing and sharing together – all of which are needed for developing caring lives. There is also the "stigma" of being homeless which invites others to label and/or perceive one as less than capable. In the absence of early intervention, many homeless families internalize a persistently low self-image of themselves (Nuñez, 1996).

How families respond to risk factors is very important, especially during the early childhood years. Influencing family responses are personal family history, available support people/resources, access to needed services, one's level of effectiveness in problem solving, financial resources, and many other factors. Combined, these forces help to shape how families respond to stressors. These are especially critical elements in the family's formative years because this is when families develop "stress reaction patterns" that once formed are very difficult to change. For example, adults who grew up in highly abusive families are more prone to being abusive in their own behavior (Groves, 2002). In effect, the social schema we learn in the early childhood years become the foundation upon which our life long social and emotional relations are developed (Goleman, 2006).

As human beings we tend to develop "patterns of functioning" based on our early relationship experiences (Bronfenbrenner, 2005). Research on the human brain indicates that the patterns of behavior we repeat become the prevailing modes of our lives (Restack, 2003; Rogoff, 2003). For example, children who are under chronic stress only "know" stress as a constant element in their lives. They may live in high-stressed ways even when stress does not exist because they have no understanding of what life is like without chronic stress (Perry, 1997). Thus, these children are always showing signs of being under heavy stress such as acting out violence or exhibiting low self-esteem behaviors (Bancroft, 2004).

How parents and other family deal with relationships and events is indeed the primary model children have as they develop their own socio-emotional lives (Hallowell, 2002). Further, families create their own system of relations that establish their ways of interacting and functioning. How stress is perceived and responded to is a key to the overall health of the family (Hanson & Lynch, 2004).

*Five insights are helpful in understanding how families experiencing heavy stress may distort their relations and actions* (Swick & Williams, 2006):

1. Chronic stress actually impedes our brain functioning, thus increasing the potential for family conflicts (Perry, 1997; Restack, 2003). Stress reduces blood flow to the brain, thus reducing its effectiveness. It also prompts us to prematurely form closure on how to relate to others in negative, ineffective ways (Goleman, 2006)

2. In trying to react to heavy stress families may scape-goat a particular family member as a means of "blaming" someone for the stress (Bancroft, 2004). Blaming someone is ineffective because the real needs of the situation are never addressed. Yet this blaming technique is adopted because it buffers the family from needed change; thus embedding them in punitive relationships (Satir, 1988; Goleman, 2006).

3. Under heavy stress families often seek solace in addictive behaviors that help them avoid dealing with the realities of their lives (Garbarino, 1992). Chemical addictions are false solutions as they only prolong and increase the stress. As noted by Hanson and Lynch (2004), addictive behaviors absorb so much energy that needed family caring rituals never get attention. Life is spent in feeding the addiction and essential caring is never achieved.

4. Chronic stress is very demanding on family energy, leaving little room for mutually nurturing relations (Swick & Williams, 2006). Families under chronic stress report that they never are able to become fully involved in life, they are constantly on the defensive.

5. Stressed families often fall victim to blaming each other as opposed to helping each other respond to the stress (Swick, 2004). It is difficult to shape caring relations when people are only seeing the deficits in each other (Bronfenbrenner, 2005).

In effect, if families lack the affective, cognitive, and social skills and support for dealing with particular stressors, they may create distorted and degrading response patterns (Swick, 2005).


## Examples of How Stress—Family Response Patterns Form: Insights for Being Effective Helpers

Families are dynamic human learning systems that rely on socio-emotional relationship patterns that sustain their daily functioning. These patterns are formed early in the family's growth and represent the "relationship map" they use in negotiating daily stressors (Swick & Williams, 2006). Three examples of families' stress reaction patterns are helpful in explicating how early childhood professionals can better understand and support families who are homeless or at very high-risk for becoming homeless.

The first case is the *Bennett family*. This is a single mother with two young children (ages 2 and 4) who is currently residing at Sister Care – an emergency shelter for abused women and their children. She escaped an abusive relationship and has been at Sister Care for a week. This is the third time in the past year that she sought shelter to escape violence. Each time the "cycle of violence" happened she returned home after her husband apologized and promised it would never happen again. But now the violence is more severe and the children are suffering more, as evidenced in the school time lost and in their overall behavior. The case manager at the shelter has outlined some steps for the mother to use in developing a plan for starting a new life apart from her spouse. These steps include: counseling for her and the children, help in finishing her college education (which she had abandoned at her husband's prompting), plans for immediate work so the family can move into a new apartment, and several other life skills and support services.

Violence has been a problem since the beginning of this family. The mother says that she noticed violence in her spouse even when they were dating but thought it would change once they got married. The children have seen a great deal of violence and the 4-year old is now acting out violent scenes in his play at school. The 2-year old is sick a great deal and developmentally delayed in several areas of development. The mother has noticed that even with just one week at the shelter that all of them are eating and sleeping better.

Reflect on the family's early involvement with violence. How has this affected their relationships? What impact is it having on everyone in the family? In what ways can we as early childhood professionals support this family in making a transition to a more peaceful way of living? Specifically, how can we help the children find our school and classrooms as safe and nurturing?

The second case is the *Roland family*. Mr. Roland has three children (ages 5, 7, and 10). They are now living in a transitional housing situation at Homes First – a social agency that seeks to help families gain permanent housing. They were living for two years with his sister who had a new baby (her third) and thus they had to find another place to live. His wife was alcoholic and left him and the children after the birth of the third child. Mr. Roland is mostly unemployed and lacks a high school diploma. He also has a drinking problem but has had control of it over the last year. He is eager to gain employment so he can care for his children more effectively. He is working with the social worker at school on some employment possibilities and getting back into school.

Consider the dynamics of Mr. Roland's life. He is trying to respond to his own needs of staying sober, returning to school, caring for his children, and gaining employment. In what ways can early childhood professionals be of help to him in his journey to become empowered?

Lastly, we have the Palmer family in which Ms. Jackson grew up as the youngest child with three siblings. Her mother was an alcoholic, provided an insecure home situation, and allowed the children to roam the streets without supervision. As a result Ms. Jackson grew up with a very defiant attitude about school, dropped out, and eventually acquired a drug habit.

Eventually the house was not big enough for both her mother's and her own drug habits, so her mother made her leave. Forced to live on the streets and with no other place to go, Ms. Jackson eventually went into an emergency shelter where she met Jacob. The relationship with Jacob lasted only briefly and he moved on. Not long afterward, she realized she was pregnant and was allowed to return to her mother's home. And once again while under her mother's roof, Ms. Jackson gives birth to a daughter.

Reflect on Ms. Jackson's challenges and ask yourself How can I, as her home visitor, assist her in becoming more skilled and confident in being a parent? How

can we help her develop more caring in her life system? How can we help her
address some of her key challenges?


## Substance Abuse and Homeless Families: A Review
## of Key Stressors

Substance abuse and homelessness have historical links that offer critical insights
into how unhealthy stress can create trauma for entire families (Banyard, 1997).
Individuals who are homeless are profoundly affected by substance abuse because
it raises the already high stress they are experiencing. It often manifests itself in
extreme dependence on others, low self-esteem, and a lack of viable and caring
social networks – mainly because of the distrust that substance abuse invites (Peled,
Jaffe, & Edleson, 1995).

*Many homeless families can point to some family member who suffered from*
*some form of drug or alcohol abuse* (Browne & Bassuk, 1997; Chassin, Pitts,
DeLucia, & Todd, 1999). Typically, the parent seeks the solace of chemical
dependence to escape the stress of trying to feed and house the family on less than
minimal income. Social isolation, illiteracy, and chaotic relations with others also
feed this process of substance abuse (Peters, McMahon, & Quinsey, 1992). This is
why we need to nurture caring relations in families and communities during the
early childhood years.

The tragedies of such abuse are many but critically, chemically dependent adults
lack the daily energy and focus to care for their children effectively (Rosier, 2000).
Unfortunately, children see the dysfunction in their parents and often internalize
this mode of living and begin the cycle over again, acting out in school and copying
the adult drug abuse behaviors as they get older (Brayden, Deitrick-MacLean,
Deitrich, Sherrold, & Altemeier, 1995).

*There is a clear link between substance abuse and continued dependence of*
*homeless families on the social service system* (Peled, Jaffe, & Edleson, 1995). The
presence of substance abuse adds to the stressors the family is already experiencing, thus increasing the likelihood of this family remaining dependent (Hanson &
Lynch, 2004). Indeed, the story of most chemically dependent homeless families is
one of total focus on maintaining the drug habit and thus all else takes lower priority
(Fals-Stewart, Fincham, & Kelley, 2004).

*Individual and total family self-esteem are negatively impacted by the substance*
*abuse life style* (Gelles & Cornell, 1985; Rosier, 2000). Three elements contribute
to this low self-esteem (Hanson & Lynch, 2004): 1) the individual/family are cognizant of their aberrant life style; 2) their social isolation reduces the supportive
help they could receive; and 3) their energy is totally focused on the drug habit.

With lowered self-esteem the chemically dependent parent adopts negative and
punitive relations with their children, thus creating a dysfunctional pattern for
nurturing children. Further this process creates barriers to healthy socialization
with other support systems. In effect, families where substance abuse is common

experience very difficult circumstances. They tend to be homeless more often and for longer periods of time, and they tend to repeat their homelessness more often (Bassuk, Dawson, & Perloff, 2001).

## Illiteracy: A Major Risk Factor for Homeless Families

Illiteracy is a powerful force in holding back families who are homeless. Literacy is indeed the energy that empowers people to carry out life's many functions. Illiteracy is a major stress area that can push a family into homelessness (Nuñez, 1996).

Without basic literacy skills, parents are unable to achieve even the most minimal educational levels (Sheppard, 2006). Thus, high illiteracy rates among homeless families are not surprising but rather alarming because a major tool for breaking the barriers to being homeless is having a good education. The trap of being limited to low-paying jobs creates a web of challenges for many parents who are homeless or on the edge of becoming homeless. The research data show that parents trapped in low-paying work have extreme difficulty surviving economically (Toro, 1999).

Illiteracy negatively impacts parents and children who are homeless. Parents suffer from several issues related to lack of literacy skills: low self-esteem, poor job skills, lack of needed life management skills, difficulty in doing the parenting roles, and many other challenges (Bassuk, Browne, & Buckner, 1996). Likewise, children suffer greatly because they are–or potentially can become–a part of intergenerational illiteracy unless there is early and continuing intervention (Brizius & Foster, 1993). Children depend on parents and other adults to guide them toward literacy skills that empower them to lead fulfilling lives.

*Early childhood professionals can empower parents and children through several literacy enhancing strategies.* A starting point is to strengthen the social and life skills of parents and children. It is important for us to help parents and children advance their skills in relating to others, solving problems, and interacting in the world in productive ways (Brizius & Foster, 1993). We must help them develop not only self-coping skills but also independent-living skills and community-living skills (Bernfield, Blasé, & Fixen, 2006).

Another strategy we can foster is collaborating with shelters for homeless families in developing literacy support resources in the shelters (Nuñez, 1996). This might be accomplished by setting up a literacy center in the shelter that is equipped with print and computer resources, tutoring, and possibly some classes for parents and the children. The goal here is to meet the socio-educational needs of the families.

Sponsoring adult education courses, after school programs, and specialized job training opportunities are excellent resources we can help to provide parents and children who are homeless. We need to pay special attention to providing child care, transportation, and other needed enabling services so the parents and children can fully utilize such services.

Ultimately we want to empower families with as many literacy skills as possible so that they can reshape their lives into being productive in terms of economic and social factors. Quality early childhood programs can indeed use many community resources to create family literacy and related parent and child empowerment resources, but it takes a partnership. Communities must have a common knowledge-base, shared goals, and an established system for maintaining their quality (Horsley & Ciske, 2005).

## Early Childhood Educator's Role: Beginning with Understanding

Because families are in the formative stage during the early childhood years, it is critical that early childhood professionals develop an authentic, sensitive, and responsive understanding of the stressors families experience and the nature of how these stressors affect young families (Pipher, 1996). The stressors families experience during these early years are powerful because they serve as the foundation upon which families craft their relationship patterns, develop responses to different stressors, and hopefully develop skills and perspectives for anticipating and resolving risk factors that may place them in very difficult situations (Swick & Williams, 2006). In particular, three roles are important for early childhood professionals to consider in their efforts to support young families: 1) awareness of the factors that place young families at-risk for homelessness; 2) understanding of how families develop relationship patterns when they are under stress; and 3) knowledge of perspectives and skills they can use to help families deal with stressors (Swick, 2004).

*Awareness* of key factors that place young families at-risk for homelessness is a key to our developing proactive skills for helping families. We need to be asking questions such as (Nuñez, 1996):

1. What are indicators of very high family stress?
2  What factors seem to lead to homelessness in young families?
3. What are some observable indicators and behaviors in young children that suggest they may be homeless or at-risk for this situation?
4. Where in the community can we gain further insight into the risk situations families of our young children face?
5. How can we make initial steps toward developing school and community resources that might address these family stressors?

*Understanding* how families respond to stress and develop relationship patterns that evidence these stressors is vital to becoming effective and sensitive helpers (Bronfenbrenner, 2005). In many cases early childhood professionals want to be helpful but lack insights into the nature of how families under heavy stress respond by altering their relationship patterns; which in turn exert a negative effect on how they function. For example, it is very common for alcoholic families to "enable" the alcoholic (changing the social and psychological ecology of the family to allow for the alcoholic to dominate people's lives) to continue their dependency behaviors (Pittman, 1987). While this enabling behavior is understandable because it seems to save the family from further dysfunction, it is actually very damaging because it prevents the family from developing healthy relations. In a similar mode, abusive spousal relations may create the "cycle of violence" where after the violence the family sinks into a "we forgive you" response system without addressing the problems fostering the violence. As early childhood professionals we need to understand why these maladaptive behavior patterns are harmful to growth and development, and we need to develop skills for helping families address these stressors, helping them find resources and support for improving their situations.

*Knowledge* of perspectives and skills for helping families under stress is also important to our total skill kit (Bancroft, 2004). As helping professionals we need to be sensitive to the multitude of factors that impinge upon the lives of high-risk families. Too often we see the situation through our professional lens that may only provide us with limited insights into our having a trusting and nurturing relationship with the family. Yet we need to understand the family perspective, see the dynamics of their daily lives as they are impacted by these events. For example, living in a very small house with four children and an alcoholic can indeed create very high stress, thus impeding the accomplishment of what may seem like small events such as being on time for school (Swick & Williams, 2006). Living in an abusive relationship may deplete the energy of the family to such a degree that many prosocial activities are abandoned so as to "hide" the abusive situation (Mills, 2003).

## Recommendations for Preventing Homelessness in Very Young Families

As the scholarly efforts noted in this paper suggest, there are several effective practices that we can use to help prevent and/or resolve homelessness and other risk factors in very young families. Helping families *address risk factors very early in their development* is a key to empowering families to form positive and supportive relations (Conard & Novick, 1996). Several rationales provide the substance for this construct of very early intervention. One of these ideas is that as families gain success in resolving risk factors like chemical dependence or abusive relations they change their behavior patterns toward more proactive and mutually strengthening relations (Bronfenbrenner, 2005). As families build upon each successful venture they create their own system of healthy, resilient interactions that further empower every aspect of their lives. Even small changes in parent-child relations toward establishing more nurturing interactions are noted to positively impact future behaviors (Brazelton & Greenspan, 2000). As one homeless parent noted, after she modified her evening routine to include reading with the children each night their ways of interacting improved greatly and they also became more caring toward each other.

Another element in this construct is that by disrupting the prevalence of risk factors early in the family's life the less damage such stressors can foster (Swick & Graves, 1993). It is the continuing degradation that risk factors support that is so powerful in creating family dysfunction.

Perhaps the most positive element in this construct is that it provides families with a set of visible ways to solve problems (Swick, 2005). For example, young parents who return to school and achieve a high school equivalency diploma, and often more education, note that they are empowered to seek solutions to many different stressors in their lives. They often seek more education and better jobs (Rosier, 2000).

Another important practice is to *engage the family in mapping solutions to the key stressors they are experiencing* (Swick & Williams, 2006). Families often have valuable insights relative to what is happening in their lives, especially when they are involved in a coaching relationship with helpers who respect and value their ideas and feelings (Hanft, Rush, & Shelden, 2004). For example, one home visitor who was trying to help a family deal with grief noted that when she took time to listen to different family members she found they were indeed beginning to put together the needed elements for handling their situation. Four steps can help shape this process into a very caring experience:

1. Involve the family in identifying the key stressors in their situation.
2. Ask the family to articulate ways they feel these stressors can best be addressed.
3. Help the family to begin to take steps to put their ideas in action.
4. Strategize with the family in a way to increase its social resilience to social and family changes through the school system (Garbarino, 1992; Hiatt-Michael, 2001).

Families need external helpers but they have many solutions to their situations when they are supported in this direction.

Homelessness among young families is a very dynamic process that requires *strategies for nurturing the long-term well being of the family* (Swick, 1997). Several stressors interact to degrade families: economic, social, educational, psychological, political, and several other factors. The prevention of homelessness among young families needs to begin with the formation of the family. Prenatal care, attention to maternal health and well being, support for having healthy marital relations, and nurturing young people toward completing optimal education and job training are examples of strategies that can indeed act to empower them in their early development as parents and families (Swick, 2004).

In addition, identifying risk factors early in the lives of parents and families is key to establishing a basis for their long term well being (Lewit & Baker, 1996). For example, research notes that adults who spent considerable time in foster care settings are more at risk for homelessness (Bassuk, Buckner, Weinreb, Browne, Bassuk, Dawson, & Perloff, 1997). Other factors such as being sexually abused as a child, being involved in an abusive relationship as an adult, and lacking essential literacy and education skills–all intensify the risk of homelessness (Bassuk, Dawson, & Perloff, 2001). Helping parents and families identify and then address risk factors early can provide the basis for long term health. Counseling, education, and appropriate support resources can empower young families to deal with potential stressors early in their lives (Connard & Novick, 1996). Families need to know the power of "past ghosts" like abuse and neglect in their lives. In this way they can begin to address risks that may impede their functioning (Kerr-Morse & Wiley, 1997).

Three additional long-term strategies that can strengthen young families are: involving them in parenting education, connecting them to supportive relations with others, and helping them gain needed educational skills (Nuñez, 1996). High quality parenting acts as a protective factor in preventing homelessness among young families (Bassuk, Buckner, Weinreb, Browne, Bassuk, Dawson, & Perloff, 1997). Effective parenting promotes positive relations within families that enable them to solve problems and position themselves to empower each other (Swick & Williams, 2006).

Encouraging and supporting families in linking up with supportive others is critical to their long-term successful functioning. Strong interpersonal relations are associated with better mental health, better job and school achievement, and more problem-solving skills – all of which are linked to the prevention of chronic problems in families (Bassuk, Dawson, & Perloff, 2001). Use parent meetings and conference times to help parents strengthen their networking skills (Powell, 1998).

Engaging young parents in attaining needed education and job skills is key to their success in maintaining adequate family functioning. Without education young families face many obstacles in maintaining housing and other life needs.

*Through the use of empowering approaches,* early childhood professionals can help families achieve quality living arrangements. A sampling of roles and strategies we can carry out are instructive of the importance of our part in helping families who are homeless or at-risk for becoming homeless.

One role is to function as a *liaison* for the children and families in your school or center. Make sure the needs of the children are being met, that staff are aware of the needs of children who are homeless, that families are receiving needed services, and that the community is connected to the school and the children in productive ways. Be an advocate for young families – seek to engage the community in empowering families.

We can all act to *remove barriers* to children's school success. For example, make sure children have the transportation needed to get to the school of their choice. We should also check to see that children have after-school transportation if needed so they can participate in other activities. Check with shelters to be sure they have arrangements where children can do homework in a comfortable and supportive place. Help the shelter if you can to provide this needed support, and advocate for better after-school programs.

Very importantly, *develop nurturing relations with the children and the entire family.* Positive supportive approaches empower the child and the parents in finding success in the school and community settings. Two ways to carry this nurturing out are: 1) tutor the children as they may need a boost to get started in setting up regular study habits; and 2) offer to hold family conferences and programs at nearby shelters (or at churches) to meet families where it is most convenient for them.

Help families *get needed counseling and support*. They may need the school counselor to simply listen to their concerns, help them initiate some problem-solving, or help them gain connections to needed community or professional resources.

*Involve parents and family in* finding ways to solve their stressors, to gain adequate housing, and to be a part of their children's education. For example, involve parents who are homeless in leadership training where they can initiate efforts to address some of their stressors while they are also helping others strengthen their lives.

*Promote school success habits* in all children and families you interact with during the school year. For example, help parents learn of the importance of "home learning" where they read with their children, talk with them about their interests and encourage them to explore their environment.

Ultimately, early childhood professionals can empower families to resolve stressors that place them at risk for being homeless or support homeless families in becoming able to move toward housing stability. Young families can create the needed stability and well being for caring relations with children when they have empowered helpers.

# References

Bancroft, L. (2004). *When dad hurts mom*. New York: G.P. Putnam Sons.
Banyard, V. (1997). The impact of childhood sexual abuse and family functioning on four dimensions of women's later parenting. *Child Abuse and Neglect, 21*, 1095–1107.
Bassuk, E. (1991). Homeless families. *Scientific American, 265*, 66–74.
Bassuk, E., Browne, A., & Buckner, J. (1996). Single mothers and welfare. *Scientific American, 275* (4), 60–67.
Bassuk, E., Dawson, R., & Perloff, J. (2001). Multiply homeless families: The insidious impact of violence. *Housing Policy Debate, 1*(3), 299–320.
Bassuk, E., Buckner, J., Weinreb, L., Browne, A., Bassuk, S., Dawson, R., & Perloff, J. (1997). Homelessness in female-headed families: Childhood and adult risk and protective factors. *American Journal of Public Health, 87*, 241–261.
Bernfield, G., Blasé, K., & Fixen, D. (2006). Towards a unified perspective on human service delivery systems. *The Behavior Analyst Today, 7*(2), 168–187.
Bhola, H. (2004). Policy implementation: Planning and actualizing. *Journal of Educational Planning and Administration, 18* (3), 295–312.
Brayden, V., Deitrich-MacLean, G., Dietrich, M., Sherrod, K., & Altemeier, W. (1995). Evidence for specific effects of childhood sexual abuse on mental well-being and physical self-esteem. *Child Abuse and Neglect, 19*(10), 1255–1262.
Brazelton, T., & Greenspan, S. (2000). *The irreducible needs of children*. Cambridge, MA: Perseus Publishing.
Brizius, J., & Foster, S. (1993). *Generation to generation: Realizing the promise of family literacy*. Ypsilanti, MI: High Scope Press.
Bronfenbrenner, U. (2005). *Making human beings human: Bioecological perspectives on human development*. Thousand Oaks, CA: Sage.
Bronfenrbrenner, U. (1979). *The ecology of human development*. Cambridge, MA: Harvard University Press.

Browne, A., & Bassuk, S. (1999). Intimate violence in the lives of homeless and poor housed women: Prevalence and patterns in an ethnically diverse sample. *American Journal of Orthopsychiatry, 67* (2), 261–278.

Chassin, L., Pitts, S., DeLucia, C., & Todd, M. (1999). A longitudinal study of children of alcoholics: Predicting young adult substance use disorders, anxiety, and depression. *Journal of Abnormal Psychology, 108* (1), 106–119.

Conard, C., & Novick, R. (1996). *The ecology of the family: A background paper for a family-centered approach to education and social service delivery.* Portland, OR: Northwest Regional Educational Laboratory.

Dail, P. (1990). The psychosocial context of homeless mothers with young children: Program and policy implications. *Child Welfare, 69* (4), 291–307.

Dubow, E., & Reid, G. (1994). Risk and resource variables in children's aggressive behavior: A two-year longitudinal study. In L. Huesmann (Ed.), *Aggressive behavior: Current perspectives (pp. 72–91).* New York: Plenum.

Dunst, C., Trivette, C., & Deal, A. (1988). *Enabling and empowering families: Principles and guidelines for practice.* Cambridge, MA: Brookline Books.

Fals-Stewart, W., Fincham, F., & Kelley, M. (2004). Substance-abusing parents' attitudes toward allowing their custodial children to participate in treatment: A comparison of mothers versus fathers. *Journal of Family Psychology, 18* (4), 666–671.

Frey, K., Fewell, R., & Vadasy, P. (1989). Parental adjustment and changes in child outcomes among families of young handicapped children. *Topics in Early Childhood Special Education, 8* (4), 38–57.

Garbarino, J. (1992). *Children and families in the social environment. Second Edition.* New York: Aldine de Gruyter.

Gelles, R., & Cornell, C. (1985). *Intimate violence in families.* Thousand Oaks, CA: Sage.

Goleman, D. (1995). *Emotional intelligence.* New York: Bantam Books.

Goleman, D. (2006). *Social intelligence.* New York: Bantam Books.

Groves, B. (2002). *Children who see too much: Lessons from the child witness to violence project.* Boston: Beacon Press.

Hallowell, E. (2002). *The childhood roots of happiness.* New York: Ballentine.

Hanft, B., Rush, D., & Shelden, M. (2004). *Coaching families and colleagues in early childhood.* Baltimore: Paul H. Brookes.

Hanson, M., & Lynch, E. (2004). *Understanding families: Approaches to diversity, disability, and risk.* Baltimore: Paul H. Brookes.

Hiatt-Michael, D. (2001). *Promising practices for family involvement in schools.* Hartford, CT: Information Age Publishing.

Horsley, K., & Ciske, S. (2005). From neurons to King County neighborhoods: Partnering to promote policies based on the science of early childhood development. *American Journal of Public Health, 95* (4), 562–567.

Karr-Morse, R., & Wiley, M. (1997). *Ghosts from the nursery: Tracing the roots of violence.* New York: The Atlantic Monthly Press.

Lewit, E., & Baker, L. (1996). Homeless families and children. *The Future of Children, 6* (2), 146–158.

Mills, L. (2003). *Insult to injury: Rethinking our responses to intimate abuse.* Princeton, NJ: Princeton University Press.

Madu, S., & Roos, J. (2006), Depression among mothers with preterm infants and their stress coping strategies. *Social Behavior and Personality, 3* (7), 877–890.

Nuñez, R. (1996). *The new poverty: Homeless families in America.* New York: Insight Books.

Oliner, S., & Oliner, P. (1995). *Toward a caring society: Ideas in action.* Westport, CT: Praeger.

Peled, E., Jaffe, P., & Edleson, J. (Eds.) (1995). *Ending the cycle of violence: Community responses to children of battered women.* Thousand Oaks, CA: Sage.

Perry, B. (1997). Incubated in terror: Neurodevelopmental factors in the cycle of violence. In J. Osofsky (Ed.), *Children, youth, and violence: The search for solutions.* New York: Guilford Press.

Peters, R., McMahon, R., & Quinsey, V. (1992). *Aggression and violence throughout the life span*. Thousand Oaks, CA: Sage.

Pipher, M. (1996). *The shelter of each other: Rebuilding our families*. New York: Ballentine Books.

Pittman, F. (1987). *Turning points: Treating families in transition and crisis*. New York: W.W. Norton and Company.

Powell, D. (1998). Reweaving parents into the fabric of early childhood programs. *Young Children, 53* (5), 60–67.

Restack, R. (2003). *The new brain: How the modern age is rewiring your mind*. New York: Roadale.

Rogoff, B. (2003). *The cultural nature of human development*. New York: Oxford University Press.

Rosier, K. (2000). *Mothering inner-city children: The early school years*. New Brunswick, NJ: Rutgers University Press.

Satir, V. (1988). *The new peoplemaking*. Mountain View, CA: Science and Behavior Books.

Shane, P. (1996). *What about America's homeless children?* Thousand Oaks, CA: Sage.

Sheppard, D. (2006). Successful African-American mathematics students in academically unacceptable high schools. *Education, 126* (4), 609–625.

Swick, (2005). Promoting caring in children and families as prevention of violence strategy. *Early Childhood Education Journal, 32* (5), 341–346.

Swick, K. (2005a). Preventing violence through empathy development in families. *Early Childhood Education Journal, 33*(1), 53–59.

Swick, K. (2004). The dynamics of families who are homeless: Implications for early childhood educators. *Childhood Education, 80*(3), 116–126.

Swick, K. (1997). Strengthening homeless families and their young children. *Dimensions of Early Childhood, 25* (2), 29–34.

Swick, K. (1993). *Strengthening parents and families during the early childhood years*. Champaign, IL: Stipes.

Swick, K., & Williams, R. (2006). An analysis of Bronfenbrenner's bio-ecological perspective for early childhood educators: Implications for working with families experiencing stress. *Early Childhood Education Journal. 33*(5), 371–378.

Swick, K., & Graves, S. (1993). *Empowering at-risk families during the early childhood years*. Washington, DC: National Education Association.

Toro, P. (1999). Homelessness in the United States: Policy considerations. *Journal of Community Psychology, 27* (2), 119–136.

Wasson, R., & Hill, R. (1998). The process of becoming homeless: An investigation of female-headed families living in poverty. *Journal of Consumer Affairs, 32* (2), 320–332.

**Dr. Kevin J. Swick,**
College of Education, Wardlaw 107,
University of South Carolina, Columbia, SC 29208.
(kswick@gwm.sc.edu).
Phone: 803-777-5278
Fax: 803-777-7970

Kevin J. Swick, Ph.D. is a Professor of Early Childhood Education in the College of Education at the University of South Carolina, Columbia.

**Reginald H. Williams** is a Doctoral Student in Early Childhood Education at the College of Education, University of South Carolina, Columbia.

# Chapter 7
# Fostering Emergent Literacy
# Through Parent/Child Reading Relationships

Natalie K. Conrad

**Abstract** This chapter reviews research pertaining to young children's emergent literacy and parental support through storybook read alouds. Characteristics of home environments and experiences that contribute to children's early literacy development are discussed. In addition, reading relationships between parents and children, such as interactions and routines while sharing storybooks, are examined.

**Keywords** emergent literacy, young children, parent involvement, reading aloud, reading relationships

## Introduction

In 1908, Huey asserted that "The secret of it all lies in parents reading aloud to and with the child" (p. 332). Nearly one hundred years later, there is a growing body of research in emergent literacy to support this claim. A great deal of language learning takes place within the home before children enter school (Brooker, 1997; Hiebert & Pearson, 2000). Families typically support children's literacy development through subtle, everyday experiences with language rather than the structured, didactic methods traditionally associated with formal schooling (Burns, Griffin, & Snow, 1999; Roskos & Christie, 2000). Although literacy practices at home may be different than those children encounter in school, learning still takes place (Janes & Kermani, 2001; Nistler & Maiers, 1999). This chapter begins with a description of emergent literacy within the context of sharing storybooks. Next, it identifies the characteristics of young children's home literacy environments that build positive reading relationships. Then it describes children who read early and the forms of support that this phenomenon entails. The chapter concludes with research-based

University of Pittsburgh at Johnstown

M.R. Jalongo (ed.), *Enduring Bonds.*
© Springer 2008

guidelines and recommendations for promoting emergent literacy within diverse family contexts.

## Emergent Literacy via Storybook Reading

*Beth shares books with her children Hannah and Matthew every day. Beth stated, "They both love to read." Beth reads to Matthew while Hannah is at school. She also reads to both of her children at bedtime and "sometimes during the day, but it usually depends on the weather—not so much in the summer." Beth described that Hannah really looks forward to the routine of reading a bedtime story. If the family returns home late in the evening, Beth said, "She [Hannah] would still make me read to her. She wouldn't fall asleep in the car." (Conrad, 2004, p. 79)*

Emergent literacy encompasses children's literacy acquisition throughout early childhood and is not merely a phenomenon that occurs when children enter school (Justice & Kaderavek, 2002; Whitehurst & Lonigan, 1998). Children are observers of literacy events in their everyday lives, and it is through these events and interactions that children construct meaning about written and spoken language (Neuman, 1999; Ortiz, 2000; Roskos & Christie, 2000). Storybook read alouds are helpful in promoting children's emergent literacy (DeBruin-Parecki, 2007; Sulzby, 1985; van Kleeck, 2003; Yarosz & Barnett, 2001). Language skills of children are developed as they share storybooks with their parents (Allor & McCathren, 2003; DeBruin-Parecki, 2007; De Temple & Snow, 2003; Taylor & Strickland, 1986).

During storybook reading with parents, children have the opportunity to listen, recall information, and share their own ideas (DeBruin-Parecki, 2007). Certain emergent literacy behaviors are demonstrated by children as they begin to read (Clay, 1991; Jalongo, 2007; Whitehurst & Lonigan, 1998). Reading aloud to children is necessary in order for them to acquire conventions of print that build literacy skills, such as turning the pages in the correct way and following text from left to right and top to bottom (Clay, 1991; Jalongo, 2007; Whitehurst & Lonigan, 1998). Emergent literacy behaviors also include recognizing familiar words, such as names, and showing interest in the text (DeBruin-Parecki, 2007; Jalongo, 2007; Whitehurst & Lonigan, 1998). Children learn that print carries a message and begin to internalize "story language" (e.g., fairytales often begin 'Once upon a time …'). Children may retell stories and pretend to read favorite storybooks, which helps to strengthen their literacy skills (Harris & Hodges, 1995; Jalongo, 2007; Sulzby, 1985; Whitehurst & Lonigan, 1998). When children appear to recite an entire story practically verbatim, they are not merely memorizing the text; children are using strategies as well as behaviors that are concept-driven to retrieve the exact text (Sulzby, 1985). Book sharing interactions between parents and children are affected by book familiarity (van Kleeck, 2003). All of these emergent literacy behaviors prepare children to become readers in the traditional sense.

## Young Children's Literacy Experiences within Their Home Environments

*Courtney described that they have a "library" in their basement. She mentioned that they buy many of their books and a great deal have been passed on to her youngest son from his older siblings. They purchase books from book sales, Goodwill, and the book orders from Trevor's school. Courtney said that they have a library card and borrow books from the library. One of Trevor's favorite books is Ed and Fred Flea (Edwards, 1999). Courtney stated, "He does like that book. We read it often. That's the one he usually picks." (Conrad, 2004, p. 101)*

Within children's home environments, storybook reading promotes literacy development (Bus, 2001b; Jordan, Snow, & Porche, 2000; Justice & Ezell, 2002; Leseman & de Jong, 1998; Neuman, 1999; Sulzby & Teale, 1987; Zeece, 2005). Parents help their children understand storybooks through discussing the content and illustrations as well as drawing attention to the print (Hammett, van Kleeck, & Huberty, 2003). There are two types of literacy experiences while reading aloud that children may be exposed to within their homes: formal and informal (Rodríguez-Brown, Li, & Albom, 1999; Sénéchal & LeFevre, 2002). An example of a formal experience would be a parent and child reading a book together and the parent discussing letter names and sounds with the child (Sénéchal & LeFevre, 2002). For example, Brenda posed questions to her son Nathan throughout the story sharing session (Conrad, 2004). If Nathan had difficulty identifying a word, Brenda pointed to illustrations or text to assist him. Brenda asked, "What letter is that?" when Nathan was confused between a "b" and a "d" (Conrad, 2004, pp. 118–119). An informal experience would include a parent and child reading together and the child asking questions about the story (Sénéchal & LeFevre, 2002). For example, as Courtney and her son Trevor read *Ed and Fred Flea* (Edwards, 1999), Trevor posed the question, "What's a 'phoney'?" in regard to the text (Conrad, 2004, p. 119). Courtney responded with the explanation, "It means he's faking it," and Trevor appeared to understand the definition of the word (Conrad, 2004, p. 119). Often parents are unaware of the formal and informal experiences that take place while sharing storybooks with their children.

Children's literacy acquisition is supported through book reading which is a main aspect of literacy environments (Bus, van IJzendoorn, & Pellegrini, 1995). In order to promote children's literacy within the home environment, parents may incorporate the following suggestions: provide a library corner, perhaps in the child's bedroom with a variety of books; discuss environmental print, such as signs and food labels; read with the child on a regular basis; and visit libraries and/or bookstores frequently (Lawhon, 2000; Morrow, 1989). Roskos and Twardosz (2004) suggest designating a quiet place to read away from traffic within the home. Comfortable seating, adequate lighting, and an area to store books are also important physical resources (Roskos & Twardosz, 2004). Keeping a basket of books in each room is beneficial and encourages spontaneous reading. Strickland and Morrow (1990) suggest that children should be read to from the first day of birth. If parents begin reading to their children at an early age, children's interest in books and literacy is likely to be sustained as they develop (Bus, 2001a). In addition, parents can connect art, dramatic play, field trips, music, and singing to the literature that they share with their children (Lawhon, 2000). Home environments have an impact on the reading relationships between parents and their young children.

A wide variety of books should be introduced to children (Partridge, 2004; Strickland & Morrow, 1990). Strickland and Morrow (1990) describe various types of books that are appropriate for children at different ages. For infants and toddlers, durable concept books with bright colors are suggested (Strickland & Morrow, 1990). Although concept books do not have a story line, they may focus on themes such as colors and shapes (Strickland & Morrow, 1990). Books made of cloth are suitable for very young children as well as soft vinyl books that can be used at bath time. Activity-oriented books that include textures for children to feel and touch are also appropriate (Strickland & Morrow, 1990). In addition, children should also be exposed to traditional literature which includes fairy tales and nursery rhymes, and picture storybooks (Strickland & Morrow, 1990). Within picture storybooks, the text and illustrations are closely associated. While sharing storybooks, children can explore both text and symbolism through the examination of written language and pictures (Sulzby, 1985).

Other types of books recommended for parents to share with their children include: realistic literature that addresses real-life problems; fables and folktales based upon traditional stories and myths; easy-to-read books with limited vocabularies which emergent readers can read by themselves; informational books on topics such as animals, plants, or famous people; and poetry (Strickland & Morrow, 1990). Books that encourage active involvement and may provide interactive features include: lift-the-flap books, slot books, and predictable books (Justice & Kaderavek, 2002). Manipulative-type storybooks may reduce adult directedness and allow children to exhibit more play-like behaviors (Kaderavek & Justice, 2005). In addition, wordless picture books are excellent resources for fostering children's vocabulary development (Jalongo, 2002). Rasinski and Fredericks (1990) recommend that parents assist their children in selecting quality literature, such as Caldecott and Newberry Award winners, to read aloud. A book's genre can have a significant impact on parents' and children's reading relationships (van Kleeck, 2003). It is vital for parents to provide and share quality literature with their children. When books are easily accessible and parents provide opportunities to build reading relationships, children's emergent literacy is enhanced.

## Characteristics of Young Children Who Read Early

*Brenda and her son Nathan, who is 5 years old, read Go, Dog. Go! (Eastman, 1976). Nathan read a large portion of the text. Brenda mentioned that she and her son discuss the books they share and talk about the illustrations. Brenda also said that she asks her son questions and praises him for appropriate responses. Brenda stated that Nathan predicts about the books they read. Brenda engaged her son by allowing him to hold the book, turn the pages, and participate in counting. Nathan also offered his own ideas about the story. Brenda helped Nathan identify the text and pointed out print that Nathan found confusing. She also assisted him in making a connection between their everyday lives and the story. (Conrad, 2004, p. 126)*

Within a literate society, children reach a key milestone as they learn to read (Whitehurst & Lonigan, 2001). Durkin (1966) describes an "early start" in reading as reading at home before attending first grade. Parents of children who read early often are willing to give their children help when the children show interest in reading, such as asking questions and when requesting assistance with reading (Durkin, 1966). Early readers display an internal desire to learn about print and are quite inquisitive. Typically, they have been read to on a regular basis (Durkin, 1966; Strickland & Morrow, 1990). (See Table 1)

Fitzgerald, Spiegel, and Cunningham (1991) describe parents' perceptions of early development as important and pivotal in providing nurturing home literacy environments. Parents, who answer their young children's questions and recognize their appeals to learn more about print (e.g., "What does that spell?"), serve as support systems for their children's early reading development. Sharing storybooks together allows children to listen to adults reading aloud fluently while enjoying close reading relationships.

**Table 1**    Positive Influences on Emergent Literacy

| ☥ Parents ☥ | 📖 Home Environments 📖 | 📚 Early Readers 📚 |
|---|---|---|
| read to children | offer regular reading routines | scribble and draw often—"paper and pencil kids" (Durkin, 1966, p. 137) |
| ask and answer children's questions | contain a variety of printed materials | take part in reading, spelling, and writing |
| display literacy modeling | provide materials based on children's interests | copy objects and letters of the alphabet |
| exhibit positive parental perceptions of early development | make pencil and paper easily accessible to children | have "interest binges" (Durkin, 1966, p. 137) e.g., copies phone book, |
| read for relaxation, information, and contentment | provide a positive, warm atmosphere | want to know how to spell words |
| help children make connections to storybooks | limit television viewing | engage in conversations about letter sounds |
| take children on frequent trips to the library and bookstore | involve all family members in literacy-related activities | read and reread material |

Adapted from: (Bus et al., 1995; Christian, Morrison, & Bryant, 1998; Durkin, 1966, 1978; Morrow & Tracey, 2007; Rodríguez-Brown et al., 1999; Strickland & Morrow, 1990)

# Recommendations on Building Reading Relationships

*Courtney and Trevor sit on the couch together to share books. They read in the evening and at bedtime. Courtney said, "Sometimes he reads to me if he's brought books home from school and other times I read to him."(Conrad, 2004, p. 97)*

According to Cuckle (1996), parents believe that reading stories aloud with their children provides an appropriate model for reading, demonstrates the belief that reading is a valuable activity, and expresses a connection between written and spoken language. When adults read to children and share positive views about literacy, children also gain positive views (Baker, Scher, & Mackler, 1997; Ortiz, 2000; Rasinski & Fredericks, 1990; Snow, Tabors, Nicholson, & Kurland, 1995). Reading aloud to children helps to prepare them to become readers by exposing them to conventions of print, various genres of books, cultural awareness, and conversational techniques regarding storybooks (De Temple & Snow, 2003). Without parental support, storybooks are only somewhat accessible to children who cannot yet read conventionally (Bus et al., 1995). When parents read storybooks with their young children, they bring the print to life while sharing one-on-one time with their children. In addition, the reading relationships between parents and their children are shaped by parental attitudes and beliefs about reading.

## *Analyze Parents' Beliefs Regarding Reading With Children*

*Courtney believes that parents who value reading offer books to their children. She said, "Parents' and children's opinions of things tend to run together. So what you value, they generally value." Courtney stated that reading to Trevor makes her happy and said, "I think it encourages a lifelong love of reading." (Conrad, 2004, p. 86)*

It is crucial to take into account the role of parental beliefs regarding children's literacy development and learning (Baker et al., 1997; van Kleeck, 2003). A study was conducted regarding parents' beliefs about their goals related to reading aloud with their preschool children (DeBaryshe & Binder, 1994). The "Parent Reading Belief Inventory" was used to measure six tenets that include: (1) conversations between adults and children are crucial to the acquisition of language skills; (2) the onset of literacy awareness occurs throughout everyday experiences before formal schooling; (3) daily book reading routines and discussion are necessary; (4) children should engage in active discussions about books; (5) book sharing sessions should be motivational and centered around the children; and (6) during the preschool years, meaning should be focused upon rather than individual code skills (DeBaryshe & Binder, 1994). The authors found that children's age and sex as well as the families' ethnic status were not related to parental beliefs. However, parents' belief scores were significantly and positively associated with children's exposure (variety and frequency) to books, parents modeling reading, strategies used by parents during read alouds, and children's reading interest (DeBaryshe & Binder, 1994). Therefore, the differences within children's home literacy environments (DeBaryshe & Binder, 1994) and children's interest in reading (Baker et al., 1997) appear to be connected to parental beliefs.

When parents were interviewed about story reading and storytelling with their preschool children, parents reported that they read to their children on a regular basis (Bloome, Katz, Solsken, Willett, & Wilson-Keenan, 2000). However, parents sometimes modify activities to align with their perceived beliefs of teachers and researchers (Bloome et al., 2000). For example, some parents stated that they discouraged their children from "reading" to them because they believed educators wanted to teach children how to read during joint storybook reading sessions (Bloome et al., 2000). During the read alouds, parents often encouraged children to ask questions and make comments (Bloome et al., 2000). Families reported reading aloud when it best fit their schedules and a variety of times were reported, such as in the mornings or at bedtime (Bloome et al., 2000). Parents' efforts to share books with their children as well as children reading to parents should be encouraged and supported.

A study was conducted of parents' beliefs and behaviors regarding how they support their preschool children's literacy development (Lynch, Anderson, Anderson, & Shapiro, 2006). Parents typically have a more holistic view of literacy, a skills-based view or a combination (Lynch et al., 2006). The parents with a holistic view focused more on their children's interests and experiences while encouraging literacy (Lynch et al., 2006). However, parents who tended to have a more skills-based view focused on literacy as isolated skills (Lynch et al., 2006). Overall, most parents within the study had a more holistic view about literacy beliefs and fostered meaningful literacy experiences for their children (Lynch et al., 2006). Parents' love of reading will undoubtedly carry over to their children. Meaningful literacy experiences shared within the home environment contribute to children's desire to read for pleasure and their understanding that print carries a message.

## *Support Conversations and Vocabulary Development While Reading Aloud*

*Julia stated, "I've always loved to read," and she loves to read to her daughter Lauren as well. Julia believes that is has helped her daughter's language skills and vocabulary development. She pointed out that Lauren, who is 3 years old, is beginning to recognize text and asks, "What does that say?" (Conrad, 2004, p. 85). Julia asked Lauren about the various illustrations in the storybook, Down at the Station (Kubler, 2002). Lauren responded by making the sounds that corresponded to each illustration. For example, Julia read, "See the engine driver pull the little handle," and Lauren responded and said, "Chug, chug, chug and off they go!" (Conrad, 2004, p. 119)*

Valuable conversations regarding literacy experiences are integral for children's learning (Bailey, 2006). The quality of the conversations that take place between parents and children while reading aloud is important to children's literacy development (Baker, Fernandez-Fein, Scher, & Williams, 1998; Jalongo, Fennimore, & Stamp, 2004; Richgels, 2003; Sulzby & Teale, 1987). While reading aloud, children are exposed to grammatical rules and vocabulary that typical conversations may not include (Bus & van IJzendoorn, 1995). Parents may scaffold, guide, and mediate while sharing books with their children (Bruner, 1990; De Temple & Snow, 2003; van Kleeck & Vander Woude, 2003). During the learning process, scaffolding may be described as the steady withdrawal of adult "support, as through instruction, modeling, questioning, feedback, etc., for a child's performance across successive engagements, thus transferring more and more autonomy to the child" (Harris & Hodges, 1995, p. 226). Scaffolding refers to building upon children's prior knowledge, whereas mediating refers to parents supporting and providing more challenges to build their children's skills while sharing books (Snow, 1983; van Kleeck & Vander Woude, 2003). Scaffolding interactions by adults in respect to the child's skill level can help the child to advance more rapidly regarding their literacy development (Fletcher & Reese, 2005; Lonigan & Whitehurst, 1998; Morrow & Tracey, 2007; Snow 1983; Strickland & Morrow, 1990).

During shared reading experiences, children typically learn to discuss stories, words, and characters as well as answer specific questions about the stories (Pellegrini & Galda, 2003). Yaden, Smolkin, and Conlon (1989) posit that children generally ask questions about the following five aspects during shared book experiences: (1) illustrations; (2) story text; (3) word meanings; (4) graphic forms, such as punctuation and letters; and (5) book conventions. In a study by Tracey and Young (2002), girls were found to participate more during conversations than boys while reading aloud with parents. Thus, while reading together at home, parents should encourage their sons to speak more often (Tracey & Young, 2002). Conversations between parents and children while sharing books are necessary for children's literacy development (Yaden, 2003).

Children's book exposure within their homes indirectly supports children's reading skills development. When a child listens to an adult reading aloud, it assists his receptive language development (Sénéchal & LeFevre, 2002; van Kleeck, 2003). Verbal language knowledge is displayed through expressive language gains (van Kleeck, 2003). For example, when a child describes his favorite storybook, he utilizes his expressive language abilities. Children's vocabulary development can be enhanced through quality shared book reading experiences and discussions (Baker et al., 1998; De Temple & Snow, 2003; Sénéchal LeFevre, Hudson, & Lawson, 1996; Taylor & Strickland, 1986; Walsh & Blewitt, 2006). Children's storybooks often contain words that may not be included in their spoken language (De Temple & Snow, 2003; Sénéchal et al., 1996). Adults' undivided attention with children during shared book experiences helps to facilitate the children's language skills (De Temple & Snow, 2003; Sénéchal et al., 1996). De Temple and Snow (2003) describe "non-immediate talk" as talk between the parent and child that includes the following regarding storybook read alouds: making predictions;

making connections to past experiences of the child, books, and/or the world; drawing inferences; analyzing information; discussing words' meanings; and offering explanations. When adults engage children in meaningful conversations related to storybooks, quality reading relationships are fostered.

## Make Shared Book Sessions Mutually Satisfying

*Linda and Christopher, who is 4 years old and in preschool, read Charlie the Caterpillar (1993) by Dom DeLuise. The dyad sat next to each other. Linda used a lively, positive tone while reading aloud to her son. She paused during the read aloud to allow Christopher to respond to repetitive text. Christopher was given the opportunity to hold the picture book and turn the pages on his own. Linda actively engaged Christopher in the story by participating in actions that correlated to the text. For example, when the text stated that the character looked to his left and looked to his right, Linda led her son in the motions of looking to the left and right. (Conrad, 2004, p. 115)*

The participation of both parents and children during interactions while sharing books is essential (DeBruin-Parecki, 2007; Hargrave & Sénéchal, 2000; Pellegrini & Galda, 2003; van Kleeck, 2003). There are various methods to actively engage both parents and children while sharing storybooks. Parents may exhibit specific behaviors during read alouds to enhance their reading relationships, such as: maintaining close physical proximity with children, adjusting their language and using positive reinforcement, allowing children to hold books, and sharing the books with children (DeBruin-Parecki, 2007). In order to promote interactive reading and comprehension while sharing books, parents' behavior may include: posing and soliciting questions about the stories' content, pointing to illustrations and words, drawing connections from the books to their children, and pausing to answer their children's questions (DeBruin-Parecki, 2007). When children are asked a greater number of appropriate questions and given feedback, they tend to increase their verbalizations (Sénéchal Cornell, & Broda, 1995). Parents may utilize literacy strategies while sharing storybooks with their children by identifying visual cues within the stories, soliciting predictions, asking questions, and elaborating on their children's ideas (DeBruin-Parecki, 2007).

Parents may alter their story sharing sessions based upon the child's age and competencies (Sénéchal et al., 1995). Ortiz, Stowe, and Arnold (2001) suggest the following interventions for parents to actively engage their child during storybook reading: allowing the child to choose what is read or selecting books based upon the child's interests; promoting inquiries; providing feedback; and not forcing the child to read if he/she is uninterested at the time. It is important that parents are responsive to their children's needs and create close reading relationships. Often, parents can create reading routines (e.g., reading before nap or bedtime) that children eagerly anticipate. Sharing books should be socially rewarding and pleasurable for both children and adults (Holdaway, 1982).

## *Understanding the Role of Interest in Motivation*

> *Linda's son Christopher retells about the books they read together. If she asks him questions about the stories, he retells and gives details. Linda stated that her son will use lines from his favorite storybooks, such as I Love Mud and Mud Loves Me (Stephens, 1994). She said, "This is one of our running jokes. When he comes in the house, I'll say, 'Christopher, why are your shoes all muddy?' and he'll say, 'Cause I love mud and mud loves me!'"*
> *(Conrad, 2004, p. 95)*

Motivation is a significant aspect of children's literacy development (Morgan & Fuchs, 2007). Parents and children sharing books on a regular basis can stimulate children's interest in literacy and foster positive attitudes (Baker et al., 1997; Bailey, 2006). However, merely reading aloud to children is not sufficient in encouraging children to learn from shared book reading experiences (Bus, 2003; Reese, Cox, Harte, & McAnally, 2003; van Kleeck & Vander Woude, 2003). The methods parents use to support their children during read alouds are important, such as being sensitive to children's interests and understandings (Bus, 2003; Frijters, Barron, & Brunello, 2000; Ortiz et al., 2001). Children's enjoyment of books is of the utmost importance (Adams, 1990; Baker et al., 1997; Partridge, 2004). Their learning depends upon parents' abilities to connect the children's world with the book's world through their personal knowledge of children's experiences, possessions, meaningful settings, and language (Bus, 2003). Parents should help their children make personal connections between family experiences and read alouds in order for children to gain meaning (Calkins, 1997; De Temple & Snow, 2003; Rasinski & Fredericks, 1990; Strickland & Morrow, 1990). For example, while reading a story about a dog, a parent could help her child make a connection to their family's pet dog. Reading relationships are built when storybooks are shared between parents and children because they not only learn about themselves, but also one another (Taylor & Strickland, 1986).

Both the quantity and quality of children's literacy experiences can be profoundly influenced by parents (Douville, 2000). The frequency and the interactions that occur during read alouds are important (DeBaryshe & Binder, 1994; Yarosz & Barnett, 2001). However, some researchers dispute the impact of storybook reading and according to Scarborough and Dobrich (1994), the frequency of reading aloud to children throughout their preschool years accounts for only approximately 8% variance of their literacy achievement in later years. Although the frequency of shared book reading experiences often has been the focus of studies, the quality has not (Ortiz et al., 2001; Yarosz & Barnett, 2001). The quality of book reading depends on the interactions between the parents and the child (Bus, Belsky, van IJzendoorn, & Crnic, 1997). Yarosz and Barnett (2001) suggest that future studies should focus on the quality of interactions through direct observations. Parental self-reports are typically used to collect data concerning parents and children reading aloud, however, observations may be more valid and reliable (Bus et al., 1995). During self-reports, parents may exaggerate their responses about shared reading to produce more socially desirable answers (Bus et al., 1995). Therefore, self-reporting may produce more biased information than observations on shared reading (Bus et al., 1995).

Frijters, Barron, and Brunello (2000) state that when children's interests about reading aloud are studied the children are rarely interviewed. When focusing on children's interest in literacy, investigators tend to rely on reports by the parents concerning the children's requests for read-alouds and the frequency of the children reading alone rather than speaking to them directly (Frijters et al., 2000). In order to gain more insight into children's thoughts about reading, the author of this chapter interviewed young children (Conrad, 2004). Children were asked, "How do you feel when you and (e.g., mom, dad, etc.) share books together?" Hannah, a 5 year old, responded, "I feel good because I learn. I love books. I've got a whole shelf of them [books], but I think I need more, especially about animals" (Conrad, 2004, pp. 109–110). Children are often well aware of their feelings and a great deal of information can be gleaned from interviews.

## Evaluate Parental Reading Styles While Sharing Storybooks With Children

*Sara and her daughter Katelyn, age 2, read My Big Dog (Crummel, 1998), which is one of Katelyn's favorite books. Katelyn sat on her mother's lap while they read aloud. Katelyn held Sara's hand during a portion of the book sharing session. Sara used various voices for the characters as they read which sustained Katelyn's interest in the book. Sara held the book in front of Katelyn in order for her to view the text and illustrations as she read aloud. (Conrad, 2004, p. 114)*

The reading styles of parents may be an important influence on children's early interest (Ortiz et al., 2001). Although parents may share storybooks with their children, not all parents exhibit the same style. Researchers have found that parents often adapt their reading styles to best meet their children's needs. Parents are likely to adjust their interaction styles based upon their children's competencies (Bus, 2001a; Pellegrini, Brody, & Sigel, 1985). They tend to use more directive language and are less demanding toward children with communicative disorders (Pellegrini et al., 1985). It appears that the communicative status of children rather than age affects the interaction styles of the parents (Pellegrini et al., 1985). As children mature, parents should ask their children higher-level questions about the books that they read, such as drawing inferences in order to foster comprehension, instead of merely asking children to describe and label illustrations.

Parents often exhibit various styles while reading aloud with their children. Styles of reading may fall under two categories: describers and comprehenders (Reese et al., 2003). Describers spend more time labeling, describing illustrations, and requesting the child's evaluations (Reese et al., 2003). The describer-like style is similar to dialogic reading (Reese et al., 2003). The comprehenders spend more time on higher-level thinking questions and evaluations as well as making connections or requesting connections to personal experiences (Reese et al., 2003). However, there is not one best style of reading for all children and parents should be aware of and accommodate to children's diverse literacy and language levels (Reese et al., 2003).


## *Focus Attention and Actively Engage Children During Shared Book Experiences*

> *Beth asked Hannah questions as they read The Very Hungry Caterpillar (Carle, 1969). Beth pointed to the illustrations throughout the reading and Hannah displayed understanding by naming the objects. Beth would sometimes begin a sentence and pause for her daughter to finish it. She read, "On Thursday he ate through _____," and Hannah responded to the cloze by saying, "four strawberries, but he was still hungry." (Conrad, 2004, pp. 117–118)*

When children are actively engaged in shared book experiences, their self-confidence and self-regulation increase (Justice & Kaderavek, 2002). Children have the opportunity to listen, recall information, and share their own ideas (DeBruin-Parecki, 2007). Children may display particular behaviors while actively engaging in sharing books with their parents, such as: maintaining close physical proximity; sustaining attention; holding the book and turning pages; and initiating and responding to book sharing (DeBruin-Parecki, 2007). In order to focus children's attention and foster comprehension while sharing books, adults should encourage children to exhibit the following behaviors: responding independently to questions; identifying words and illustrations; making personal connections to the story; and asking questions about the book (DeBruin-Parecki, 2007). Asking children questions socializes them to display their knowledge verbally which is a common classroom practice in formal schooling (Watson, 2001).

Research indicates that children are more likely to respond to parental prompts than to parental comments while reading together aloud (Justice, Weber, Ezell, & Bakeman, 2002). A prompt is a parent's print reference that obligates a response from the child, whereas, a comment does not obligate the child to respond (Justice et al., 2002). Literacy experiences of young children strongly depend upon their parents' abilities to actively involve their children in such experiences (Bus & van IJzendoorn, 1995; Ortiz et al., 2001; Strickland & Morrow, 1990; Whitehurst, Epstein, Angell, Payne, Crone, & Fischel, 1994).


## *Appreciate the Value of Repeated Readings*

> *Linda described that she and her son Christopher sometimes take part in activities related to the books that they share. She stated, "he has a favorite book Bread, Bread, Bread (Morris, 1989). So when we read that [book], we have to go make a bagel. Last night we read it and he had to have an English muffin." (Conrad, 2004, pp. 102–103)*

When you ask a child who has been read to regularly if she has a favorite storybook, you will more than likely receive a positive response. However, when you ask the child's parent(s) the same question regarding their child's favorite storybook, you more than likely will hear, "Yes, we must have read that book a hundred times!" Holdaway (1982) states that children's favorite storybooks are "loved so much that they pestered people to read to them again and again. These are the books which they played at reading to themselves, puzzled and pored over with aggressive curiosity about the devices of print" (p. 293). Repeated readings play a formative role in children's literacy development (Jalongo, 2007; Kaderavek & Justice, 2005; Lawhon, 2000; Martinez & Roser, 1985; Partridge, 2004; Yaden, 1988). Although it is beneficial for adults to expose children to many different types of books, it is also important to understand the value of repeated readings (Martinez & Roser, 1985).

Sulzby's (1985) research has focused on the reading attempts of children reenacting or reading books that are often considered favorites. In a study conducted by Robinson and Sulzby (1983) regarding children's favorite storybooks, the researchers found that children show specific behaviors related to conventional reading before formal reading begins. Parent-child reading relationships are reflected through their sociocultural norms, unique interpersonal styles, and past storybook reading experiences (Bus, 2001b). The findings of Robinson and Sulzby (1983) include the following: children often request parents to reread favorite storybooks repeatedly; children correct parents if they read text differently from that which is printed; and children attempt to "read" their favorite books to siblings, pets, dolls, or themselves. Within interviews, several parents mentioned that they tire of rereading a particular book over and over; however, children's internal desire promotes interest (Robinson & Sulzby, 1983). As children become increasingly familiar with particular books, they internalize different information (Bus, 2003; Holdaway, 1982; van Kleeck, 2003). When familiar rather than unfamiliar books are shared with children, certain differences are likely to occur (Martinez & Roser, 1985). First, children tend to speak more often during shared reading while using familiar storybooks (Martinez & Roser, 1985). Children may ask questions about the illustrations, word meanings, or story events (Yaden, 1988). Second, children comment more during repeated readings. Third, children often focus on various aspects of the storybooks (e.g., story detail or story elements) as they are read repeatedly (Martinez & Roser, 1985). Last, children appear to gain deeper insights about the storybooks that are familiar (Martinez & Roser, 1985; Yaden, 1988).

Revisiting storybooks also helps children learn to use vocabulary that is more sophisticated (De Temple & Snow, 2003; Sénéchal et al., 1996). When parents repeatedly reread books to their young children (before 14 months), it appears that those children are better able to internalize the language and story structure to a greater extent during the preschool years than children who were not read to at an early age (Bus, 2003). Children, who often heard repeated readings of books, used phrases from the stories to retell and they were able to relate knowledge to new books (Bus, 2003). Rich exposure to books immerses children in new vocabulary (Holdaway, 1982). During interviews, parents expressed specific behaviors they use while sharing books with their children such as, pointing things out to help the child understand the story, following cues of the child (i.e., child acts as teacher), engaging in dramatic play and changing the story's text intentionally to check listening skills (Robinson & Sulzby, 1983). Bus (2003) states, when children internalize the stories' events and the typical phrasings of storybooks, they are better prepared to identify structures and events in new text. Although parents may tire of reading particular storybooks aloud, children's vocabulary knowledge is richer due to these experiences (Holdaway, 1982; De Temple & Snow, 2003).

## Seek Training Methods and Materials to Enhance Reading Relationships

*Beth and her children often borrow books from the library. She mentioned that Hannah and Matthew participated in the story hour at the library as well. They also buy books from the bookstore and the used bookstore. Beth described, "A lot of times we'll just order them online." (Conrad, 2004, p. 99)*

Parents' perceptions regarding the role they play in the education of their children is the main factor to predicting parental involvement (McDermott & Rothenberg, 2000). Parents need to feel that they have a bond with the school and that they are helpful and contribute to their child's instructional programs at school (Hughes, Schumm, & Vaughn, 1999). When schools and families work together, children's literacy and learning experiences are supported. Books and literacy materials may be made available to parents and children through a parent resource center. Parents should also be encouraged to participate in workshops and programs offered at local libraries in order to strengthen young children's literacy development (Lawhon, 2000).

Although parents may be willing to assist and help their children read, they may lack the confidence about how to proceed (Cuckle, 1996; Faires, Nichols, & Rickelman, 2000; Fitzgerald, Spiegel, & Cunningham, 1991; Persampieri, Gortmaker, Daly, Sheridan, & McDurdy, 2006). There are a variety of initiatives and programs to encourage parent participation in children's learning (Barbour, 1998). Programs may include teaching parents to effectively utilize a certain methods while reading with their children, such as repeated readings, modeling, and performance feedback (Persampieri, et al., 2006). In addition to teaching parents how to use certain methods correctly, parents' should be provided with supportive feedback (Persampieri et al., 2006).

Certain methods are beneficial for children with language impairments. The Complete Reading Cycle (CRC) is a reading routine taught to adult caregivers of preschoolers who displayed language impairments (Crowe, Norris, & Hoffman, 2004). CRC helps caregivers engage children in interactive storybook reading (Crowe et al., 2004). Training caregivers to use specific procedures and techniques with their children who have language impairments appears to produce positive outcomes (Crowe et al., 2004).

   Dialogic reading, a specific technique that is based upon the premise that children are active participants during joint book reading sessions, is one method of reading that involves both children and adults (Crowe et al., 2004; Whitehurst et al., 1994; Zevenbergen & Whitehurst, 2003). During dialogic reading, adults provide scaffolding during shared book experiences with children (Zevenbergen & Whitehurst, 2003). Zevenbergen and Whitehurst, (2003) suggest the following seven points for adults to follow: (1) ask children "what" questions; (2) follow children's answers with questioning techniques; (3) repeat what children say; (4) assist the child as necessary (e.g., provide difficult vocabulary and ask children to repeat); (5) encourage and praise children; (6) respond to children's interests; and (7) have fun while reading. Dialogic reading focuses on five types of prompts used while reading aloud with children: (1) completion prompts (such as fill-in the blank), (2) recall prompts, (3) open-ended prompts, (4) wh-prompts (such as why, where, when), and (5) distancing prompts (such as making personal connections to the text) (Whitehurst et al.,1994). Whitehurst et al. (1994) concluded when dialogic reading was incorporated by both parents and teachers, children's language skills were enhanced.

   Literacy bags are excellent tools to provide children and their families with quality materials to share within their homes (Barbour, 1998; Grande, 2004; Lawhon, 2000). A literacy bag typically contains a parent letter, a checklist of materials, a journal, and various books and activities related to a particular theme (e.g., shapes, the alphabet, etc.). Educators of young children prepare the literacy bags for children to take home for approximately one week on a rotating basis. Parents and children have the opportunity to share books, write and draw in the journal, and utilize the activities.

   Considering a social-constructivist viewpoint regarding shared reading without intensive support from adults young children may not find books as comprehensible and enjoyable (Bus, 2001a). The social interactions between adults and children while sharing books ultimately affect children's interest in books and determines whether or not shared reading experiences will be included within their daily routines (Bus, 2001a, 2003). Failure to engage children in shared book experiences may cause them to maintain dependency on their parents in order to understand stories, rather than elicit book interactions and become actively engaged (Bus, 2003).


## Conclusion


Historically, book reading has been a common family routine (Bus, 2001a). A mutual enjoyment, between children and parents sharing books, is important to create a positive, responsive, and emotionally supportive atmosphere (Bus, 2001a; Fletcher, Perez, Hooper, & Clausen, 2005). The literacy knowledge gained within the home becomes the foundation for formal reading instruction within the school (Ortiz et al., 2001; Whitehurst & Lonigan, 2001). In order to support parent/child reading relationships, the following recommendations are suggested: support book reading routines within families' home environments with consideration in regard to the availability to printed materials (Roskos & Twardosz, 2004); time and space, aside from printed materials, should also be viewed as resources within the home (Roskos & Twardosz, 2004); support children's motivation to read by focusing on their interests (Frijters et al., 2000); and encourage interactive read alouds which support pleasurable reading relationships between parents and children (Allor & McCathren, 2003; DeBruin-Parecki, 2007; De Temple & Snow, 2003; Taylor & Strickland, 1986; Zevenbergen & Whitehurst, 2003). Therefore, informal literacy experiences in out-of-school settings exert a powerful influence not only on children's emergent literacy, but also on lifelong academic achievement.

# References

Adams, M. J. (1990). *Beginning to read: Thinking and learning about print*. Cambridge, MA: The MIT Press.

Allor, J. H., & McCathren, R. B. (2003). Developing emergent literacy skills through storybook reading. *Intervention in School and Clinic, 39*(2), 72–79.

Bailey, L. B. (2006). Examining gifted students who are economically at-risk to determine factors that influence their early reading success. *Early Childhood Education Journal, 33*(5), 307–315.

Baker, L., Fernandez-Fein, S., Scher, D., & Williams, H. (1998). Home experiences related to the development of word recognition. In J. L. Metsala & L. C. Ehri (Eds.), *Word recognition in beginning literacy* (pp. 263–287). Mahwah, NJ: Lawrence Erlbaum Associates.

Baker, L., Scher, D., & Mackler, K. (1997). Home and family influences on motivations for reading. *Educational Psychologist, 32*(2), 69–82.

Barbour, A. C. (1998). Home literacy bags promote family involvement. *Childhood Education, 75*(2), 71–75.

Bloome, D., Katz, L., Solsken, J., Willett, J., & Wilson-Keenan, J. (2000). Interpellations of family/community and classroom literacy practices. *The Journal of Educational Research, 93*(1), 155–162.

Brooker, M. (1997). Bringing parents into the schools. *Reading Today, 15*(1), 13.

Bruner, J. S. (1990). *Acts of meaning*. Cambridge, MA: Harvard University Press.

Burns, M. S., Griffin, P., & Snow, C. E. (Eds.). (1999). *Starting out right: A guide to promoting children's reading success*. Washington, DC: National Academy Press.

Bus, A. G. (2001a). Joint caregiver–child storybook reading: A route to literacy development. In S. B. Neuman & D. K. Dickinson (Eds.), *Handbook of early literacy research* (pp. 179–191). New York: The Guilford Press.

Bus, A. G. (2001b). Parent-child book reading through the lens of attachment theory. In L. Verhoeven & C. E. Snow (Eds.), *Literacy and motivation* (pp. 39–53). Mahwah, NJ: Lawrence Erlbaum Associates.

Bus, A. G. (2003). Social-emotional requisites for learning to read. In A. van Kleeck, S. A. Stahl, & E. B. Bauer (Eds.), *On reading books to children: Parents and teachers* (pp. 3–15). Mahwah, NJ: Lawrence Erlbaum Associates.

Bus, A. G., Belsky, J., van IJzendoorn, M. H., & Crnic, K. (1997). Attachment and book reading patterns: A study of mothers, fathers, and their toddlers. *Early Childhood Research Quarterly, 12*(1), 81–98.

Bus, A. G., & van IJzendoorn, M. H. (1995). Mothers reading to their 3-year-olds: The role of mother-child attachment security in becoming literate. *Reading Research Quarterly, 30*(4), 998–1015.

Bus, A. G., van IJzendoorn, M. H., & Pellegrini, A. D. (1995). Joint book reading makes for success in learning to read: A meta-analysis on intergenerational transmission of literacy. *Review of Educational Research, 65*(1), 1–21.

Calkins, L. (with Bellino, L.). (1997). *Raising lifelong learners: A parent's guide.* Cambridge, MA: Perseus Books.

Clay, M. (1991). *Becoming literate.* Portsmouth, NH: Heinemann.

Christian, K., Morrison, F. L., & Bryant, F. B. (1998). Predicting kindergarten academic skills: Interactions among child care, maternal education, and family literacy environments. *Early Childhood Research Quarterly, 13*(3), 501–521.

Conrad, N. K. (2004). Emergent literacy case studies: Attitudes, beliefs, and interactions of rural children and their parents/guardians during storybook read alouds. (Doctoral Dissertation, Indiana University of Pennsylvania, 2004). Dissertation Abstracts International. (UMI No. 3137067)

Crowe, L. K., Norris, J. A., & Hoffman, P. R. (2004). Training caregivers to facilitate communicative participation of preschool children with language impairment during storybook reading. *Journal of Communication Disorders, 37*(2), 177–196.

Cuckle, P. (1996). Children learning to read–exploring home and school relationships. *British Educational Research Journal, 22*(1), 17–32.

DeBaryshe, B. D., & Binder, J. C. (1994). Development of an instrument for measuring parental beliefs about reading aloud to young children. *Perceptual and Motor Skills, 78*(3), 1303–1311.

DeBruin-Parecki, A. (2007). *Let's read together: Improving literacy outcomes with the Adult-Child Interactive Reading Inventory (ACIRI).* Baltimore, MD: Brookes Publishing Co.

De Temple, J., & Snow, C. E. (2003). Learning words from books. In A. van Kleeck, S. A. Stahl, & E. B. Bauer (Eds.), *On reading books to children: Parents and teachers* (pp. 3–15). Mahwah, NJ: Lawrence Erlbaum Associates.

Douville, P. (2000). Helping parents develop literacy at home. *Preventing School Failure, 44*(4), 179–180.

Durkin, D. (1966). *Children who read early: Two longitudinal studies.* New York: Teachers College Press.

Durkin, D. (1978). *Teaching them to read* (3rd ed.). Boston: Allyn and Bacon.

Faires, J., Nichols, W. D., & Rickelman, R. J. (2000). Effects of parental involvement in developing competent readers in first grade. *Reading Psychology, 21*, 195–215.

Fitzgerald, J., Spiegel, D. L., & Cunningham, J. W. (1991). The relationship between parental literacy level and perceptions of emergent literacy. *Journal of Reading Behavior, 23*(2), 191–213.

Fletcher, K. L., Perez, A., Hooper, C., & Claussen, A. H. (2005). Responsiveness and attention during picture-book reading in 18-month-old to 24-month-old toddlers at risk. *Early Child Development and Care, 175*(1), 63–83.

Fletcher, K. L., & Reese, E. (2005). Picture book reading with young children: A conceptual framework. *Developmental Review, 25*(1), 64–103.

Frijters, J. C., Barron, R. W., & Brunello, M. (2000). Direct and mediated influences of home literacy and literacy interest on prereaders' oral vocabulary and early written language skill. *Journal of Educational Psychology, 92*(3), 466–477.

Grande, M. (2004). Increasing parent participation and knowledge using home literacy bags. *Intervention in School and Clinic, 40*(2), 120–126.

Hammett, L. A., van Kleeck, A., & Huberty, C. J. (2003). Patterns of parents' extratextual interactions during book sharing with preschool children: A cluster analysis study. *Reading Research Quarterly, 38*(4), 442–468.

Hargrave, A. D., & Sénéchal, M. (2000). A book reading intervention with preschool children who have limited vocabularies: The benefits of regular reading and dialogic reading. *Early Childhood Research Quarterly, 15*(1), 75–90.

Harris, T. L., & Hodges, R. E. (Eds.). (1995). *The literacy dictionary: The vocabulary of reading and writing.* Newark, DE: International Reading Association.

Hiebert, E. H., & Pearson, P. D. (2000). Building on the past, bridging to the future: A research agenda for the center for the improvement of early reading achievement. *Journal of Educational Research, 93*(3), 133–144.

Holdaway, D. (1982). Shared book experience: Teaching reading using favorite books. *Theory Into Practice, 21*(4), 293–300.

Huey, E. B. (1908). *Psychology of reading.* Norwood, MA: Norwood Press.

Hughes, M. T., Schumm, J. S., & Vaughn, S. (1999). Home literacy activities: Perceptions and practices of Hispanic parents of children with learning disabilities. *Learning Disability Quarterly, 22*(3), 224–235.

Jalongo, M. R. (2007). *Early childhood language arts* (4th ed.). Boston: Allyn & Bacon.

Jalongo, M. R. (with Dragich, D., Conrad, N. K., & Zhang, A.). (2002). Using wordless picture books to support emergent literacy. *Early Childhood Education Journal, 29*(3), 167–178.

Jalongo, M. R., Fennimore, B., & Stamp, L. (2004). The acquisition of literacy: Reframing definitions, paradigms, ideologies, and practices. In O. Saracho & B. Spodek (Eds.), *Contemporary perspectives on language education and language policy in early childhood education* (pp. 65–86). Greenwich, CT: Information Age Publishing.

Janes, H., & Kermani, H. (2001). Caregivers' story reading to young children in family literacy programs: Pleasure or punishment? *Journal of Adolescent & Adult Literacy, 44*(5), 455–463.

Jordan, G. E., Snow, C. E., & Porche, M. V. (2000). Project EASE: The effect of a family literacy project on kindergarten students' early literacy skills. *Reading Research Quarterly, 35*(4), 524–546.

Justice, L. M., & Ezell, H. K. (2002). Use of storybook reading to increase print awareness in at-risk children. *American Journal of Speech-Language Pathology, 11*(1), 17–29.

Justice, L. M., & Kaderavek, J. (2002). Using shared storybook reading to promote emergent literacy. *TEACHING Exceptional Children, 34*(4), 8–13.

Justice, L. M., Weber, S. E., Ezell, H. K., & Bakeman, R. (2002). A sequential analysis of children's responsiveness to parental print references during shared book-reading interactions. *American Journal of Speech-Language Pathology, 11*(1), 30–40.

Kaderavek, J. N., & Justice, L. M. (2005). The effect of book genre in the repeated readings of mothers and their children with language impairment: A pilot investigation. *Child Language Teaching and Therapy, 21*(1), 76–92.

Lawhon, T. (2000). Creating language and print awareness environments for young children. *Contemporary Education, 71*(3), 5–9.

Leseman, P. P. M., & de Jong, P. F. (1998). Home literacy: Opportunity, instruction, cooperation and social-emotional quality predicting early reading achievement. *Reading Research Quarterly, 33*(3), 294–318.

Lonigan, C. J., & Whitehurst, G. J. (1998). Relative efficacy of parent and teacher involvement in a shared-reading intervention for preschool children from low-income backgrounds. *Early Childhood Research Quarterly, 13*(2), 263–290.

Lynch, J., Anderson, J., Anderson, A., & Shapiro, J. (2006). Parents' beliefs about young children's literacy development and parents' literacy behaviors. *Reading Psychology, 27*(1), 1–20.

Martinez, M., & Roser, N. (1985). Read it again: The value of repeated readings during storytime. *The Reading Teacher, 38*(8), 782–786.

McDermott, P., & Rothenberg, J. (2000). Why urban parents resist involvement in their children's elementary education. *The Qualitative Report, 5*(3/4). Retrieved November 2, 2002, from http://www.nova.edu/ssss/QR/QR5-3/mcdermott.html

Morgan, P. L., & Fuchs, D. (2007). Is there a bidirectional relationship between children's reading skills and reading motivation? *Teaching Exceptional Children, 73*(2), 165–183.

Morrow, L. M. (1989). *Literacy development in the early years: Helping children read and write.* Englewood Cliffs, NJ: Prentice Hall.

Morrow, L. M., & Tracey, D. H. (2007). Best practices in early literacy development in preschool, kindergarten, and first grade. In L. B. Gambrell, L. M. Morrow, & M. Pressley (Eds.), *Best practices in literacy instruction* (pp. 57–82). New York: The Guilford Press.

Neuman, S. B. (1999). Books make a difference: A study of access to literacy. *Reading Research Quarterly, 34*(3), 286–311.

Nistler, R. J., & Maiers, A. (1999). Exploring home-school connections. *Education & Urban Society, 32*(1), 3–17.

Ortiz, C., Stowe, R. M., & Arnold, D. H. (2001). Parental influence on child interest in shared picture book reading. *Early Childhood Research Quarterly, 16*(2), 263–281.

Ortiz, R. W. (2000). The many faces of learning to read: The role of fathers in helping their children to develop early literacy skills. *Multicultural Perspectives, 2*(2), 10–17.

Partridge, H. A. (2004). Helping parents make the most of shared book reading. *Early Childhood Education Journal, 32*(1), 25–30.

Pellegrini, A. D., Brody, G. H., & Sigel, I. E. (1985). Parents' book-reading habits with their children. *Journal of Educational Psychology, 77*(3), 332–340.

Pellegrini, A. D., & Galda, L. (2003). Joint reading as a context: Explicating the ways context is created by participants. In A. van Kleeck, S. A. Stahl, & E. B. Bauer (Eds.), *On reading books to children: Parents and teachers* (pp. 321–335). Mahwah, NJ: Lawrence Erlbaum Associates.

Persampieri, M., Gortmaker, V., Daly, E. J., III, Sheridan, S. M., & McCurdy, M. (2006). Promoting parent use of empirically supported reading interventions: Two experimental investigations of child outcomes. *Behavioral Interventions, 21*(1), 31–57.

Rasinski, T. V., & Fredericks, A. D. (1990). The best reading advice for parents. *The Reading Teacher, 43*(4), 344–345.

Reese, E., Cox, A., Harte, D., & McAnally, H. M. (2003). Diversity in adults' styles of reading books to children. In A. van Kleeck, S. A. Stahl, & E. B. Bauer (Eds.), *On reading books to children: Parents and teachers* (pp. 37–57). Mahwah, NJ: Lawrence Erlbaum Associates.

Richgels, D. J. (2003). Emergent literacy. In A. DeBruin-Parecki, & B. Krol-Sinclair (Eds.), *Family literacy: From theory to practice* (pp. 28–48). Newark, DE: International Reading Association.

Robinson, F., & Sulzby, E. (1983). *Parents, children, and "favorite" books: An interview study.* (Report No. PS 014 214). Evanston, IL: Northwestern University. (ERIC Document Reproduction Service No. ED 241 169)

Rodríguez-Brown, F. V., Li, R. F., & Albom, J. B. (1999). Hispanic parents' awareness and use of literacy-rich environments at home and in the community. *Education and Urban Society, 32*(1), 41–57.

Roskos, K. A., & Christie, J. F. (Eds.). (2000). *Play and literacy in early childhood: Research from multiple perspectives.* Mahwah, NJ: Lawrence Erlbaum Associates.

Roskos, K. A., & Twardosz, S. (2004). Resources, family literacy, and children learning to read. In B. H. Wasik (Ed.), *Handbook of family literacy* (pp. 287–304). Mahwah, NJ: Lawrence Erlbaum Associates.

Scarborough, H. S., & Dobrich, W. (1994). On the efficacy of reading to preschoolers. *Developmental Review, 14,* 245–302.

Sénéchal, M., Cornell, E. H., & Broda, L. S. (1995). Age-related differences in the organization of parent-infant interactions during picture-book reading. *Early Childhood Research Quarterly, 10*(3), 317–337.

Sénéchal, M., & LeFevre, J. (2002). Parental involvement in the development of children's reading skill: A five-year longitudinal study. *Child Development, 73*(2), 445–460.

Sénéchal, M., LeFevre, J., Hudson, E., & Lawson, E. P. (1996). Knowledge of storybooks as a predictor of young children's vocabulary. *Journal of Educational Psychology, 88*(3), 520–536.

Snow, C. E. (1983). Literacy and language: Relationships during the preschool years. *Harvard Educational Review, 53*(2), 165–189.

Snow, C. E., Tabors, P. O., Nicholson, P. A., & Kurland, B. F. (1995). SHELL: Oral language and early literacy skills in kindergarten and first-grade children. *Journal of Research in Childhood Education, 10*(1), 37–48.

Strickland, D. S., & Morrow, L. M. (1990). Family literacy: Sharing good books. *The Reading Teacher, 43*(7), 518–519.

Sulzby, E. (1985). Children's emergent reading of favorite storybooks: A developmental study. *Reading Research Quarterly, 20*(4), 458–481.

Sulzby, E., & Teale, W. H. (1987). *Young children's storybook reading: Longitudinal study of parent-child interaction and children's independent functioning.* Final report to The Spencer Foundation. Ann Arbor, MI: University of Michigan.

Taylor, D., & Strickland, D. S. (1986). *Family storybook reading.* Portsmouth, NH: Heinemann.

Tracey, D. H., & Young, J. W. (2002). Mothers' helping behaviors during children's at-home oral-reading practice: Effects of children's reading ability, children's gender, and mothers' educational level. *Journal of Educational Psychology, 94*(4), 729–737.

van Kleeck, A. (2003). Research on book sharing: Another critical look. In A. van Kleeck, S. A. Stahl, & E. B. Bauer (Eds.), *On reading books to children: Parents and teachers* (pp. 271–320). Mahwah, NJ: Lawrence Erlbaum Associates.

van Kleeck, A., & Vander Woude, J. (2003). Book sharing with preschoolers with language delays. In A. van Kleeck, S. A. Stahl, & E. B. Bauer (Eds.), *On reading books to children: Parents and teachers* (pp. 58–94). Mahwah, NJ: Lawrence Erlbaum Associates.

Walsh, B. A., & Blewitt, P. (2006). The effect of questioning style during storybook reading on novel vocabulary acquisition of preschoolers. *Early Childhood Education Journal, 33*(4), 273–278.

Watson, R. (2001). Literacy and oral language implications for early literacy acquisition. In S. B. Neuman & D. K. Dickinson (Eds.), *Handbook of early literacy research* (pp. 43–53). New York: The Guilford Press.

Whitehurst, G. J., Epstein, J. N., Angell, A. L., Payne, A. C., Crone, D. A., & Fischel, J. E. (1994). Outcomes of an emergent literacy intervention in Head Start. *Journal of Educational Psychology, 86*(4), 542–555.

Whitehurst, G. J., & Lonigan, C. J. (1998). Child development and emergent literacy. *Child Development, 69*(3), 848–872.

Whitehurst, G. J., & Lonigan, C. J. (2001). Emergent literacy: Development from prereaders to readers. In S. B. Neuman & D. K. Dickinson (Eds.), *Handbook of early literacy research* (pp. 11–42). New York: The Guilford Press.

Yaden, D. (1988). Understanding stories through repeated read-alouds: How many does it take? *The Reading Teacher, 41*(6), 556–560.

Yaden, D. B., Jr. (2003). Parent-child storybook reading as a complex adaptive system: Or "An Igloo Is a House for Bears." In A. van Kleeck, S. A. Stahl, & E. B. Bauer (Eds.), *On reading books to children: Parents and teachers* (pp. 336–362). Mahwah, NJ: Lawrence Erlbaum Associates.

Yaden, D. B., Jr., Smolkin, L. B., & Conlon, A. (1989). Preschoolers' questions about pictures, print conventions, and story text during reading aloud at home. *Reading Research Quarterly, 24*(2), 188–214.

Yarosz, D. J., & Barnett, W. S. (2001). Who reads to young children?: Identifying predictors of family reading activities. *Reading Psychology, 22*(1), 67–81.

Zeece, P. D. (2005). Using literature to support low literate parents as children's first literacy teachers. *Early Childhood Education Journal, 32*(5), 313–320.

Zevenbergen, A. A., & Whitehurst, G. J. (2003). Dialogic reading: A shared picture book reading intervention for preschoolers. In A. van Kleeck, S. A. Stahl, & E. B. Bauer (Eds.), *On reading books to children: Parents and teachers* (pp. 177–200). Mahwah, NJ: Lawrence Erlbaum Associates.

# Children's Literature Cited

Carle, E. (1969). *The very hungry caterpillar*. New York: Scholastic Inc.
Crummel, S. S. (1998). *My big dog*. New York: Random House Inc.
DeLuise, D. (1993). *Charlie the caterpillar*. New York: Simon & Schuster.
Eastman, P. D. (1976). *Go, dog. Go!* New York: Random House Inc.
Edwards, P. D. (1999). *Ed and Fred flea*. New York: Hyperion Books for Children.
Kubler, A. (2002). *Down at the station*. New York: Child's Play International.
Morris, A. (1989). *Bread, bread, bread*. New York: Lothrop, Lee, & Shepard Books.
Stephens, V. (1994). *I love mud and mud loves me*. New York: Scholastic Inc.

**Natalie K. Conrad, D.Ed.**
University of Pittsburgh at Johnstown
149B Biddle Hall
450 Schoolhouse Road
Johnstown, PA 15904
814-269-7273 (office)
814-736-9386 (home)
E-mail: nconrad@pitt.edu
FAX: 814-269-7084

Natalie Conrad is an Assistant Professor in the Division of Education at the University of Pittsburgh at Johnstown. She taught preschool, kindergarten, and elementary grades before completing her doctorate at Indiana University of Pennsylvania. Her research and writing focuses on literacy, early childhood, and parent/family involvement.

# Chapter 8
# Grandparents in the Lives of Young Children

## Redefining Roles and Responsibilities

**Laurie Nicholson with Pauline Davey Zeece**

**Abstract** Grandparents have played significant roles in the lives of young children throughout history. But grandparenting has changed over the last 50 years to include a variety of newly defined roles and potential responsibilities. This chapter synthesizes much of the literature on the history of grandparenting, the many ways in which grandparents support young children's development, and the new challenges confronting grandparents in contemporary society.

**Keywords** grandparent, grandchild, grandchildren, intergenerational relationships, family relationships, extended family, divorce, parenting, child rearing

## Introduction

> In 1960, when I was three, my daddy's father was 80. But my grandfather still lived on his own and drove his farm tractor the few miles to town daily to get his groceries and do his banking. He had asked my mother repeatedly to let me ride with him, and my mother had always put him off, fearful that he was not really strong or alert enough to manage an active 3-year-old. But one day she gave in and she let my father lift me onto his dad's lap on the old Farm All tractor. "Do you think they'll be all right?" she asked, taking my Dad's hand and watching as we sputtered slowly away. "Oh they'll be fine," my father smiled. "She can't talk, and he can't hear."

Demographic characteristics have shifted significantly since the 1960s. Improved disease control and medical innovations have expanded life expectancy and quality. Even twenty years ago, a discussion of grandparents conjured images of persons who were old-fashioned, frail, doddering, and out of touch with contemporary society. For decades, "grandparent" was a synonym for elderly, but the American concept of "old age" has shifted. To illustrate, in 2000, one-third of American parents were baby boomers (Longeno & Earle, 1996). By 2030, this cohort of poten-

Indiana University of Pennsylvania

University of Nebraska - Lincoln

M.R. Jalongo (ed.), *Enduring Bonds.*

tial grandparents will be 66 to 84 years old and comprise 20% of the total population (Simon-Rusinowitz & Kroch, 1996). Contemporary grandparents are younger at their first grandchild's birth, and are more likely to be financially secure, healthier, and to have a living spouse than grandparents of bygone eras (Aldous, 1995). With replaced hips, artificial knees, and hearts repaired through bypass surgeries, grandparents have a new lease on an active and involved lifestyle with their grandchildren. Clearly, social, political, and technological changes in the United States during the twentieth century have greatly increased the number of living grandparents potentially available to young children (Clingempeel, Colyar, Brand & Hetherington, 1992). Contemporary grandparents may be kick-boxers or knitters, cross country runners or crossword puzzle workers; GED candidates or retired professors. Yet one thing they share with all others who precede them is grandchildren. Grandparents answer to the young child's developing version of the words grandma and grandpa; whether it is nana, grammy, pap, nona, pappa, or big mama these names signify the universally powerful and complex relationship of grandparents and grandchildren and indicate the bonds of deep care and connection between young children and grandparents. The parents of parents frequently exert an important influence on the upbringing of their children's children and remain significant figures into the adulthood of the grandchild (Mills, Wakeman, & Fea, 2001).

Grandparents are an important source of help, advice, and support (Ferguson, 2004). It is critical to note that there has never been a time in history when so many adults have lived long enough to get to know most of their grandchildren. A person born in 1870 had less than a 50% chance of surviving to age 65, while comparable projections for persons born in 1930 reveal that 63% of men and 77% of women reached at least age 65 (Cherlin & Furstenberg, 1986). In the late 1800s, most families gave birth to more than 4 children. This often meant that there were still children in the home when the first child in the birth order had a child of his or her own, thus overlapping the parent and grandparent role. In 1900, half of all 50-year-old women still had children under 18, but by 1980, only 25% of 50-year-old women were still actively parenting minor age children. As the contemporary birth rate is much lower than it was fifty years ago, families have generally finished raising their own children and experienced some empty nest years prior to the arrival of grandchildren.

A 1998 report stated that 75% of 30 year-olds had at least one living grandparent, while almost 10% of 20 year-olds had all four grandparents. This contrasted sharply with just 3% of 20-year-olds in 1960 having four living grandparents (Uhlenberg & Kirby, 1998). As the lifespan increases, more and more young children will enjoy the potential for long relationships with grandparents, and may anticipate spending up to four decades of their own lives in the grandparent role (Waldrop & Weber, 2001).

Historically, America's agricultural families shared common acreage, with second and third generations building houses or remodelling the "home place" as family members grew up, established households of their own, and passed away;

leaving the property to the next generation. But family life has shifted from this model to one of families who may be geographically dispersed. Children may grow up across the country or even on a different continent than their grandparents, due to parents' professional choices and family configuration. Nevertheless, geographic proximity continues to be a key factor in grandparents' involvement in children's lives. Without a doubt, the role of grandparents is changing in significant ways.

## Grandparenting: Historical and Contemporary Perspectives

Most adults are in their 40s or 50s when they become grandparents, an event that is typically associated with a time of great joy and satisfaction. As adult children marry and become parents themselves, a strong sense of family continuity is established (Hagestad, 1985). A mother's relationship with her own mother is documented as a contributing factor to the quality of this relationship. According to Feldman and Elliott (1990), the transformation of the mother daughter relationship is developmental and evolves from adolescence through young adulthood. Daughters move from dependency on their mothers to more equal peer-like relationships, but retain an emotional connection. Kara, a 25-year-old mother of a 3-month-old, shared these impressions.

> I wanted my mother in the birthing suite with my husband and me. She encouraged me and helped him to stay calm also. She saw her first grandchild's birth, and as they weighed Bailey and cleaned her up, I just remember holding my mother's hand and looking at her face. I had never seen her so happy! She told us how much she loved us and how proud she was. Then, she left us alone just to be a little family together. When she came back later and held Bailey for the first time she said, "I've been waiting a long time to meet you!" I felt so close to my mother that day ... in an entirely new way. All of a sudden I had a new understanding about how much she loved me. She's the best grandmother in the world!

The mother-grandmother relationship frequently is especially relevant in young African American families. Many young African American mothers rely on kin networks, and may involve their mothers in co-residence or child care arrangements (Wakschalg, Chase-Lansdale, & Brooks-Gunn, 1996). Navigating the task of moving from the daughter role to the mother role involves adjusting to being behaviorally and emotionally autonomous at a time when the need for both physical and emotional assistance may be heightened.

Research on grandparents has typically focused on the types of aid they provided to their grandchildren, their geographic propinquity, the nature and frequency of their family contact, and their styles of interaction (Block, 2000). The literature on grandparents is replete with positive effects of the triadic relationship; transmission of knowledge and values across generations (Kennedy, 1992), a sense of the heritage and stability of the family (Kornhaber, 1996), and advice and guidance in childrearing (Szinovacz, 1998).

## *Perceptions of Grandparents*

The earliest research regarding intergenerational relationships focused almost entirely on the perception of the grandparents. Researchers have expanded their view of intergenerational relationships, and note shifts in health, mortality, income, and level of education across the "history" of grandparenting. Over four decades ago, Neugarten and Weinstein (1964) sought to understand the meaning of grandparenthood. Their seminal study identified five styles of grandparenting behavior: fun-seeking, formal, distant figures, reservoirs of family wisdom, and surrogate parent. These researchers also proposed three dimensions of the grandparent's role: comfort, significance, and style. More recently, Mueller and colleagues (2002) suggested similar categories and grouped grandparents into influential, supportive, passive, authority oriented, and detached styles (Thiele & Whelan, 2006). Clearly, the role of grandparents involves multiple relational aspects. Kivnick (1982) proposed that each grandparent derives multiple sources of meaning related to their grandparenting role. Grandparents are influenced by how much the role is tied to their sense of identity (centrality), their need to be remembered into the future as an admired figure (valued elder), their need to provide generational continuity within a family (immortality through clan), the value they place on being allowed to spoil and be lenient with their grandchildren (indulgence), and the importance of reliving their own or their parents' early life experiences (reinvolvement with personal past). These dimensions of meaning were significantly interrelated, suggesting that they were not independent of one another (Hayslip, Henderson, & Shore, 2003). Clearly, relationships between children and their grandparents evolve, both in terms of individual lifespan and historical time. Szinovacz (1998) suggests that the grandparent role is multifaceted and as such should be considered in the context of cultural norms and the individual characteristics of each grandparent. Hurme (1991) proposes several aspects of the grandparenting role, including attitudes and expectations, behaviors, and the symbolic meaning of grandparenthood (Thiele & Whelan, 2006).

## *Attitudes and Expectations of Grandparents*

Certainly, grandparents have very little, if any, influence over the timing of becoming grandparents. Yet, they have significant control over their level of emotional investment. The age at birth of grandchild, life stage, and general life circumstances all affect the grandparent role in the life of the young child. Additionally, birth order of grandchildren and the total number of grandchildren that an individual grandparent has may affect the quality of relationship. Research suggests that the birth of each subsequent grandchild decreases the interaction time with a grandparent by 6 to 9% (Myers & Perrin, 1993).

Mid-life grandparents may still be active in the work force, and may have less time to devote to active grandparenting of an infant or energetic toddler (Myers

& Perrin, 1993). Yet, midlife adults are in a developmental phase which Erikson (1963) characterized through the psychosocial crisis of generativity. Concerned with contributing something of value to the next generation, and with assisting their children to become happy, healthy adults, these grandparents may struggle with the lure of the empty nest and future freedom from childrearing responsibilities. Grandparenting may not be a role for which they feel ready (Myers & Perrin, 1993). Older grandparents may have more discretionary hours to devote to active grandparenting. Their central psychosocial task is the achievement of ego integrity (Erikson, 1963). The examination of whether their lives have been lived in a satisfying way leads many older grandparents to refocus on the quality of their family relationships. With both the available time and the desire, they are likely to establish strong relationships as their grandchildren are born. The evidence suggests that individuals are far more accepting of the grandparent role when it occurs "on time" for them, although grandparents and grandchildren hold some normative expectations for each other regarding the roles each will play (Thiele & Whelan, 2006). Szinovacz (1998) argues that specific obligations and expectations surrounding the grandparent role are negotiated within individual families. Some researchers indicate that grandparenthood is frequently viewed as a role without any definitive characteristics because there are no explicit or set expectations (Fuller-Thomson, Minkler, & Driver, 1997).

## Quality of Grandparenting Relationships

The interaction of grandparent and grandchild can be placed on a continuum of involvement from totally detached to extensively involved. These interactions may range from occasional holiday visits to regular babysitting, infrequent written contact to daily e-mails or telephone calls. Interaction may also include financial assistance, advice on parenting, and the stabilizing function that grandparents can provide to young families (Edwards & Daire, 2001).

Five elements of quality in the grandparent/grandchild relationship were identified in the 1990's (Kennedy, 1992), suggesting that grandparents would consider themselves successful in the role if these characteristics were present in their relationships:

* The grandchild felt close to them
* The grandchild felt known and understood by them
* The grandchild knew and understood the grandparents
* The grandparents had a positive influence on the grandchildren
* The grandchildren viewed their relationship with the grandparents as an authentic friendship rather than an obligatory association held together by parents as intermediaries

Several additional characteristics of involved grandparents are documented in the literature (Mueller & Elder, 2003).

- Involved grandparents generally live closer to their grandchildren than their less involved peers.
- Maternal grandparents tend to be more involved than paternal grandparents.
- Involved grandparents live in closer proximity to grandchildren than their less involved peers.
- They are younger
- Their grandchildren are younger

Research also indicates that the level of involvement changes across the lifespan of the child, with the most intense involvement in the early childhood years, and a lessening of grandparent-grandchild interaction as the child grows older. As grandchildren approach adolescence, their focus on peer relationships is intensified and the grandparent-grandchild relationship becomes "asymmetrical" in nature (Cherlin & Furstenberg, 1985). One grandmother characterized it in this way.

> It's just not the same as when they were small. We used to go to everything at their school, have supper together each week; always see them on the weekends. Now that Nathan is 10 and Josh is 12, they're always on the run. Soccer, ice hockey, basketball ... they're so busy! I don't know how my daughter and son-in-law keep up. I'll call from time to time just to speak to the kids if I haven't seen them, but I'm realistic about it. Josh and Nathan love us, but we're not as much fun to hang around with as their friends are.

Shifting the focus to grandchildren's perceptions of the role, Kornhaber and Woodward (1981) characterized five roles of the grandparent from the grandchild's perspective.

- Historians
- Mentors
- Role Models
- Wizards
- Nurturers or "great parents"

Grandparents may function in these roles independently or simultaneously across a grandchild's development.


## *Building Positive Relationships*

Being exposed to a nurturing grandparent in early childhood increases the chance that an individual will become an engaged grandparent in adulthood (King, Elder, & Conger, 2000). Research indicates that children form their ideas about aging, older persons, and their value through intergenerational contact. Parents control the amount of exposure that young children have to grandparents and other older adults, and their attitudes are powerful messages to children (Block, 2000). Parents who are actively involved with their own parents create a positive context for meaningful relationships between grandparents and grandchildren (Hodgson, 1992) and allow children to see their grandparents as repositories of family wisdom, history, and tradition.

Gratton and Haber (1996) posit that grandparents have been traditionally viewed in both positive and negative ways; as figures of authority, burdens on the family and society, and companions. When encouraged to see grandparents as figures of authority, children derive a perception of aging as a process of gaining wisdom. Families who encourage children to see grandparents as companions allow grandchildren to consider aging adults as healthy and active individuals who have much to offer to the family and to society in general. But parents who focus primarily on the burdens of dealing with their own parents may teach their children that aging is only about loss of independence, economic instability, and declining function (Block, 2000).

Grandparents can also have an impact on parent-child relationships. In some cases, grandparents provide a degree of financial support which can significantly affect the quality of life for grandchildren (Tinsley & Parke, 1984). Grandparents can also be "stress buffers" or arbiters of family disagreements (Myers & Perrin, 1993). Grandchildren are entertained by grandparents' tales of "when your dad was five and got in trouble for …" and grandparents may provide tremendous emotional support for grandchildren during marital or family conflicts.

But grandparents may also have a negative effect on grandchildren through their relationships with parents, either individually, or through their impact on marital relationships. Tension may be created in families when grandparents are disapproving of parental decisions, or when grandparents interfere in parental discipline of grandchildren (Myers & Perrin, 1993). Perhaps most significantly, grandparents can exacerbate conflict between parents in the case of divorce, when visitation may become a hotly contested issue.

## Parenting Grandchildren

Divorce is a family disruption that occurs in 50% of all families in America. More than 60% of these families have minor children. One common element of divorce is the severance or modification of some family relationships such as the relationship between grandparents and grandchildren (Myers & Perrin, 1993). Even families with close relationships between parents and grandparents may struggle with the shock of divorce. In a 1986 study, fewer than half of grandparents were aware of a separation before it occurred. The effect of divorce on grandparents is far reaching, and may place the grandparents at odds with their religious beliefs or social mores. Conflict about where "fault" for the divorce lies, as well as genuine grief about loss of relationship with a family member must also be faced by grandparents in a fractured marital relationship (Myers & Perrin, 1993). Divorce can also provide opportunities for grandparents to deepen relationships with parents and grandchildren. Child care, advice, support, and material assistance may be provided by grandparents. But access to casual visits may become restricted as custody awards are disputed.

Sadly, grandparents' choices may be forced when a marital fracture occurs. The situation may strain grandparents financially, emotionally, and in terms of values, as they must react to a new and perhaps more permissive lifestyle with their own adult children. Should an adult child remarry, the grandparent is forced once again to adjust; with a "new" set of step-grandparents potentially added to the family. Research indicates that the age of a child at parents' remarriage has impact on the bonding that may occur with step-grandparents; the younger the child, the greater the opportunity for development of a meaningful relationship.

> I'm an only child, so I inherited my grandparents' wedding bands. They were married for 57 years and were totally devoted to each other. I spent every summer that I can remember at their farm. After my parents divorced, while my mom was getting her college degree, her parents really were my stability. There was never any question about who loved me or would be there for me. We went on long walks, went fishing, and did chores. I'm a gardener today because of helping Pap in the garden, and Nan always let me help her in the kitchen, even when I was so little that I had to kneel on a stool to reach the counter. I always felt secure with them. They taught me to want a life like that, with a partner I loved and respected. When JoAnn and I got engaged, I took their two rings and had them melted down. The jeweler blended some new gold with the old to create two rings for us. I think of Nan and Pap every time I look at my ring. Without them, I doubt I ever would have thought that marriage was a good idea. My folks fought like crazy and ended up hating each other and used me as a weapon against each other after their divorce. I'd like to think that my marriage can be as solid as my grandparents'. I look forward to having my own children so that I can be there to support them; and to having grandchildren, so that I can love them the same way Nan and Pap loved me.

## Grandparents as Primary Caregivers

Perhaps the most challenging role that a grandparent can play occurs when children's parents are not available or able to care for them. Consider the story of Jake and Betty.

> Jake is 64 and his wife Betty is 60. They retired a few years ago after Jake had worked in the steel mill outside Pittsburgh for 40 years. They had saved a little, and their house was paid for. All four of their kids were grown with families of their own, but then Ava, their only daughter, was arrested with stolen prescription slips that she had been forging. Jake explains, "Eva and the kids' dad had divorced six years ago, and he's remarried with a new family now out in Oregon. When we heard from Eva the day she was arrested, she told us that Conor and Tracy would be put in foster care." His eyes fill with tears as he says, "I just couldn't let that happen". Betty is now working part time as a cashier and they juggle taking the kids to school and church activities. Jake laughs. "I'm the oldest 'dad' at everything at their school, but I want them to feel like other kids, and know that they matter to somebody." What will happen when Eva is out of jail? "I don't know. She's mine and I love her, but she's hurt these kids bad. The stories they've let slip since coming to us make me think she was leaving them alone a lot at night, having to fend for themselves. Conor didn't trust anybody when he got here, and Tracy got frantic if her big brother was out of her sight. I don't want to give up my relationship with my daughter, or be crossways with her in court, but some things are going to have to be different before those kids go back to living just with her. Maybe we'd have to try it with all of us living together for her to get back on her feet. I just don't know."

Stories such as this one are becoming more prevalent in the 21$^{st}$ century. In 2000, 6.3% of children in the United States lived with a grandparent. Since 1990 the fastest growing category of household has been the grandparent-headed household, in which neither parent is in co-residence (Bryson, 2001). In the 1990's alone, grandparent headed households increased by about 19% (Bullock, 2004). More than 3 million grandparents were raising grandchildren in 1997. Of that number 2.3 million were grandmothers (Lugaila, 1998). These women are more likely to be poor, to be receiving public assistance, and less likely to have adequate health insurance (Casper & Bryson, 1998). Why has this occurred?

## Determining Factors in Custodial Care

This increasing trend has been driven by a number of societal factors. The death of one or both parents, the high incidence of divorce, parental abandonment, parental substance abuse or addiction, physical and mental illness; and parental incarceration all contribute to the increase in the number of families headed by grandparents (Sands & Goldberg-Glen, 2000). While African American grandparents are more likely to assume the parental role on a temporary or supplemental basis, many grandparents take on the role with the idea that it is short term, and that all will return to normal soon.

The United States Census data on skipped generation families profiles them as 68% White, 60% female-headed, 76% married, with a median age of 57. Raising grandchildren is an extreme stressor, and grandparents may have health issues which are exacerbated by new found responsibilities. These grandparents may also be a part of the sandwich generation, caring for their own parents or other adult relatives, and may also be enjoying their own retirement when pressed into the role of raising a child (Chalfie, 1994). The 2000 United States Census was the first time that "grandparental care giving" was included as a household category. Over 5.8 million children were reported at that time to be in the sole care of grandparents, with 39% of those caregivers having been responsible for grandchildren for five or more years. Many grandparents state that taking on the rearing of a grandchild offered new meaning to life. Custodial grandparents identify some of the positives of the arrangement as the love and companionship of the child, the opportunity to nurture family legacies, and a "second chance"; an opportunity to use their accumulated wisdom and life experience to raise a child (Madden, 2006).

## Challenges of Raising Grandchildren

Grandparents faced with raising their grandchildren may be confronted with harsh economic realities. Their retirement savings, planned to be sufficient for two, may dwindle very quickly when stretched to include food, clothing, medical insurance, and all of the attendant expenses of childrearing. Additionally, grandparents who have not yet retired may find themselves needing to reduce their hours at work, seek part time employment, or leave the work force all together in order to provide care and supervision for the children joining the household (Roe & Minkler, 1999).

Grandparents may have anticipated a time when they could travel, explore new hobbies, downshift their careers, relocate to a smaller space or to a community that is more oriented to retirement living than raising a family (Madden 2006), Certainly, assuming responsibility as a custodial grandparent can change all of those dreams very quickly. Additionally, "taking in" the grandchildren may upset other adult children in the family, and may complicate an already strained relationship with the grandchild's parent.

Taking on the parent role requires "surrendering" the grandparent role. Even with all of the loss of freedom associated with this, many grandparents accept the task (Madden, 2006). Common stressors for grandparents raising grandchildren are varied and numerous.

- Fatigue – Grandparents may be faced with strenuous physical tasks of lifting, carrying, and bathing a young child. Increasing physical demands.
- Limited social contact with peer networks – Because their lives and schedules are so drastically altered by having a child in the home, social contacts tend to lessen. Likewise, peers no longer have as much in common.
- Health concerns – If health conditions are present, stress may exacerbate existing conditions.
- Financial strain – Food, clothing, toys, school expenses, and child care are an enormous expense for middle aged grandparents. Additional costs such as health care may add to the burden.
- Lack of privacy and time – Grandparents may have forgotten that taking an uninterrupted bath or shower, or having a later dinner are challenges with young children in the home.
- Lack of community support – Services may be difficult to locate and access. Custody issues may also complicate obtaining services.
- Legal issues – Legal custody requires time, energy, and the will to risk severing the relationship with an adult child.

Harrison, Richman, and Vittimberga (2000) indicate that many grandparents who find themselves in custodial roles report that becoming a parent again is "difficult, life altering, and stressful" (p. 263). Even grandparents who acknowledge a level of satisfaction in raising their grandchildren often experience an odd mix of anger, disappointment, blame, and guilt. They may have feelings of gratitude and resentment as they cope with the "loss" of their own child, even when the assumption of responsibility for the grandchild is clearly in the child's best interest. As relationships become more strained, resentment may deepen for all three generations. Many families struggle with years of unresolved estrangement (Rothenberg, 1996). Support groups for custodial grandparents can provide focus on assisting with refreshing understanding about child development, parental rights, parenting skills, and improving communication with a child who may be emotionally hurt and grieving.

## *Housing Challenges*

Housing a grandchild presents a critical challenge to some families. Many grandparents have already downsized their homes as they transitioned to the "empty nest". The retirement home that was comfortable for one or two adults may not be adequate or appropriate for a family with children.

> Dorothy Wade had been a single mother, and had sacrificed a lot to stay in a neighborhood that allowed her son Trey to go to a "safe school". The house she had rented in those years was in poor repair, and the neighborhood had become even more run down after Trey left home. With only herself to care for, Dorothy had applied for a small apartment in Crafton Towers, a public housing complex. The apartment was small but adequate, and Dorothy enjoyed the security and friendship of having other retired persons as her neighbors. Much as she loved Trey and his son Quinn, she had to admit that she enjoyed the quiet of a more "adult" building. But Dorothy found herself in a different situation when Trey started calling her late at night, begging her for money, and asking her to keep Quinn for him more and more. One Sunday, Trey did not return to pick up Quinn as planned, and an attempt to call her former daughter-in-law only confirmed what Trey had been telling her. Trey's mother had moved out of the city several months prior, and was living with a new boyfriend. She told Dorothy that she couldn't be tied down with the baby. Frustrated, Dorothy had bathed Quinn and placed his pillow and blanket on the couch in the small living room to rest until his father returned but Trey never came back. When he was found two days later, Trey had been shot and killed over a huge gambling debt. Suddenly, Dorothy was a parent again, and her comfortable, efficient apartment was no longer the right home.

Many American grandparents face parallel dilemmas. Individuals living in public housing must often follow strict guidelines about the number of persons or the family configuration inhabiting an apartment. Failure to comply may mean eviction, and then the grandparent suddenly has to find appropriate, affordable housing–often at a premium. One approach to dealing with this chronic problem among adults raising grandchildren has been the development of specialized housing.

In 1998, GrandFamilies House opened in Boston. The 26 apartments in the complex include units with two, three, or four bedrooms, so that families can be appropriately accommodated. The building is also suited to the needs of aging grandparents as well as children. There are ramps and grab bars in the rest rooms for the aging tenants, as well as outlet covers and child-proof windows to protect the youngest inhabitants. A staff assists with coordinating services such as van transportation for shopping and medical appointments, and there is both an onsite preschool and after school care program facilitated by the local YMCA. Such housing is a possibility because of the American Dream Down Payment Act, signed into law in 2003. This legislation is responsive to the housing needs of grandparents raising grandchildren across the United States. Similar projects are in various stages of planning and implementation in 13 states (AARP, 2004).

## *Additional Challenges for Custodial Grandparents*

Some of the challenges that grandparents raising children face are behavioral. Never did these adults confront so many cultural and materialistic challenges when raising their own children. Generational differences in values may cause conflict, and grandparents may find themselves having to shift from a loving, spoiling role, to being much firmer (Stokes & Greenstone, 1981).

When confronted with the choice of assuming responsibility for a child or children, grandparents may be faced with a three-pronged no-win choice: take over the childrearing, accept having the child continue to live in a neglectful or dangerous environment, or have the child go to foster care (Stokes & Greenstone, 1981). Strong ethnic and cultural traditions influence the care of a grandchild. African American culture has always been rife with family tradition, with one of the most notable traditions of the family system being to see that its youngest and most elderly members are appropriately cared for (Sudarkasa, 1996). Many grandparents accept grandchildren into their homes only because they are the only available persons to keep the child out of the public foster care system (Cox, 2000). The National Family Caregiver Support Program was established as part of the Older Americans Act Amendments (PL 106–50) in 2001 to provide money to states to partner with the area agencies on aging and community service providers to provide information, assistance in accessing supportive services, counselling, respite care, and supplemental services to family caregivers. In a study of grandparents raising grandchildren, the adults were asked to recall their initial thoughts about what they were getting into. One third of those questioned expected to raise the child to adulthood when they took the child in, but that figure rose to 77% after the child had come into their home (Cox, 2000). The issues that necessitate a grandparent's assumption of the parental role are not easily or quickly resolved, and if not resolved, may cause skipped generation families to lack cohesion.

Kinship care, such as grandparents raising children provide, requires multiple competencies. A grandparent must understand child development, behavior management, cultural diversity, and the philosophy and practicality of permanency planning for this child (Lawrence-Webb, 2003). Grandparents often have parenting skills that worked well a generation ago, but to parent children in the 21$^{st}$ century requires that those skills be modified or retooled. Skills may also need to be expanded to include those necessary to address contemporary concerns (Berrick, 1997).

## *A Complex Grief*

An additional stressor for the grandparent, which is not often discussed, is the impact of accepting that one's own child cannot, for whatever reason, parent.

Raising grandchildren may be perceived as an indicator of one's own failure or that of one's children and may compound, negatively affecting the emotional health of the grandparent, and threatening the health of the relationship with the child. Grandparents who are struggling with their guilt over their own children may find that these feelings become more overwhelming, forcing them to doubt their ability to successfully raise their grandchildren. Former associates and friends, or other potentially supportive networks may evaporate as a result of the new found demands of parenting. (Sands & Goldberg-Glen, 2000).

Kelley and Damato (1995) indicate that grandparents may experience conflicting loyalties and emotions as they struggle to balance the needs and desires of their adult children with the best interest of the grandchildren. As a result, the literature suggests that grandparents raising children are twice as likely as their non-custodial peers to experience depression (Fuller-Thompson, Driver, & Minkler, 1997).

For some grandparents, the role of employee must be reduced substantially or relinquished entirely to fully assume the role of parent. As a result of this, many grandparents are faced with uncertainty, ambiguity of their role, personal conflict, and stress overload (Burnette, 1999).

After nearly half a century of research findings, it is clear that there is no singular, unequivocal description of the grandparent role. Discussion with any group of adults supports the notion that the role of grandparent can be carried out in a variety of ways. One grandchild depicted the lasting influence of his grandfather this way:

> When I was growing up, I loved to go downtown with my Grandfather. He was the pastor of the AME Zion Church in the community where we lived, and he knew everybody by name. I was always so proud to be with him, and see how people stopped him on the street to talk to him. He was a political leader in the community, and worked hard to assist folks in the neighborhood when there was a crisis or trouble in the family. He was not a "soft" man. I don't remember any hugs or kisses, or being told that he loved me. But I knew by his care. I had clean clothes to wear, and my own bed. He expected a lot of me, and wasn't afraid to reprimand me or discipline me when I needed it. My mother's situation as the pregnant, unwed daughter of the pastor must have been a real hardship for him in the community, but he never showed that to me. I think I decided when I was about 5 that I wanted to be just like him ... to be someone that people looked up to and trusted. He's the reason I'm involved in the community today. And he's definitely the reason I'm a responsible parent.

## Conclusion

Clearly, grandparenting is a multi-faceted role, with many permutations in the 21$^{st}$ century family. Whether as traditional grandparents providing care and support, or as full-time caregivers or surrogate parents, grandparents are situated in a family system. The implications of this extend into future generations, when the young children who have been lovingly grandparented become the "gatekeepers of intergenerational exchange" (Mueller & Elder, 2003, p. 405).

# References

Aldous, J. (1995). New views of grandparents' intergenerational context. *Journal of Family Issues,(16),* 104–122.

American Association of Retired Persons. (2004, September 1). Help for grandparents raising grandchildren: Housing Issues. Retrieved from http://www.aarp.org/families/grandparents/raising_grandchild/a2004-09-01-grandparents-housingissues.html

Berrick, J. D. (1997). Assessing quality of care in kinship and foster family care. *Family Relations, 46,* 273–281.

Block, C.E. (2000). Dyadic and gender differences in perceptions of the grandparent-grandchild relationship. *International Journal of Aging and Human Development, 51* (2), 85–104.

Bryson, K.R. (2001). New Census Bureau data on grandparents raising grandchildren. Paper presented at the 54th annual scientific meeting of the Gerontological Society of America, Chicago, November 10.

Bullock, K. (2004). The changing role of grandparents in rural families: The result of an exploratory study in Southeastern North Carolina. *Families in Society: The Journal of Contemporary Social Services, 85*(1), 45–54.

Bullock, K. (2005). Grandfathers and the impact of raising grandchildren. *Journal of Sociology and Social Welfare, xxxii,*(1), 43–59.

Burnette, D. (1999). Social relationships of Latino grandparents. A role theory perspective. *The Gerontologist, 39,* 49–59.

Casper, L.M., & Bryson, K.R. (1998). *Co-resident grandparents and their grandchildren: Grandparent maintained families.* Washington, DC: Population Division, U.S. Bureau of the Census.

Chalfie, D. (1994). *Going it alone: A closer look at grandparents rearing grandchildren.* Washington, DC: American Association of Retired Persons.

Cherlin, A., & Furtenberg, F. (1985). Styles and strategies of grandparenting. In V. Bingston and J. Roberts (Eds.), *Grandparenthood* (pp. 97–116). London: Sage Publications.

Cherlin, A.J., & Furstenberg, F. (1986). *The new American grandparent.* New York: Basic Books.

Clingempeel, W., Colyar, J., Brand, E., & Hetherington, M. (1992). Children's relationships with maternal grandparents: A longitudinal study of family structure and pubertal status effects. *Child Development, 63*(6), 1404–1422.

Cox, C. B. (2000). Why grandchildren are going to and staying at grandmother's house and what happens when they get there. In C.B. Cox (Ed.), *To grandmother's house we go and stay: Perspectives on custodial grandparenting* (pp. 3–19). New York: Springer.

Edwards, O.W., & Daire, A.P. (2001). School age children raised by their grandparents: Problems and solutions. *Journal of Instructional Psychology, 33*(2), 113–119.

Erikson, E. (1963). *Childhood and society.* New York: Norton.

Feldman, S. & Elliott, G. (Eds.). (1990). *At the threshold: The developing adolescent.* Cambridge, MA: Harvard University Press.

Ferguson, N. (2004). Children's contact with grandparents after divorce. *Family Matters, 67,* 36–41.

Fuller-Thomson, E., Minkler, M., & Driver, D. (1997). A profile of grandparents raising grandchildren in the United States. *Gerontologist, 37*(3), 406–411.

Gratton, B., & Haber, C. (1996). Three phases in the history of American grandparents: Authority, burden, companion. *Generations, 20,* 7–12.

Hagestad, G. (1985). Demographic change and the life course: Some emerging trends in the family realm. *Family Relations, 20*(10), 17–23.

Harrison, K.A., Richman, G.S., & Vittimberga, G.L. (2000). Parental stress in grandparents versus parents raising children with behavior problems. *Journal of Family Issues, 21,* 262–270.

Hayslip, B., Henderson, C.E., & Shore, R.J. (2003). The structure of grandparental role meaning. *Journal of Adult Development, 10*(1) 1–11.

Hodgson, L.G. (1992). Adult grandchildren and their enduring bond. *International Journal of Aging and Human Development., 34*, 209–224.

Hurme, H. (1991). Dimensions of the grandparent role in Finland. In P. Smith (Ed.) *The psychology of grandparenthood* (pp.19–31). London: Routledge.

Jehlen, A. (2006). Second time around. *NEA Today. 24*(7), 21.

Kelley, S.J., & Damato, E.G. (1995). Grandparents as primary caregivers. *Maternal and Child Nursing, 20*, 326–332.

Kennedy, G.E. (1992). Quality in grandparent/grandchild relationships. *International Journal of Aging and Human development. 35*, 83–96.

King, V., Elder, G.H., & Conger, R.D. (2000). Wisdom of the ages. In G.H. Elder, Jr., & R.D. Conger (Eds.), *Children of the land: Adversity and success in rural America*. Chicago: University of Chicago Press.

Kivnick, H. (1982). Grandparents: An overview of meaning and mental health. *The Gerontologist, 22*, 59–66.

Kornhaber, A. (1996). *Contemporary grandparenting*. London: Sage.

Kornhaber, A., & Woodward, A.L. (1981). *Grandparents/grandchildren: The vital connection*. New York: Anchor Press/Doubleday.

Lawrence-Webb, C., Okundaye, J.N., Haffner, G. (2003). Education and kinship caregivers: Creating a new vision. *Families in Society, 84*(1), 135–142.

Longeno, C., & Earle, J. (1996). Who are the grandparents at century's end? *Generations, 20*(1), 13–17.

Lugaila, T. (1998). *Marital status and living arrangements*. Bureau of the Census, Current Population reports. Washington, DC: US Government Printing Office.

Madden, L. (2006). Taking it all in. *Children and Libraries, 4*(1), 15–16.

Mills, T.L., Wakeman, M.A., & Fea, C.B. (2001). Adult grandchildren's perceptions of emotional closeness and consensus with their maternal and paternal grandparents. *Journal of Family Issues, 22*(4), 427–455.

Mueller, M.M., & Elder, G.H., Jr. (2003). Family contingencies across the generations: Grandparent-grandchild relationships in holistic perspective. *Journal of Marriage and Family, 65*,404–417.

Mueller, M., Wilhelm, B., & Elder, G. (2002). Variations in grandparenting. *Research on Aging, 24*, 360–388.

Myers, J.E., & Perrin, N. (1993). Grandparents affected by parental divorce: A population at risk? *Journal of Counseling and Development, 72*, 62–66.

Neugarten, B., & Weinstein, K. (1964). The changing American grandparent. *Journal of Marriage and the Family, 26*, 199–204.

Roe, K.M., & Minkler, M. (1999). Grandparents raising grandchildren: Challenges and responses. *Generations* (Winter), 1998–1999, 25–32.

Rothenberg, D. (1996). *Grandparents as parents: A primer for schools*. ERIC Clearinghouse on Elementary and Early Childhood Education, Urbana, IL. (ERIC Document Reproduction Service No. ED 401044)

Sands, R.G., & Goldberg-Glen, R.S. (2000). Factors associated with stress among grandparents raising their grandchildren. *Family Relations, 49*, 97–105.

Simon-Rusinowitz, L., & Krach, C. (1996). Grandparents in the workplace: The effects of economic and labor trends. *Generations, 20*(1), 41–45.

Stokes, J., & Greenstone, J. (1981). Black grandparents and child rearing. *Child Welfare, 60*, 691–701.

Sudarkasa, N. (1996). Interpreting the African heritage in Afro-American family organization. In H.P. McAdoo (Ed.). *Black families* (pp. 37–53). Beverly Hills, CA: Sage.

Szinovacz, M. (1998). Research on grandparenting: Needed refinement in concepts, themes, and methods. In M. Szinovacz (Ed.) *Handbook on grandparenthood* (pp.1–20). Westport, CT: Greenwood Press.

Thiele, D., & Whelan, T. (2006). The nature and dimensions of the grandparent role. *Marriage and Family Review, 40*(1), 93–108.

Tinsley, B.R., & Parke, R.D. (1984). Grandparents as support and socialization agents. In M. Lewis (Ed.), *Beyond the dyad* (pp. 161–194). New York: Plenum Press.

Uhlenberg, P., & Kirby, J.B. (1998). Grandparenthood over time: Historical and demographic trends. In M.E. Szinovacz (Ed.), *Handbook on grandparenthood* (pp. 23–39). Westport, CT: Greenwood Press.

Wakschlag, L.S., Chase-Lansdale, P.L., & Brooks-Gunn, J. (1996). Not just "Ghosts in the nursery": Contemporaneous intergenerational relationships and parenting in young African American families. *Child Development, 67,* 2131–2147.

Waldrop, D.P., & Weber, J.A. (2001). From grandparent to caregiver: The stress and satisfaction of raising grandchildren. *Families in Society, 82*(5), 461–472.

**Laurie Nicholson** lnichols@iup.edu is Associate Professor in Professional Studies in Education at Indiana University of Pennsylvania. Her research interests include children's arts experiences and family engagement in literacy development.

**Pauline Davey Zeece** pzeece1@unl.edu is a Professor in the Department of Child Youth and Family Studies at the University of Nebraska-Lincoln. Her research and teaching activities include issues related to lifespan development, child development, children's literature, and quality programming and community partnerships related to Head Start and Early Head Start.

# Part Three
# Relationships in Child Care and School Settings

# Chapter 9
# Building Positive Relationships in the Lives of Infants and Toddlers in Child Care

**Mary Beth Mann and Russell N. Carney**

**Abstract** Positive relationships are critical for the healthy development of infants and toddlers. This chapter provides an overview of familiar theories of child development, and brain-based research that supports this view. We then provide practical suggestions for building positive relationships in the lives of infants and toddlers in child care.

**Keywords** relationships, attachment, infants, toddlers, babies, child care, group care, caregiver, development, developmental theory, psychoanalytic theory, psychosocial theory, sociocultural theory, attachment theory, humanistic theory, Piaget, Bronfenbrenner, Maslow, Vygotsky

Now, more than ever, professionals studying young children have convincing evidence of the importance of relationships in the lives of infants and toddlers. While past theories and research relied primarily on observations to assess the impact of relationships, science now has the tools necessary to actually measure changes taking place in the child's developing brain (e.g., Skontoff & Phillips, 2000). As has been suggested, babies seem to be born "wired" for social relationships (Masten & Coatsworth, 1998). That is, they seem to be genetically programmed "to seek out significant relationships through which they can be nurtured and protected, and to use relationships to learn appropriate and inappropriate ways of relating to others" (Lally & Mangione, 2006, p. 15). These early relationships have a profound and lasting effect on the developing child. Indeed, the young child's achievements in social development, self-regulation, language, and learning all take place in the context of close relationships with parents and others involved in the life of the child, such as caregivers in child care settings (Shonkoff & Phillips, 2000).

Missouri State University

Missouri State University

M.R. Jalongo (ed.), *Enduring Bonds.*
© Springer 2008

In 2000, the proportion of working mothers with infants and toddlers in child care stood at about 61 percent (Children's Defense Fund, 2003). The need for child care for this vulnerable age group has increased with this growing number of young mothers in the labor force. The rate of participation for mothers with children under 12 months of age is 55 percent. This is down, somewhat, from the highest figure of 59 percent in 1998. Nevertheless, both figures are about double that of 1976 when such rates were first reported. Given the societal impact of organized child care over the past half century and given that ever more mothers are going back to work sooner after the birth of their babies, we have chosen to focus our discussion of relationships on out-of-home child care.

In this chapter, we first survey a number of familiar theories of child development as they relate to infants and toddlers (ages zero to three), with a focus on the role that relationships play in children's lives. These theories underscore the critical nature of early nurturance, and have implications for the caregiver and for the child care setting. We go on to describe the unique environment of infant toddler child care. Finally, we close with practical suggestions for promoting healthy relationships between caregiver and child in the child care setting.

## The Role of Relationships in Theories of Child Development

### Psychoanalytic Theory

Theories of child development have long emphasized the importance of relationships on the developing child. For example, Sigmund Freud's research dating from the late 1800s suggested that the emotional problems of adults stemmed from their childhood experiences–particularly their relationships with their mothers. Rather than viewing early childhood as a time of "benign emptiness," Freud felt that successful passage through his stages was crucial to the healthy emotional development of the individual. Experiences (via relationships) in these early stages laid the foundation for relatively permanent personality characteristics (Mann & Carney, 1999).

### Psychosocial Theory

As with Freud's perspective, other theories of child development have relationships at their heart. Erik H. Erikson extended and modernized Freud's work. As a young man, Erikson underwent psychoanalysis with Anna Freud in Vienna, and later brought his psychoanalytic training and credentials to the United States. Here, he developed his eight-stage life-cycle theory of psychosocial development

(Friedman, 1999). In Erikson's view, at each stage the child faces a developmental crisis. Each crisis should be viewed as not so much "a debilitating conflict but rather a period of vulnerability and potential" (Hopkins, 1995, pp. 796–797). His first two stages focus on the infant and toddler: "trust vs. mistrust" (ages 0 to 1.5 years) and "autonomy vs. shame and doubt" (1.5 to 3 years). In both cases, relationships with caregivers are central to positive outcomes for the child (i.e., trust and autonomy).

In the trust vs. mistrust stage, the principal task of the child is the development of trust in his environment and relationship with caregivers. Consistent and responsive relationships between child and parent or caregiver should lead to the development of trust in the infant. Likewise, in the autonomy vs. shame and doubt stage, the relationship with the caregiver is again critical. Here, responsive care continues to be important; however, at the same time, the caregiver must allow the child the freedom to develop autonomy by doing things on his own. "Developmental theories derived from Erikson and Vygotsky's work acknowledge that young children need a safe, predictable base for exploration. Healthy infant-caregiver attachment leads to development of autonomous thinking and positive relationships with others" (Vacca & Bagdik, 2005, p. 10).

## Attachment Theory

Closely related to Erikson's notion of trust is Mary Ainsworth's concept of attachment security. Attachment security has to do with the type of relationship (and subsequent behaviors) the child has with her principal caregivers. Over the years, attachment theory has become "the dominant approach to understanding early socioemotional and personality development during the past quarter-century" (Thompson, 2000, p.145). Ainsworth and her colleagues (e.g., Ainsworth, Blehar, Waters, & Wall, 1978) utilized what was termed the "strange situation" procedure. In this procedure, researchers observed children's exploratory behavior in the presence of the mother, in her absence, and upon her return to the room. Researchers (e.g., Ainsworth et al., 1978; Main & Solomon, 1990) have identified one type of secure attachment and three types of insecure attachment (avoidant, resistant, and disorganized/disoriented). Optimally, the securely attached infant or toddler "explores comfortably in the presence of his or her caregiver, keeps track of and seeks proximity with the caregiver, happily and eagerly seeks contact after having been separated, and, in general, shows signs of trust and delight in the caregiver's presence" (Shonkoff & Phillips, 2000, p. 231). While other factors are involved–such as the baby's temperament and family circumstances–nurturing relationships in which the mother (or other caregiver) has been warm, sensitive, responsive and consistent should lead to the more desirable secure attachment.

## *Sociocultural Theory*

Lev Vygotsky's (1978) sociocultural theory emphasized the social nature of development. Unlike his contemporary, Jean Piaget, who conceptualized the child as a "little scientist working alone," Vygotsky stressed the role that others, such as parents, caregivers, and peers, play in the child's development. One of his tenets was that learning can lead development. He felt that social interactions are not just simple influences on development. Rather, interactions with others actually build the child's cognitive structures (Palinscar, 1998). Along these lines, researchers have found that when mothers guide their infant's attention and activities, the infants end up more advanced in terms of language, play, and problem-solving skills (e.g., Belsky, Goode, & Most, 1980; Tamis-LeMonda & Bornstein, 1989).

## *Humanistic Theory (Hierarchy of Needs)*

A classic theory of motivation with implications for the child's relationships is Maslow's seven-level hierarchy of needs (1968). Maslow's humanistic theory suggested that children are motivated by a set of inner needs, and that lower level needs must be satisfied in order for the higher order needs to emerge. From the base, his theory posits the following seven needs in order: survival (e.g., hunger, thirst), safety (e.g., security, stability), belongingness and love, self-esteem, intellectual achievement, aesthetic appreciation, and self-actualization. Of these, the first four "deficiency" needs seem most obviously related to infants and toddlers. The mother and other caregivers ideally go beyond meeting the child's basic physical needs necessary for survival to satisfy the child's needs for safety, belonging, and self-esteem. "Bowlby proposed that the earliest emotional experiences have a lifelong effect. The baby is an active participant in trying to get her needs met through her early relationships. Through these interactions, the child develops a mental image of herself and of her expectations of relationships. She uses this mental image in all later relationships" (Wittmer & Petersen, 2006, p. 53).

## *Brain-Based Research*

Brain-based research has documented the importance of relationships in the lives of young children. With new techniques, such as brain imaging and the capacity to measure brain activity, scientists can learn much about brain functioning. For example, we now know that with each action, a circuit or pathway is made in the brain. With experience and practice, this circuitry is reinforced and becomes permanent. "As this connecting process is repeated across many cells, pathways of interconnection develop throughout the brain and body, allowing us to think, remember, and to act" (Butterfield, Martin, & Prairie, 2004, p. 23). We know that brain wiring depends upon the child's experience and nurturance during this critical time – which underscores the child's need for responsive relationships during the first three years of life.

## *Relationship-Based Theory*

Finally, a theory of development that fits squarely with this chapter's relationship theme is the relationship-based theory of child development (e.g., Emde & Robinson, 2000; Hinde, 1992b). Hinde (1992a) has suggested that "a relationship approach involves the recognition that children must be seen not as isolated entities, but as forming part of a network of social relationships; and requires a delicate balance between conceptions of the child as an individual and as a social being" (p. 1019). While the mother-child relationship is usually primary, relationships outside the home, such as those with caregivers in child care settings, are becoming ever more important (Shonkoff & Phillips, 2000). A relationship-based theory views the child as developing in a supportive network of relationships, and would "create a structure of teacher schedules and group sizes that would provide opportunities for relationships to develop over time" (Wittmer & Petersen, 2006, p. 59).

## Recommendations on Supporting Positive Relationships in Child Care Settings

Out of home care is a way of life in the United States. Given that infants and toddlers spend so much time in non-parental care situations, the focus of this chapter is on fostering positive relationships with caregivers in the child care setting. Broadly, the term *caregiver* "refers to all adults who are in a caring relationship with infants, regardless of the setting" (Lally & Mangione, 2006, p. 14). In the child care setting, the environment, the staff, programming, and family relationships all play vital roles in facilitating healthy emotional development in infants and toddlers.

## *Recognize the Unique Environment of Infant Toddler Child Care*

For infants and toddlers, establishing environments that are stable and predictable is most likely to enhance healthy relationships. However, this can be difficult in infant toddler programs. For example, one caregiver may be assigned to several infants, as opposed to a one-on-one relationship (such as the one-on-one relationship between mother and child). Further, caregivers, albeit well meaning, may lack the necessary training and skills required to work with this age group, and may have a high rate of turnover due to stress and burnout. Hurried parents may drop off and pick up their children abruptly, with little or no time for exchanges about the child. Along these lines, Lally and Mangione (2006) have suggested that infant toddler settings differ markedly from preschools, and require a unique approach in order to meet these children's emotional needs. The following practical suggestions are made as means of building healthy caregiver-child relationships in infant toddler settings.

## *Maintain a Consistent Routine for Each Child*

For example, the youngest infants should be on individual schedules. This allows their routine care needs to be met on a similar schedule to that which they experience at home. Such individualized care respects the uniqueness of each child while considering the desires of the family, and interfaces with the internal rhythms of the infant. As the infant matures neurologically, similar patterns for eating, sleeping, and diapering may emerge such that the routines of two or three children may be on the same schedule and may be cared for as a small group. During these periods of routine care, caregivers must adopt a calm, leisurely pace and tune in to opportunities for positive one-on-one interaction with each infant.

Greenman (1986) suggested the use of a "primary care system" in which one adult is assigned to the main care of an infant and gets to know that child intimately on a one-on-one basis. The primary caregiver concept is viewed as a means of establishing continuity between home and center. Each caregiver is assigned to care specifically for four or fewer babies at a given time. The advantages of this system are that the caregiver can intentionally become very familiar with each baby, get to know that child's likes and dislikes, and his or her preferences for care. The caregiver can also develop a close relationship with the family with the smaller number of children. In some cases, as many as eight babies may be in one group, cared for together and assigned to two teachers. Rather than each teacher trying to get to know all eight babies, they get to know four babies and their families on a much more intimate basis. Once the infant has become comfortable with the caregiver and the setting, then the other caregiver can take on more responsibility for the care and well being of the infant. Such a system of caregiving is much more conducive for developing intimate relationships than one in which the caregivers have to know eight infants and their families concurrently. Of course, this is not to say that the teachers do not get to know all the children, because they do. Rather, their closest relationship will be with the small group of four or fewer children and their families.

Taking this concept a step further is the notion of keeping the same caregiver with this same small group of children from infancy through preschool. This concept in known as "continuity of care." The advantages are the same as those for the system for primary caregiving. Further, by keeping the group small and limiting the number of staff with this group, the classroom itself can be adapted to meeting the changing needs of these children as they get older. Keeping the same caregiver and classroom will enhance the sense of security for the children.

One study found that when environments were safe, and when numbers of children cared for were low, caregivers smiled at children more and were much more willing to allow them to explore. There were fewer "no" and "don't" statements and more positive, encouraging exchanges. As Maslow might have suggested, make the environment safe for children first of all. Then, make it interesting to the baby depending upon developmental level.

## *Strive for Stable and Predictable Child/Staff Interactions*

Caregivers should "model caring, responsive, thoughtful relationships with children and other adults" (Edwards & Raikes, 2002). The smaller the number of children per adult, the better. Licensing requirements vary from state to state, but a majority of states require a ratio of no more than three children to one adult.

Strive to minimize turnover. Stress and burnout are major factors in staff turnover. The National Association for the Education of Young Children (2001) states that staff turnover in child care is 30 percent annually. In comparison to about 8–9% for teaching jobs in public schools, 30 percent seems exceptionally high. Staff turnover costs the child care industry for training new personnel to mention just one cost. An unstable teaching staff is hard on children who need consistency in their daily schedules and consistent adults who know them to ensure that children's needs for security are met. In this regard, well trained caregivers are less likely to experience stress and burnout.

Staffing patterns can be adjusted so that caregivers' shifts are staggered and that they work a 9-hour shift requiring an hour off for lunch. In a classroom with two teachers, one would take the early shift and the other would come in late enough to be present when the children leave in the evening. This is especially important so that a person who has been with the child all day is there to visit with the parent at the end of the day. One program we know gives their staff the option to work 10-hour shifts four days per week. This enables the caregiver to have an additional full day off from work each week. This particular program staffs with four full-time teachers who are motivated to make it work. All in the unit must be in agreement to participate in such a system.

Keep groups of infants and toddlers small and intact for as long as possible instead of the more common practice of switching a child from group to group. The latter approach is usually based on economic concerns and staffing convenience, rather than on what is best for the child. Family style or multi-age grouping is another way to ensure that groups can stay small and familiar. In this arrangement, if the age range of the children is expanded in the group, fewer children will be moving in and out of the group. Should it be necessary to move a child from one group to another, the child will benefit most if the move can be made with her caregiver or with a peer. This familiarity with another person will help with the separation from the group. Best practice would indicate that what is best for children is to limit such moves.Keeping the same person with the infant for as long as possible is best. "What is ideal is for the caregiver and the small group of children to stay together from infancy through preschool" (Lally, 1995, p. 59). As infants develop, move the adult along with the child and her small group of peers as transitions are needed.

People working with infants and toddlers are more likely to better meet the child's needs if they are knowledgeable and understand what is considered normal development and behavior for young children. Trained caregivers are more likely to be sensitive to an individual child. Erikson (1963) viewed adults who trust in themselves as being loving and facilitative and thereby, sensitive and responsive to an infant's signals. With more knowledge, caregivers are likely to be more confident and, thus, more likely to nurture trust in infants.

## *Monitor and Improve Program Quality*

Develop policies and procedures with an eye toward the goal of optimizing relationship building. Children and families will benefit as a result. The following are some ways to insure optimal programming.

Enroll children staggered by age and balance ages within a group. As suggested previously, try to enroll children within broad age ranges. Such enrollment strategies allow the children to develop relationships with their peers similar to that within a family. Children learn as much from each other as much as they do from adults. Knowing their peers and caregivers well helps the children learn what to expect from each other and to predict the behavior of others. This adds to their sense of security and well being.

Adopt policies to insure that each day has a consistent schedule and a consistent staff member for the child. Children are very dependent upon that consistency for their sense of security and belonging. Consistent routines are beneficial to staff, as well. Successful transitioning of a child who has been at home (or in a single care setting) to a group setting can be enhanced with careful planning. Prior to moving from one care setting to another, plan enough time for a smooth transition allowing the child to gradually to become comfortable in the new setting. For example, the family could begin by driving by the new center on the route to and from home commenting to the baby about "your new school." Then, encourage the parent to come into the classroom in the new setting with the baby. Have the child first come at the end of the day when fewer children might be present. This allows the baby to become familiar with the classroom and the new caregiver while the parent serves as a "secure base." A family might even want to come when *all* the children are out of the classroom, such as at the end of the day, so that the caregiver can focus upon the new child in a non-threatening manner. The visits might evolve to where the parent leaves the child for a few hours a few days in a row. Then, the length of the separation would gradually increase over time so that the baby is staying for longer and longer periods of time. Again, allowing a generous amount of time for the transition is optimal for both the child and the family.

## Build Positive Relationships with Families

A system of communication between staff and families is essential to developing healthy relationships. Regular communication between the family and the center will facilitate a smooth transition of the infant from home to school. Such communication might include verbal and written systems of daily slips, charts, and logs. Such systems would be designed in such a way as to convey the family's desires and needs, the child's experience, and the program concerns for the infant (Greenman, 1986).

One suggestion for written communication is for parents to fill out a brief intake form each morning that outlines the routines of the infant at home. During the day, the staff can chart the infant's activities and then parents receive the form or chart each evening. This written communication allows for continuity of care from school to home. The parent will know what time the baby had snack, food, was diapered, and so forth. The intake information is particularly useful on days when the infant may have had multiple caregivers. That slip of paper may be all the parent has to rely on for information about the child's day.

Many parents prefer daily informal back and forth conversations about their child at arrival and departure times. For this reason, it is especially important to stagger staff schedules so that someone who has been with the child a good portion of the day is available to visit with the parent at the end of the day. Families should also be encouraged to telephone the caregiver as desired to inquire about their child's well-being. This may be particularly reassuring to families who are new to out of home care and may have had to leave their baby crying.

## Concluding Remarks

As theories of child development attest, the relationships that take place during the first few years of life are crucial for the healthy development of the child. As more and more children spend these early years in child care, it is important to optimize the relationship between the child, family, and caregiver. Our practical suggestions should help to make the most of those relationships, so that desired outcomes such as trust, self-regulation, secure attachment, autonomy, and positive self-image are attained with the youngest children in group care: infants and toddlers.

## References

Ainsworth, M. D. S., Blehar, M. C., Waters, E., & Wall, S. (1978). *Patterns of attachment.* Hillsdale, NJ: Erlbaum.

Belsky, J., Goode, M. K., & Most, R. K. (1980). Maternal stimulation and infant exploratory competence: Cross-sectional, correlational, and experimental analysis. *Child Development, 51,* 1163–1178.

Butterfield, P. M., Martin, C. A., & Prairie, A. P. (2004). *Emotional connections: How relation-ships guide early learning*. Washington, DC: Zero to Three Press.

Children's Defense Fund (2003). Infants and toddlers are particularly vulnerable: Good child care and early education can play a vital role in their development from *Child Care Basics 2005* retrieved from the Internet at http://www.childrensdefense.org/site/PageServer?pagename=res earch_early_ childhood on March 22, 2007.

Edwards, C. P., & Raikes, H. (2002). Extending the dance: Relationship-based approaches in infant-toddler care in education. *Young Children, 53* (3), 73–79.

Emde, R. H., & Robinson, J. L. (2000). Guiding principles for a theory of early intervention: A developmental-psychoanalytic perspective. In J. P. Shonkoff & S. J. Meisels (Eds.), *Handbook of early intervention*. (pp. 160–178). New York: Cambridge University Press.

Erikson, E. (1963). *Childhood and society*. New York: Norton.

Friedman, L. J. (1999). *Identity's architect: A biography of Erik H. Erikson*. New York: Scribner.

Greenman, J. (1986, Winter). Grouping infants and toddlers. *Caring for Infants and Toddlers*, 11–14.

Hinde, R. (1992a). Developmental psychology in the context of older behavioral sciences. *Developmental Psychology, 28*, 1018–1029.

Hinde, R. (1992b). Ethological and relationship approaches. In R. Vasta (Ed.), *Six theories of child development: Revised formulations and current issues* (pp. 251–285). London: JKP Press.

Hopkins, J. R. (1995). Erik Homburger Erikson (1902–1994). *American Psychologist, 50*, 796–797.

Lally, J. R. (1995). The impact of child care policies and practices on infant/toddler identity for-mation. *Young Children, 51*(1), 58–67.

Lally, J. R., & Mangione, P. (2006). The uniqueness of infancy demands a responsive approach to care. *Young Children, 61*(4), 14–20.

Main, M., & Solomon, J. (1990). Procedures for identifying infants as disorganized/ disoriented during the Ainsworth Strange Situation. In M. Greenberg, D. Cicchetti, & M. Cummings (Eds.), *Attachment in the preschool years: Theory, research, and intervention* (pp. 121–160). Chicago: University of Chicago Press.

Mann, M. B., & Carney, R. N. (1999). Emotional development. In T. C. Jefferson (Ed.), *Children's health* (pp. 250–255) [2 vols.]. Pasadena, CA: Salem Press.

Maslow, A. H. (1968). *Toward a psychology of being* (2nd ed.). New York: Van Nostrand.

Masten, A. S., & Coatsworth, J. D. (1998). The development of competence in favorable and unfavorable environments: Lessons from research on successful children. *American Psychologist, 53*, 205–220.

National Association for the Education of Young Children (2001). *Financing the early childhood education system. A policy brief*. Retrieved from the Internet at http://www.naeyc.org/ece/pdf/ financing-policybrief.pdf#xml=http://naeychq.naeyc.org/texis/search/pdfhi.txt?query=staff+tu rnover+in+child+care&pr=naeyc&prox=sentence&rorder=750&rprox=500&rdfreq=1000&r wfreq=1000&rlead=1000&sufs=2&order=r&cq=&id=452256bf19 on April 10, 2007.

Palinscar, A. S. (1998). Social constructivist perspectives on teaching and learning. In J. T. Spence, J. M. Darley, & D. J. Foss (Eds.), *Annual review of psychology* (pp. 345–375). Palo Alto, CA: Annual Reviews.

Shonkoff, J. P., & Phillips, D. A. (Eds.). (2000). *From neurons to neighborhoods: The science of early development*. Washington, DC: National Academy Press.

Tamis-LeMonda, C. S., & Bornstein, M. H. (1989). Habituation and maternal encouragement of attention in infancy as predictors of toddler language, play, and representational competence. *Child Development, 60*, 738–751.

Thompson, R. A. (2000). The legacy of early attachments. *Child Development, 71*, 145–152.

Vacca, J., & Bagdik, A. (2005). Relationships for life: Supporting the emotional health of infants and toddlers. *Dimensions of Early Childhood, 33*(1), 9–16.

Vygotsky, L. (1978). *Mind in society: The development of higher psychological processes*. Cambridge, MA: Harvard University Press. (Original works published 1930, 1933, and 1935)

Wittmer, D. S., & Petersen, S. H. (2006). *Infant and toddler development and responsive program planning: A relationship-based approach*. Upper Saddle River, NJ: Pearson.

**Mary Beth Mann, Ph.D.**
Associate Professor
Department of Early Childhood and Family Development
Missouri State University
901 South National Avenue
Springfield, MO 65897
417-836-6339
MaryBethMann@missouristate.edu

Mary Beth Mann has been a teacher and director primarily in university settings for nearly thirty years. Her research interests are in the areas of infant development, attachment, continuity of care and parent education. She has been at Missouri State University in the Child and Family Development Program since 1994 as a faculty member teaching infant toddler development, program administration, and child development.

**Russell N. Carney, Ph.D.**
Professor
Department of Psychology
Missouri State University
901 South National Avenue
Springfield, MO 65897
417-836-5833
RussellCarney@missouristate.edu
2266 E. Barataria
Springfield, MO 65804
Home: 417-882-1410

Russell N. Carney taught junior high math prior to receiving his doctorate in educational psychology. He worked as a school psychologist before coming to the Psychology Department at Missouri State University in 1988. He teaches child development, educational psychology, and tests and measurements. His research interests are in developmental psychology and cognitive strategies.

# Chapter 10
# Fostering Relationships Between Infants, Toddlers and Their Primary Caregivers in Child Care Centres in Australia

**Marjory Ebbeck and Hoi Yin Bonnie Yim**

**Abstract** The chapter provides a synthesis of theory and research in relation to relationships between babies, toddlers and their caregivers in child care centres. The themes addressed includes attachment theory and how this is taken account of by caregivers, the importance of secure relationships that recognize and build on the first transition from home to child care centre. In addition, the use of primary caregiving groups is investigated whereby the caregiver establishes close reciprocal relationships with babies, toddlers and their families.

**Keywords** babies, toddlers, infants, attachment, primary caregiving, relationships, child care programs, group care, Australia, child care centers

## Introduction

The fostering of positive relationships between infants, toddlers and their caregivers in child care centres continues to be an area of interest and concern to everyone involved in the care, education and welfare of this age group. Families, as the most important stakeholders, have foremost in their minds the long term interests of their infants and toddlers. Indeed, in countries that have accreditation systems operating for children's care services, the fostering of positive relationships is, in most cases, the most important criterion in assessing service quality.

University of South Australia

University of South Australia

M.R. Jalongo (ed.), *Enduring Bonds.*
© Springer 2008

# Background

In Australia, statistics of 2006 show that 45% of the workforce is comprised of women whose youngest child was aged under 5 years (Australian Bureau of Statistics). This example points to a re-employment trend that has considerable ramifications for early childhood services provision.

Australian statistics further show that the proportion of families with at least one parent employed using a care arrangement and this increased from 56% in 2002 to 61% in 2005. The form of care, that is the context, varies from informal care by grandparents, other relatives to formalised long day care which is the most commonly used form of care. In addition, the hours of care used by parents varies greatly from approximately 14–50 hours a week (Australian Bureau of Statistics, 2006b; Harrison & Ungerer, 2005).

Taylor (2004) cites findings that over 300,000 children aged 0–5 years are currently attending long day child care in Australia (p. 3). A further 95,000 are currently cared for in family day care. Taylor adds that the impetus for the development of a quality assurance system in long day care in Australia includes the finding that the average amount of time an individual child spends in child care has increased. A child can spend up to 12,500 hours in child care before starting school (based on attendance of 50 hours per week for 5 years). This is only 500 hours less than the amount a child will spend in lessons during the whole 13 years of schooling (Taylor, 2004, p.3).

One implication of the findings cited by Taylor (2004) is that infants and toddlers may be spending more waking time with caregivers than with parents. This implication is not confined to Australia. It is also an important point to note that in many countries there is huge diversity in the cultural background of the families using some form of child care service, be it formal or informal.

When mothers return to the workforce after the birth and early care of their infant or toddler, whatever the country or context, access to quality child care services is a prime requirement for families. Winter (2003, p. 14), looking at quality care from the perspective of adequate funding and support, argued that low-quality early childhood services are actually harmful for young children. This finding has been supported by other researchers (Australian Institute of Family Studies, 2005; Elliott, 2006; Harrison & Ungerer, 2005,; NICHD Early Child Care Research Network, 2005; Press & Hayes, 2000; Sims, Guilfoyle, & Parry, 2005). There is a view that where there is optimum investment and support leading to high quality early childhood services, positive outcomes with lasting cognitive and social benefits for children and their communities can happen (Press & Hayes, 2000; Sylva, Melhuish, Sammons, Siraj-Blatchford, Taggart, & Elliot, 2003). However, an important study conducted in three national contexts suggested a need for more complex estimates of how both quality and quantity of child care may influence a range of children's developmental outcomes (Love, Harrison, Sagi-Schwartz, van IJzendoorn, Ross C. Ungerer, Raikes, Brady-Smith, Boller, Brooks-Gunn, Constantine, Kisker, Paulsell, & Chazan-Cohen, 2003).

What most policy makers, educators and parents hope is that a child's development needs not be undermined if he or she is placed in a high quality environment, well resourced with well qualified staff (Elliott, 2006; NICHD Early Child Care Research Network, 2000, 2001, 2005).

## Foundations for Positive Relationships

Balaban (2006, pp. 14–15) states that attachment and separation are the stuff of which life is made. Feelings about saying goodbye are not restricted to child care situations. Separation from someone we love and care about is a lifelong experience that affects every one of us!

When investigating the foundations for positive relationships with such a young age group the issue of attachment theory arises consistently. Professionals and families need to take serious account of attachment when making provision for infants and toddlers who will spend time away from their primary caregivers, who is usually the mother. Bowlby's attachment theory is very well known and was presented in his three classic papers (1958; 1959; 1960) and his attachment trilogy ([1969] 2000; [1973] 2000; [1980] 2000).

Bowlby ([1969] 2000) stated that infants and young children should experience a warm, intimate, and continuous relationship with their mother (or permanent mother substitute) in which both find satisfaction and enjoyment. He also argued that an infant's attachment to the mother (or permanent mother substitute) is "a biological need, a survival mechanism, and as such, is critical to the child's emotional well-being", which is also the foundation for the "role of lasting relationships in human development" (Harrison, 2003, p.2).

## Attachment Theory

### Some Definitions

Intrigued by Bowlby's theory, researchers began to enrich and refine the definitions of attachment. Most researchers focus on the linkage between attachment and bonding. Harrison (2003), for instance, regards attachment as "our unique human ability to form lasting relationships with others, and to maintain these relationships over time and distance" (p. 1). Berk (2006) describes attachment as a "strong, affectionate tie we have with special people in our lives that leads us to feel pleasure when we interact with them and to be comforted by their nearness during times of stress" (p. 419). Attachment also can be described as a "strong emotional bond between an infant or young child and a caring adult who is part of the child's everyday life" (Honig, 2002, p. 2). As Dixon (2003) states the idea of attachment lies at the centre of almost all contemporary thinking about children's emotional growth.


## Patterns of Attachment

Watson, Watson and Wilson (2003, p. 102) present a useful summary of patterns of attachment drawing on the work of Ainsworth et al. (1978) and Main and Solomon (1990) as follows:

- Secure attachment is defined as when the infant uses a parent as a secure base, strongly prefers the parent over a stranger, actively seeks contact with the parent and is easily comforted by the parent after absence.
- Avoidant attachment is defined as when the infant is usually not distressed by parental separation and may avoid parent or prefer a stranger when the parent returns.
- Resistant attachment is defined as when the infant seeks closeness to the parent and resists exploring the environment, usually displays angry behaviour after the parent returns and is difficult to comfort.
- Disoriented attachment is defined as when the infant shows inconsistent attachment and reacts to the parent returning with confused/contradictory behaviour such as looking away when held.

Each of these patterns of attachment can be referred back to the "attachment behavioural system" in the early work of Miller, Galanter, & Pribram, 1960 and all are important for caregivers who need to be able to recognise and respond appropriately to identified patterns of attachment in the children they care for. It does need to be recognised however, that attachment can be thought of as a continuum, as some children may make a gradual transition from insecure to secure attachment.

A related characteristic to attachment mentioned by Watson, Watson and Wilson (2003, p. 102) drawing on the work of Kagan, Kearsley and Zelazo (1978) is that of separation anxiety which appears to be a normal developmental experience since all children across cultures express such behaviour around six months of age to approximately 15 months.

Attachment theory raises the issue of who really are the significant attachment figures in the life of the infant and toddler. What does the theory mean for the development of positive relationships? Parent(s) and close family member(s) are usually a child's main attachment figures. Among these family figures, the bond between a child and his/her parent(s) tends to be a strong one. Although the majority of attachment studies has focused on mothers, because mothers tend to fill this role most often, there is evidence that children are capable of forming attachments with "more than one adult" (Honig, 2002, p.3) in order to form hierarchy of attachment figures. Therefore, other caregivers such as fathers, grandparents, siblings, child care workers, caregivers, and family day caregivers, who are in a position to work with children on a long-term basis and to form lasting relationships with them, also play an important role in a child's attachment network (Harrison, 2003; Howes, Rodning, Galuzzo, & Myers, 1988; Schaffer & Emerson, 1964; Sullivan, 1999).

A child can also include objects, such as pacifiers, blankets and special toys, into his/her hierarchy of attachment figures (Gowrie Training and Resource Centre, 2001b, p.1). Attachment theory is relevant to all significant relationships in a child's life, not just those between parent and child. In addition, all individuals including children of a very young age have the ability to develop cognitive schemas, or internal representations about the relative degree of safety afforded by attachment figures (Ainsworth et al., 1978).

Hutchins (1995) reminds us that early research on attachment was limited to considering the importance of attachment between parents, particularly the mother, and young children. Further literature on attachment points to the important role played by secondary attachments, that is alternative caregivers (Maier, 1994).

## The Importance of Attachment for Child Care Centres

The importance of understanding attachment cannot be understated for it has to be an underpinning principle not only when considering quality in child care, but also in the development of the child care curriculum. It is important that a definition of curriculum in child care includes all those activities and experiences that happen to a child's every minute of the day he/she is in care. Research has indicated that attachment provides a "secure base" (Cookman, 2005, p. 530) for a child to positively cultivate, for example, his/her subsequent developmental issues:

- sense of self (Howes, 1999; van IJzendoorn, Sagi, & Lambermon, 1992),
- confidence in exploration (Bell & Ainsworth, 1972; Gowrie Training and Resource Centre, 2001a; Harrison, 2003),
- mental health (Honig, 1984, 1993; Matas, Arend, & Sroufe, 1978)
- self-regulation (Braungart-Rieker, Garwood, Power, & Wang, 2001; Shore, 1997; L. Alan Sroufe, 1979),
- verbal fluency (Main, Kaplan, & Cassidy, 1985),
- personality (Honig, 2002; Karen, 1994), and
- social competence (Ainsworth & Bell, 1974; Aren, Gove, & Sroufe, 1979; Erickson, Korfmacher, & Egeland, 1992; Scroufe, 1995; Troy & Sroufe, 1987; Turner, 1991).

Moreover, and as an aside, some researchers found that early attachment experiences could influence one's future relationships with romantic partners (Crowell & Waters, 1994; Hazan & Shaver, 1987) and even parenting styles (Benoit & Parker, 1994; Bretherton, 1992; De Wolff & van IJzendoorn, 1997; Kretchmar & Jacobvitz, 2002; Main & Goldwyn, 1992).

Consequently, early attachment experiences serve not only as templates for one's holistic development, but are also the hub around a person's life – from an infant or a toddler through to adolescence and the years of maturity, and into old age (Bowlby, [1980] 2000).

## Is Attachment Universal Across all Cultures?

Berk (2006, p. 435) states that cultural conditions must be considered when interpreting the meaning of attachment patterns. Other sources stress that attachment theory has always been open to 'culture-specific influences and idiosyncrasies' (van IJzendoorn & Sagi, 1999, p. 714). The underlying reasoning is that the formation of attachment relationships is universal across all cultures. This reasoning about the universality of attachment in childhood, however, does not deny the fact that the particular culture into which a child is born influences the way relationships are moulded and expressed. Van IJzendoorn and Sagi (1999) argue further that the theory does not imply that secure attachment theory would be the norm in every culture or community (Rolfe, 2004, p. 184). However, as Grossmann (1995) has proposed "attachment relationships constitute the very foundation for the child's entry and socialization into the qualitatively specific type of engagements between people – emotional, communicative, and supportive — that is characteristic of a given culture" (p. 186). Along similar lines, Balaban makes some very timely comments (2006) when she writes, "…we need to understand the importance of cultural beliefs and what separation means to families of diverse cultures" (p. 18).

## Enhancing the Bonds Between Infants/Toddlers and their Caregivers in Child Care

The quality of both primary and secondary attachment relationships between infants, toddlers and their caregivers is of critical importance to their overall development (Gonzalez-Mena, 1997; Honig, 1993; Hutchins, 1995; Mardell, 1992; Winder, 2003). Cassidy (2000, p. 88) proposes that emotions linked to caregiving may be as powerful as any experience throughout life. Many child care centres in Australia are focusing on the emotional availability of caregivers and this appears to help infants and toddlers form strong bonds with their caregivers (Lady Gowrie Child Centre Adelaide, Interviews, 16 February 2007).

Another issue for consideration is the temperament of the infant or toddler. Some individuals settle very easily and are adaptable, others take much longer. The Australian Temperament Project (ATP) (1983–2005) has followed children from the age of 4 months to 20 years, mapping their temperament and its relationship to well-being. Findings confirm the importance of the development of resilience (www.aifs.gov.au/atp). Berk (2006, p. 411) states that researchers have become increasingly interested in temperamental variations amongst children and she cites two models of temperament, the well known one by Thomas and Chess (1977) and one by Rothbart (2003). Parents and caregivers have first hand experience of the differences in temperament amongst infants and toddlers and how this trait impacts on the interaction patterns as they work towards helping children achieve emotional self-regulation.

The following five strategies may provide inspiration for caregivers to delve more deeply into the significance of important bonds and reconsider their practices in light of new understandings gained.

## Programmatic Recommendations

### *Implement a Primary Caregiving System*

An adoption of a primary caregiving system that is founded on the view that curriculum for infants and toddlers is attachment, could be one of the many ways to establish enduring bonds between infants/toddlers and the child care staff. A primary caregiving system is "one designed to ensure that each child is linked to one special person who assumes major responsibility for their care. This person also becomes the main contact person for communication between the child's family and the child care service" (Richardson, 2000, p. 1). Primary caregiving is premised on secure attachment behaviour when a child seeks closeness and contact in order to feel more secure (Department of Education and Children's Services, 2005; Greenman & Stonehouse, 1996; Watson et al., 2003).

The fundamental principles of the primary caregiving system are:

Firstly, primary caregiving helps centres to establish true partnerships with parents. These partnerships are based on a professional relationship with common goals for the infant and toddler. In addition, partnerships are also "developed over time with families which foster their confidence as parents and involve them in planning for their child" (Gowrie Training and Resource Centre, 2001a, p. 8; Honig, 2002).

Secondly, a primary caregiving system also helps the infant/toddler to settle much more easily into care as one of the features of primary caregiving is that "staff interact and involve infant in everyday routines and activities in much the same way as a parent would do at home" (Gowrie Training and Resource Centre, 2001a, p.7).

Thirdly, the primary caregiving system is especially beneficial to the infants/toddlers of working women. As some working women can only nurture the development of an intimate emotional relationship with their child part of their time, then it is crucial in the care setting that one or two familiar people be available to the child, in order to encircle the child with love (Baker & Manfredi-Petitt, 1998; Honig, 1985).

Lastly, for those infants/toddlers whose homes do not provide the love, comfort, and attention necessary for secure attachment, the nurturing support of a skilled, stable and caring provider may also make all the difference (Honig, 2002).

The Department of Education & Children's Services in South Australia promotes as its policy in child care the use of primary caregiving practices stating
(2005, p. 17) that it fosters secure attachments and is characterised by the following
practices:

- Each child has one primary caregiver
- There is continuity and consistency
- The primary caregiver takes responsibility for most of the child care nurturing
  and communication with the parents/family
- Each child's personal care is attended to by their primary caregiver
- The primary caregiver advocates for the child
- Children have secure attachments to their primary caregiver
- The primary caregiver–in collaboration with colleagues–observes, monitors,
  plans, evaluates and reports on the child's experiences, learning and
  development
- There is reciprocity between the primary caregiver and child
- The primary cargiver is appropriately responsive and 'in tune' with the child
- There are sustained interactions between the child and caregiver

Greenman and Stonehouse (1996, p. 88) are strong proponents of the primary
caregiver system but make an important point in stating that 'primary' does not
mean 'exclusive' and that other staff develop warm relationships with the child
also. "The child should not become totally dependent on the presence of one person
in order to have a good day" (p. 88).

When assigning infants and toddlers to caregivers, directors of child care centres
need to consider compatibility of parent, staff, and child's characteristics. Culture
and values are particularly relevant characteristics to consider (Greenman &
Stonehouse, 1996). This consideration is echoed also by Gonzalez-Mena (1997)
who proposes that cultural pluralism has to be taken into account, where staff working in child care must have a clear understanding of cultural differences in families.
She believes that these differences show up in the way the needs of infants are met
as they are raised to be members of their culture. Specifically, in relation to attachment, Gonzalez-Mena (1997) emphasized the dramatic differences in child rearing
practices amongst various cultures depends on their value systems – individual,
familial and cultural.

## Use Attachment Theory as a Basis for Observing Infants & Toddlers

It has been mentioned earlier in this Chapter that an 'attachment curriculum' rec-
ognises the fundamental needs of infants and toddlers for security, continuity and
stability. As Hutchins (1995) proposes "babies and toddlers need to know that there
is mutual respect and understanding between their primary caregivers and the child
care staff, and that individual family differences are considered and welcomed.

In addition, the interactions that occur between babies, toddlers and their caregivers are extremely important" (p. 7).

## Make Positive Interactions the Foundation of Relationships

Child care staff's respectful and sensitive interactions with the infant and toddler are fundamental for building positive relationships. These responsive interactions will take account of the needs, temperament and emotional availability of the caregiver. Some daily interactions, during routines and rituals such as nappy changing, dressing and feeding times, are undoubtedly times for developing and/or bridging relationships. Greenman and Stonehouse (1996) term these rituals and routines as "prime times", stressing the critical importance of positive one-to-one interactions (p. xiii). A parenting project at the University of Chicago, titled "Circle of Security", which has operated successfully for fifty years in the USA (Figure 1) (www. circleof-security.org/) and audiovisual resources "Infant Cues: A Child's First Language" (www.ncast.org/), for example, provide relevant information for adults on how to interact with young children in a respectful and sensitive way.

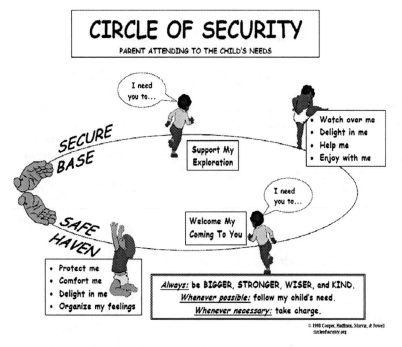

**Figure 1** Circle of Security: Secure Base and Haven of Safety (© Cooper, Hoffman, Marvin, & Powell, 1998)

This Circle of Security (COS) model (Marvin, Cooper, & Hoffman, 2002) has been incorporated into other programs in child care designed to assist in the development of secure relationships. For example, in Australia, a Government funded initiative started and expanded from the Lady Gowrie Child Centre, Adelaide, South Australia and offers a program for parents called *Through the Looking Glass* (http://www.gowrie-wa.com.au/home.cms). This program is designed to support families where there is a parent/child relationship under stress. This program is designed to support referred families by providing free child care relief of 2 days per week with an 18 weeks group program for mothers conducted by a child care centre coordinator and a social worker. The program has a primary caregiver basis but, in addition, focuses on assisting parents to develop skills, learn about parenting relationships and increase parents' knowledge of child development. The program, in effect, helps parents to cope with the everyday struggles of parenting. It has been in operation for some 8 years and evaluations show that relationships between mother and infant have improved as a result of this intervention. Staff who have worked in this program are overwhelmingly supportive of it and stress that being emotionally available to children is the key to its success. Dolby and Warren (2006) in reporting on the application of the circle of security state that "children require the support of an emotionally available adult, a special person who is always kind and stronger, older and wiser than themselves" (p. 24).

## Develop Sound Parent-Caregiver Interactions

When a child's parents shows confidence in the caregiver and the setting, the child is more likely to feel confident as well. Caregivers, likewise, should communicate their respect for the parents (Honig, 2002, p. 54). We need to find out what parents want for their children, for example, what their goals and caregiving practices are. This means encouraging staff to talk with parents, sharing, asking questions, thus communicating and allowing opportunities to build relationships with parents. "We can learn from families themselves if we listen well and do not rush to judge practices that are different from our own" (Balaban, 2006, p. 18).

## Understand Children's Separation Anxiety

Adults' understanding of the need for patience and empathy with children's separation anxiety could also be another important element for building positive bonds with both infants and toddlers (Ramsburg, 1998). During some difficult times in a child care situation, such as separation and reunion periods, adults' preparation and responses could directly influence in a short period of time the quality and quantity of children's relationships with both human and objects. One way that early child-hood practitioners seek to foster positive relationships is to utilise strategies that assist the child in understanding what we know to be "object permanence". Some simple and traditional games like Peek-a-boo or hide-and-seek, for exam-ple, can assist the development of this object permanence concept namely that things and people continue to exist when out of sight (Gowrie Training and Resource Centre, 2001b). Ball play with infant can "emphasize the concept of secure base behaviour as it produces going away and coming back behaviours" (Gowrie Training and Resource Centre, 2001b, p.9). These games, when played over time, can assist infants and toddlers to understand that "Mummy will come back!"

## Recommendations for Caregivers

### *Be Aware of the Importance of Attachment Items/Transition Objects*

It is important in infant and toddler rooms to support the use of attachment items or transition objects. Children develop attachments to certain objects such as ted-dies, pacifiers and blankets, which make the transition process from home to child care centre easier and help the child to make the connections. Hutchins (1995) pro-poses that infants and toddlers in group care should never be forced to 'give up' their attachment objects.

In order to build and maintain children's sense of security, it is a good prac-tice to have photos of the parents placed in the room at children's eye level where they can go touch, point to, in order to help them remember that their parents have not vanished from their lives (Gowrie Training and Resource Centre, 2001b, p. 10).

Sometimes, infants settle better when they have an item of clothing that their parent has worn the day before. The smell reminds the infant of the parent and helps them to feel secure (Gowrie Training and Resource Centre, 2001b, p. 10).

Caregivers can arrange the environment to promote a child's ease and com-fort with being in child care. Soft pillows, mattresses with washable covers, areas carpeted with rugs – these are some of the furnishings, textures, and materials that lend a feeling of coziness and warmth to a child care facility or family child care home. Traditional 'home play' toys in the care environment help the infant to make a connection between home and child care. Utensils used in the home activities all help the child to remember familiar objects and home routines. Holding a child in a rocking chair is also a good way to ease an infant's entry into a care program or a preschooler's anxiety when upsetting feelings sweep over him or her (Honig, 2002, pp. 36–37).

## *Be Aware of the Importance of Providing Routines in the Child Care Contexts*

To support and promote secure attachments, children need to have their needs met sensitively and appropriately. Routine times make up a significant part of a young child's day and routines provide an opportunity for the primary caregiver to spend time with an individual child, getting to know him/her and their individual routines (Gowrie Training and Resource Centre, 2001b, p. 5). If possible, routines in child care should complement those from the home such as if the infant or toddler is used to a sleep at around 11 am then this should be continued in the child care context. The methods used for the infant to self-soothe should also be continued in child care. For example, if the infant is used to soothing by rocking then this can be accommodated. Predictability of routines is important for infants and toddlers and helps to develop a sense of security and provides for individualised care (Greenman & Stonehouse, 1996, p. 98).

Encouraging parents to establish a separation ritual, such as blowing kisses to the child, is a good practice. Likewise, a ritual for pickup time smooths the parent-child reunion later in the day. As with all experiences caregivers need to plan carefully according to the needs of children (Honig, 2002, p. 53).

## *Assist the Infant and Toddler to Prepare for and Adapt to Child Care*

The role of the adult is a critical one in helping the child gain group entry skills so that ultimately they have social acceptance and can make and maintain friendships. Without specific adult assistance, some children may use inappropriate or inept behaviours, acting bossy or aggressive or grabby (Honig & Thompson, 1994). This social acceptance may take time for children who have not had any experience of group care. Suddenly to be part of a group does make emotional demands on an infant, toddler and even a pre-schooler, who often need adult support. However, a responsive caregiver will be well experienced in meeting a range of individual needs.

## *Provide Physical Contact for Infants and Toddlers*

Hutchins (1995, p. 47) emphasizes the importance of the closeness of proximity between infants and toddlers and their caregivers so as to ensure that they are given as much physical comfort as possible and when needed. She states that holding and cuddling facilitates the development of secondary attachment in almost all young children. Dolby and Warren (2006, p. 24) mention the need for staff to sit down rather than move around, each staff member brings an activity to their play space that they can share with children.

Some staff working in child care environments that cater for immigrant families strive to adopt elements of child rearing practices of the families' homeland. For example, a group of Sudanese mothers explained the traditional ways of how to tie the infant close to the body with fabric. The child care staff, when introduced to this method, became comfortable in carrying the infant this way especially so as to provide the needed physical comfort. The mothers in this context were delighted to have their cultural practice continued in the child care environment.

## Reflections of Parents and Caregivers on Relationships with Infants and Toddlers

A series of interviews was conducted in 2007 with parents and child care staff, including some directors, in Australia, who were asked the questions in Table 1. These examples above are but a few of the many interviews conducted with parents and child care staff in the hope of gaining a better understanding of the practical ways of fostering secure relationships with infants and toddlers. The interviews showed that these participants were sensitive to the needs of infants and toddlers – there was agreement that relationships were of prime importance!

**Table 1** How can a mother/father/caregiver/child care staff foster a secure relationship with their infant or toddler?

| mother/father/ caregiver | • "…Respond to the child's needs, create a sense of trust, give affection and respond to the child's cues. Recognise that even a young infant is capable of initiating interactions and of being a partner in a reciprocal relationship". |
|---|---|
| | • "…Spend quality time playing, teaching and nurturing. Respond to needs as soon as possible so that the child is not frustrated for long periods". |
| | • "…Create a loving bond with the child, responding to needs and enjoying interactions. Realise that trust, affection and responsiveness are fundamental to any enduring relationship". |
| | • "…Recognise that infancy and childhood are such a short time and make the most of every day, in spite of the struggles of parenthood the joys outweigh all else". |
| | • "…Ensure that the environment is safe, not just physically but emotionally and socially as well". |

(continued)

**Table 1** (continued)

| | |
|---|---|
| **Child care staff** | • "…Implement a primary caregiving system whereby all staff, including trained and untrained, have specific responsibility for designated children – the number depends on the age and licensing regulations. All communication with the family is via the primary caregiver. All transition visits are carried out by the designated primary caregiver. Work with the staff to ensure that they are "emotionally available" to the children they care for. Work with staff so that team leaders are able to support one another. Recognise that primary caregiving does not create a dependent relationship and they move out from their secure base as their confidence, trust, and competence increases. It is a joy to see a secure bond develop between child and caregiver one that eventually assists children to become resilient, confident, and secure in all relationships". (Director of a child care centre) |
| | • "…We have a large number of children from very diverse cultures and we aim to bridge the cultures in many ways. We believe that the primary caregiving system allows us to quickly develop a trusting relationship and understand better the child's needs. Our child care staff have continued to investigate child rearing practices of diverse cultures and to promote continuity wherever possible. We try to avoid situations where children cry for long periods due to differing practices from the home. We make provision for breast feeding by mothers if this is their preference and our staff usually get to know the entire family over time. We frequently send digital photos to parents and this assists in reassuring them that their child has settled". (Director of a child care centre) |
| | • "…I could never consider working in any other way than in a primary caregiver system". (child care primary caregiver) |
| | • "…To me attachment and primary caregiving are synonomous. The satisfaction that I get from my job is tied to the caregiving system I work in". (child care primary caregiver) |
| | • "…Being emotionally available and helping children eventually achieve emotional self-regulation is one of the most fulfilling elements of my teaching/care role with a primary care group of toddlers". (child care primary caregiver) |

## Conclusion

The development of positive relationships that are enduring bonds between infants/toddlers and their caregivers, is an essential activity in many child care centres today. Such positive development is especially aided when the program is founded on the primary caregiver concept. This concept is aided by an understanding and application of attachment theory as it is best interpreted today.

Whilst acknowledging the seminal work of Bowlby ([1969] 2000); Ainsworth and Wittig (1969) and others, it is evident that children can form significant secondary attachments beyond the mother, father and other family members. Caregivers can form significant relationships with their infants and toddlers and assist in the development of a secure, positive and enduring relationship. Parents need to be reassured and be confident that their child can be left in child care and that relationships will not be undermined when the environment offers a quality attachment curriculum. However, it has to be acknowledged that forming secure attachments is a never-ending activity in child care, where the distinct qualities of child-adult, child-child, and adult-adult attachment relationships are crucial to successful care-giving (see Ainsworth (1989). As well, the interplay between the care given in child care environments and that given within the family system (Byng-Hall, 1985; Marvin & Stewart, 1990), has also to be acknowledged.

The most important focus in planning programs for infants/toddlers is to build and maintain a secure attachment relationship with a primary caregiver. It is essential that infant and toddler staff understand attachment theory, as children's attachments evolve over time, depending on circumstances. By constantly planning for each child's attachment, assessing the quality of the caregiver/child relationship, and talking with parents, child care staff can contribute positively to the long term emotional well-being of young children (Gowrie Training and Resource Centre, 2001b, pp. 8–9). As Elliot echoed (2006) "of all the findings from attachment studies, the most enduring and influential in terms of early childhood education policy and practice was that more secure attachments were linked to better quality child care" (p. 27).

The future of our infants and toddlers cannot be left to chance; their well-being depends on the development of secure, positive relationships with a range of caring, responsive adults. It is clear from the research reviewed in this Chapter that caregiver/infant/toddler interactions are extremely significant especially given the trend nowadays to use many forms of child care service for what must be considered long periods of time. As Stanley (2004) eloquently states "there is overwhelming evidence that the first five years of life can affect an individual's whole life course – how they cope with school, relate to others, and how they deal with stress" (p.9). Effective primary caregiving can help to develop those bonds which will endure for many years to come.

# References

Ainsworth, M. (1989). Attachments beyond infancy. *American Psychologist, 44*, 709–716.

Ainsworth, M., & Bell, S. (1974). Mother-infant interaction and the development of competence. In K. J. Connelly & J. Bruner (Eds.), *The growth of competence* (pp. 97–118). London and New York: Academic.

Ainsworth, M., Blehar, M. C., Waters, E., & Wall, S. (1978). *Patterns of attachment.* Hillsdale, NJ: Lawrence Erlbaum Associates.

Ainsworth, M., & Wittig, B. A. (1969). Attachment and exploratory behavior of one year-olds in a strange situation. In B. M. Foss (Ed.), *Determinants of infant behavior* (Vol. 4, pp. 111–136). London: Methuen.

Arend, R. A., Gove, F. L., & Sroufe, L. A. (1979). Continuity of individual adaptation from Infancy to Kindergarten: A predictive study of ego-resiliency and curiosity in preschoolers. *Child Development, 50*(4), 950–959.

Australian Bureau of Statistics. (2006a). *4102.0 - Australian Social Trends, 2006.* Retrieved 18 February, 2007, from http://www.abs.gov.au/ausstats/abs@.nsf/ 7d12b0f6763c78 caca257061001cc588/858badad39afb98dca2571b000153d73!OpenDocument

Australian Bureau of Statistics. (2006b). *4402.0 - Child Care, Australia, Jun 2005 (Reissue)*. Retrieved 18 February, 2007, from http://www.abs.gov.au/AUSSTATS/ abs@.nsf/ProductsbyCatalogue/ 03D307053D1CECA5CA2571730011452E?OpenDocument

Australian Institute of Family Studies. (2005). *Growing up in Australia: The Longitudinal Study of Australian Children: 2004 Annual Report*. Melbourne.

Baker, A. C., & Manfredi-Petitt, L. A. (1998). *Circle of love: Relationships between parents, providers and children in family child care*. St. Paul, MN: Redleaf.

Balaban, N. (2006). *Everyday goodbyes: Starting school and early care-A guide to the separation process*. New York: Teachers College Press.

Bell, S. M., & Ainsworth, M. D. S. (1972). Infant crying and maternal responsiveness. *Child Development, 43*, 1171–1190.

Benoit, D., & Parker, K. C. H. (1994). Stability and transmission of attachment across three generations. *Child Development, 65*(5), 1444–1456.

Berk, L. E. (2006). *Child development* (7th ed.). Boston: Pearson/Allyn and Bacon.

Bowlby, J. (1958). The nature of the child's tie to its mother. *International Journal of Psychoanalysis, 39*, 350–373.

Bowlby, J. (1959). Separation anxiety. *International Journal of Psycho-Analysis, 41*, 1–25.

Bowlby, J. (1960). Grief and mourning in infancy and early childhood. *The Psychoanalytic Study of the Child, 60*, 3–39.

Bowlby, J. ([1969] 2000). Attachment. In *Attachment and loss* (Vol. 1). New York: Basic Books.

Bowlby, J. ([1973] 2000). Separation: Anxiety and anger. In *Attachment and loss* (Vol. 2). New York: Basic Books.

Bowlby, J. ([1980] 2000). Loss: Sadness and depression. In *Attachment and loss* (Vol. 3). New York: Basic Books.

Braungart-Rieker, J. M., Garwood, M. M., Power, B. P., & Wang, X. (2001). Parental sensitivity, infant affect, and affect regulation: Predictors of later attachment. *Child Development, 72*(1), 252–270.

Bretherton, I. (1992). The Origins of Attachment Theory: John Bowlby and Mary Ainsworth. *Developmental Psychology, 28*(5), 759–775.

Byng-Hall, J. (1985). The family script: a useful bridge between theory and practice. *Journal of Family Therapy, 7*, 301–305.

Cassidy, J. (2000). Adult romantic attachments: A development perspective on individual differences. *Review of General Psychology, 4*, 111–131.

Cookman, C. (2005). Attachment in older adulthood: Concept clarification. *Journal of Advanced Nursing, 50*(5), 528–535.

Crowell, J. A., & Waters, R. (1994). Bowlby's theory grown up: The role of attachment in adult love relationships. *Psychological Inquiry, 5*, 31–34.

De Wolff, M. S., & van IJzendoorn, M. H. (1997). Sensitivity and attachment: A meta-analysis on parental antecedents of infant attachment. *Child Development, 68*, 571–591.

Department of Education and Children's Services. (2005). *We can make a difference: learning and developing in childcare*. Australia: Author.

Dixon, W. E. (2003). *Twenty studies that revolutionized child psychology*. Upper Saddle River, NJ: Prentice Hall.

Dolby, R., & Warren, E. (2006). Circle of Security and child care practice. *Every Child, 12*(1), 24.

Elliott, A. (2006). Challenges ahead for universal preschool. *Every Child, 12*(2), 2.

Erickson, M. F., Korfmacher, J., & Egeland, B. (1992). Attachments past and present: Implications for therapeutic intervention with mother-infant dyads. *Development and Psychopathology, 4*, 495–507.

Gonzalez-Mena, J. (1997). *Multicultural issues in child care* (2nd ed.). Mountain View, CA: Mayfield Pub. Co.

Gowrie Training and Resource Centre. (2001a). Primary caregiving: Working toward secure attachments in childcare [videorecording]. Adelaide, South Australia: Gowrie Adelaide.

Gowrie Training and Resource Centre. (2001b). Secure attachments: the foundation of relationships in childcare programs [videorecording]. Adelaide, South Australia: Gowrie Adelaide.

Greenman, J., & Stonehouse, A. (1996). *Prime times: A handbook for excellence in infant and toddler care*. St. Paul, MN: Redleaf Press.

Grossmann, K. (1995). The evoluation and history of attachment research and theory. In S. Goldberg, R. Muir & J. Kerr (Eds.), *Attachment Theory: Social, developmental and clinical perspectives* (pp. 85–122). Hillsdale, NJ: The Analytic Press.

Harrison, L. (2003). *Attachment: Building secure relationships in early childhood*. Watson, A. C.T.: Australian Early Childhood Association.

Harrison, L., & Ungerer, J. (2005). What can the Longitudianl Study of Australian Children tell us about infants' and 4 to 5 year olds' experiences of early childhood education and care? *Family Matters* (72), 26–35.

Hazan, C., & Shaver, P. (1987). Romantic love conceptualized as an attachment process. *Journal of Personality and Social Psychology, 52,* 511–524.

Honig, A. S. (1984). Secure attachment: Key to infant mental health. *Infant Mental Health Journal, 9*(2), 181–183.

Honig, A. S. (1985). Research in Review: Compliance, control, and discipline - Part 1. *Young children, 40*(2), 50–58.

Honig, A. S. (1993). Mental health for babies: What do theory and research teach us? *Young Children, 48*(3), 69–76.

Honig, A. S. (2002). *Secure relationships: nurturing infant/toddler attachment in the early care settings*. Washington, DC: National Association for the Education of Young Children.

Honig, A. S., & Thompson, A. (1994). Helping toddlers with peer group entry skills. *Zero to Three, 14*(5), 15–19

Howes, C. (1999). Attachment relationships to multiple caregivers. In J. Cassidy & P. Shaver (Eds.), *Handbook of attachment: Theory, research, and clinical applications* (pp. 671–687). New York: The Guilford Press.

Howes, C., Rodning, C., Galuzzo, D. C., & Myers, L. (1988). Attachment and child care: Relationships with mother and caregiver. *Early Childhood Research Quarterly, 3,* 403–416.

Hutchins, T. (1995). *Babies need more than minding: Planning programs for babies and toddlers in group settings*. Watson, A.C.T.: Australian Early Childhood Association.

Kagan, J., Kearsley, R. B., & Zelazo, P. R. (1978). *Infancy: Its place in human development*. Cambridge, MA: Harvard University Press.

Karen, R. (1994). *Becoming attached: Unfolding the mystery of the infant-mother bond and its impact on later life*. New York: Warner.

Kretchmar, M. D., & Jacobvitz, D. B. (2002). Observing mother-child relationships across generations: Boundary patterns, attachment, and the transmission of caregiving. *Family Process, 41*(3), 351–374.

Love, J. M., Harrison, L., Sagi-Schwartz, A., van IJzendoorn, M. H., Ross C.Ungerer, J. A., Raikes, H., Brady-Smith, C., Boller, K., Brooks-Gunn, J., Constantine, J., Kisker, E. E., Paulsell, D., & Chazan-Cohen, R. (2003). Child care quality matters: How conclusions may vary with context. *Child Development, 74*(4), 1021–1033.

Maier, H. W. (1994). Attachment development is 'in'. *Journal of Child and Youth Care, 9*(1), 35–51.

Main, M., & Goldwyn, R. (1992). *Interview-based adult attachment classifications: Related to infant-mother and infant-father attachment*. Unpublished manuscript, Department of Psychology, University of California, Berkeley.

Main, M., Kaplan, N., & Cassidy, J. (1985). Security in infancy, childhood, and adulthood: A move to the level of representation. In I. Bretherton & E. Waters (Eds.), *Growing points of attachment theory and research* (Vol. 50). (pp. 66–104). Chicago: University of Chicago Press.

Main, M., & Solomon, J. (1990). Procedures for identifying infants as disorganized/disoriented during the Ainsworth Strange Situation. In M. Greenberg, D. Cicchetti & M. Cummings (Eds.), *Attachment in the preschool years: Thoery, research, and intervention* (pp. 121–160). Chicago: University of Chicago Press.

Mardell, B. (1992). A practitioner's perspective on the implications of attachment theory for day-care professionals. *Child Study Journal, 22*(3), 201–229.

Marvin, R., Cooper, G., & Hoffman, K. (2002). The Circle of Security project: Attachment-based intervention with caregiver-pre-school child dyads. *Attachment & Human Development, 4*(1), 107–124.

Marvin, R., & Stewart, R. B. (1990). A family systems framework for the study of attachment. In M. Greenberg, D. Cicchetti & E. M. Cummings (Eds.), *Attachment in the preschool years: Theory, research, and intervention* (pp. 51–86). Chicago: University of Chicago Press.

Matas, L., Arend, R. A., & Sroufe, L. A. (1978). Continuity of adaptation in the second year: the relationship between quality of attachment and later competence. *Child Development, 49*(3), 547–556.

Miller, G. A., Galanter, E., & Pribram, K. H. (1960). *Plans and the structure of behavior.* New York: Holt, Rinehart and Winston.

NICHD Early Child Care Research Network. (2000). Characteristics and quality of child care for toddlers and preschoolers. *Applied Developmental Science*(4), 116–135.

NICHD Early Child Care Research Network. (2001, 19 April). *Early child care and children's development prior to school entry.* Paper presented at the Biennial meeting of the Society for Research in Child Development, Minneapolis, Minnesota.

NICHD Early Child Care Research Network. (2005). *Child care and child development: Results from the NICHD Study of Early Child Care and Youth Development.* New York: Guilford Press.

Press, F., & Hayes, A. (2000). *OECD Thematic Review of Early Childhood Education and Care policy. Australian Background Report.* Canberra: Department of Education, Training and Youth Affairs, Australian Government Printing Service.

Ramsburg, D. (1998). *Separation anxiety in young children.* Retrieved 24 January, 2007, from http://www.parentwatch.com/content/display.asp?c=c_0176

Richardson, S. (2000). *Primary caregiving systems for infants and toddlers.* Retrieved 2 February, 2007, from http://www.rch.org.au/ecconnections/media/pdf/2000Nov.pdf

Rolfe, S. A. (2004). *Rethinking attachment for early childhood practice: Promoting security, autonomy and resilience in young children.* Crows Nest, N.S.W.: Allen & Unwin.

Rothbart, M. K. (2003). Temperament and the pursuit of an integrated developmental psychology. *Merrill-Palmer Quarterly, 50,* 492–505.

Schaffer, H., R., & Emerson, P. F. (1964). The development of social attachments in infancy. *Monographs of the Society for Research in Child Development, 29*(3).

Shore, R. (1997). *Rethinking the brain: New insights into early development.* New York: Families and Work Institute.

Sims, M., Guilfoyle, A., & Parry, T. (2005). What cortisol levels tell us about quality in child care centers. *Australian Journal of Early Childhood, 30*(2), 29–39.

Sroufe, L. A. (1979). The coherence of individual development: Early care, attachment, and subsequent developmental issues. *American Psychologist, 34*(10), 834–841.

Sroufe, L. A. (1995). *Emotional development: The organisation of emotional life in the early years.* Cambridge: Cambridge University Press.

Stanley, F. (2004, 13 August 2004). *The Australian,* p. 9.

Sullivan, J. R. (1999). Development of father-infant attachment in fathers of preterm infants. *Neonatal Network, 18*(7), 33–39.

Sylva, K., Melhuish, K., Sammons, P., Siraj-Blatchford, I., Taggart, B., & Elliot, K. (2003). *The effective Provision of Preschool (EPPE) Proejct: Findings from the pre-school period.* Retrieved 18 February, 2007, from http://www.ioe.ac.uk/cdl/eppe/pdfs/eppe_brief2503.pdf

Taylor, D. (2004). *Development of Standards and Measurement Tools for Quality Assurance Systems in Australian Children.* Paper presented at the Early Childhood Development and Education International Conference: Questions of Quality: Defining, Assessing & Supporting Quality in Early Childhood Care and Education, Dublin, Ireland.

Thomas, A., & Chess, S. (1977). *Temperament and development.* New York: BrunneryMazel.

Troy, M., & Sroufe, L. A. (1987). Victimization among preschoolers: The role of attachment relationship history. *Journal of the American Academy of Child Psychiatry, 26,* 166–172.

Turner, P. J. (1991). Relations between attachment, gender, and behavior with peers in preschool. *Child Development, 62*, 1475–1488.

van IJzendoorn, M., & Sagi, A. (1999). Cross-cultural patterns of attachment: Universal and contextual dimernsions. In J. Cassidy & P. R. Shaver (Eds.), *Handbook of attachment: Theory, research and clinical applications* (pp. 713–734). New York: The Guilford Press.

van IJzendoorn, M., Sagi, A., & Lambermon, M. (1992). The multiple caregiver paradox: Data from Holland and Israel. In R. Pianta (Ed.), *Beyond the parent: the role of other adults in children's lives* (pp. 5–27). San Francisco: Jossey-Bass.

Watson, L. D., Watson, M. A., & Wilson, L. C. (2003). *Infants & toddlers: Curriculum and teaching* (5th ed.). Clifton Park, NY: Thomson/Delmar Learning.

Winter, P. (2003). *Curriculum for babies and toddlers: an evaluation of the first phase of the South Australian curriculum, standards and accountability framework in selected childcare centres in South Australia.* Unpublished Ph.D. Dissertation, University of South Australia, Adelaide.

**Professor Marjory Ebbeck**
University of South Australia
School of Education, Room G1–23
Magill Campus
St Bernards Road
Magill SA 5072
Australia
Phone: +61 8 8302 4432
Fax: +61 8 8302 4394
Email: Marjory.Ebbeck@unisa.edu.au

Marjory Ebbeck is Professor of Early Childhood Education at the University of South Australia. She is program director of transnational early childhood programs in Singapore and Hong Kong.

**Hoi Yin Bonnie Yim**
University of South Australia
School of Education, Room G1-68
Magill Campus
St Bernards Road
Magill SA 5072 Australia
Phone: +61 8 8302-4132
Fax: +61 8 8302-4394
Email: HoiYin.Yim@postgrads.unisa.edu.au

Hoi Yin Bonnie Yim is a part-time lecturer at the University of South Australia in arts education and practitioner research in early childhood education. She is also a PhD candidate.

# Chapter 11
# Working With Recently Immigrated Young Children:

## Perspectives, Challenges, and Implications for Practice

**Jacqueline Onchwari, Nurun Begum, and Grace Onchwari**

**Abstract** In this chapter the immigrant child in the early childhood classroom is examined. The chapter starts out by outlining relevant notions that inform our understanding of immigrant children; demographics, cultural competence, and theoretical perspectives. The chapter proceeds to looking at some major challenges immigrant children face and concludes with suggestions to support these children in their adjustment in the classroom. Specifically, the role of teacher training is revisited, and several practical strategies for working with immigrant children are offered.

**Keywords** young children, immigrant children, cultural competence, diversity, English Language Learners, culturally responsive, cultural awareness, inclusion, renaming, teacher preparation, preservice teachers, inservice teachers, collaboration with families, Bronfenbrenner, Vygotsky

## Immigrant Children in Julia's Classroom: A Prologue

Julia is a second grade teacher who recently got married and moved to California from a small rural town in Pennsylvania. In her 10 years of teaching young children she has never encountered the proportion of student diversity like that of her new school. In addition to the several African American students in her classroom she also has 3 immigrant children in her classroom: Ben from China, Iffa, from Somali, and Ahmed, from Iran. Ben just moved to America and has very limited English proficiency. He is also very shy. Sometimes he does not respond when called by his name, something that the teacher finds rather strange. Later Julia comes to know

University of Minnesota, Duluth

East Stroudsburg University

University of NorthDakota

M.R. Jalongo (ed.), *Enduring Bonds.*
© Springer 2008

that Ben's Chinese name is Ming and that he is not acquainted with his recently given English name yet; his parents have renamed him in hopes of helping him to be accepted into the new culture.

Julia is really confused as to how she would approach Ben's situation. Julia has observed that Ben spends most of his time at the science and math center and does not attempt to work or play at the other centers. She also notices that he spends much of his time alone absorbed in individual pursuits.

Iffa, the Somali girl, has been in the USA for a year. Even though she can speak English fairly well, she struggles with reading and writing. Her parents can hardly speak any English, making Iffa their main interpreter. Julia really wishes she could have a private conversation with Iffa's parents to share her concerns with them. Iffa often seems aloof and preoccupied. Once, Julia observed Iffa interacting so warmly with one of the Somali boys in third grade. She wanted to see more of that Iffa in her classroom.

Ahmed, an Iranian boy, seems very bright but is also one of the most aggressive children in Julia's classroom. His classmates often complain about his behavior. The teacher has found it challenging to change Ahmed's unpopular behavior. Recently his father came to see him and was furious about children calling Ahmed a terrorist and telling him to go back to his country. Julia was appalled and knew she needed to figure out a way to change not only the children's behavior but also the attitudes underlying that behavior. During the meeting, Ahmed's father also shared his concerns about Ahmed's declining academic performance.

In her effort to improve the situation of the immigrant children in her classroom, Julia approaches Mrs. Hopps, an experienced teacher next door, for tips on teaching immigrant children. Mrs. Hopps advises her to go about her teaching as usual as these children will pick up eventually. If they don't, at the end of the year, Mrs. Hopps' solution is to recommend that they repeat the grade. Julia leaves feeling dissatisfied and even more determined to look for other strategies to help these children thrive.

This chapter takes us through a journey which Julia, a second grade teacher described in the above case, takes as she professionally seeks to understand and help her immigrant students. We begin with the concept of teachers' cultural competence and the effects of changing immigrant demographics on education. Next, we present multiple perspectives on understanding immigrant children and finally, we conclude with recommended ways of working more effectively with young immigrant children in early childhood classrooms.

## Understanding Teachers' Cultural Competence

The premise of this chapter is that teachers' cultural competence is foundational to working effectively with diverse groups of students. Cultural competence is "the ability to effectively teach cross-culturally" (Diller & Moule, 2005, p. 12). It is an ideal to which every teacher or practitioner should aspire. According to Cross, Bazron, Dennis, & Isaacs (1989) in order for one to develop this ability he or she should continually work on 5 basic components: 1) awareness and acceptance of difference, 2) self-awareness, 3) understanding the dynamics of difference, 4) knowledge of the students' cultures, and 5) adaptation of teaching skills to accommodate cultural diversity. Acquiring these skills/components require that teachers continuously seek knowledge as well as examine their own attitudes, values, and beliefs regarding the rights and uniqueness of others (Banks & Banks, 2001). Cultural competence might be viewed by many as an ethical decision and a choice; however, it has become a requisite skill in today's multicultural society. Without cultural competence teachers like Julia find it difficult to succeed as professional educators. In order to promote the practice of inclusion, every teacher has to go through the process of self-searching and knowledge acquisition in order to effectively work with all students, particularly those who are comparatively new to the dominant culture.

## A Rationale for Enhancing Teachers' Cultural Awareness

Situations like Julia's are becoming the norm rather than the exception. Immigrant children are the fastest growing segment in the U.S. child population (Capps, Fix, Murray, Host, Pasel, & Hernandez, 2006; Reid, 2001; Landale & Oropesa, 1995; Takanishi, 2004). It is estimated that around 1 million immigrants enter the US each year, with many not only being at the child-bearing age but also having high fertility rates (Portes & Rumbaut, 2001; Reid, 2001). In the schools, 1 in 5 children are immigrants (Capps et al., 2006). This is more the case in some states and urban areas. In California, for example, up to 20% of school age children are English Language Learners. Usually, immigrant children are defined as children who were born outside the United States and are first-generation immigrants who have not attended USA schools for more than three academic years (United States Department of Education, 2007; Shorr, 2006). However, it has been found that many second-generation immigrant children (those whose parents are non USA born) share similar characteristics and challenges as the first- generation immigrant children (Capps et al., 2006). Interestingly, about 75% of immigrant children are native-born, meaning their parents are first generation immigrants (Capps et al., 2006), yet they have almost similar struggles as those born in their native countries.

These changing demographics and their implications call for urgent understanding of the plight of immigrant children (Landale & Oropesa, 1995; Shorr, 2006). The next section explains the immigrant children's situation and possible solutions, both from perspective of theories of child learning and development, and from relevant research.

## Perspectives on the Immigrant Child

A number of child development theories provide a framework for understanding the immigrant child and give implications for practice. As an individual the immigrant child has both similarities and differences with a typical white-middle-class child. Looking at the child from these perspectives can help guide practice with immigrant children.

### *The Child as a Universal Being*

Piaget maintains that there are universal stages of cognitive development (Siegler, 1991; Piaget, 1960) (assuming the environment within which the development took place was conducive). As such, even though an immigrant child might have the language barrier, he or she is cognitively as capable as his or her peers in the new land. Piaget also views language as a tool for cognitive development but not necessarily a totally indispensable tool. Assessing an immigrant child's performance and retaining him or her based on tasks that heavily rely on knowledge of English language is therefore inappropriate practice. Retention as a practice also places the child with peers who are at different levels cognitively and might provide the immigrant child less challenging cognitive tasks, and compromise more relevant support he or she might need. Of course we have to keep in mind Vygotsky's notion on the role of language as an indispensable tool for thought (Portes, 2000). Language is a major mechanism for gaining more cognitive flexibility and sophistication. If we can focus on language as a tool we can support the development of the home language that the child has mastered and used for thought while gradually and respectively introducing English.

### *The Child as a Unique Individual*

This notion has been used heavily in today's educational and other service practices putting aside the "melting pot" notion. Among other theories Vygotsky's theory and Howard Gardner's theories support this view.

The immigrant child brings a totally different cultural world view into the classroom. It can be very confusing and frustrating for this child to be in a classroom that does not acknowledge the fact that, for instance, this child may have never eaten, or seen an apple (even though it is assumed that "A" for "apple" is contextualized instruction). This child may never have encountered a bear yet might be asked to get plastic bear manipulative from the shelf and add 5 + 5 bears. Background information that might be rightfully assumed as common knowledge to an American child may be totally new to the immigrant child who has to second guess almost everything that is presented in the classroom. The adaptive demands on the immigrant child are great and this can undermine academic success if the situation is not handled skillfully by educators. Vygotsky maintains that learning occurs within a cultural context (Couchenour & Chrisman, 1999). Using Vygotsky's notion of the zone of proximal development, teachers have the challenge of learning about the child's culture, or at least helping them find meaning of concepts from their past experiences. In this case the role of parents as partners in mediating the child's knowledge becomes critical. Also, using more capable peers or giving the immigrant child a chance to be the more capable peer would help a great deal. Imagine what a difference it would make if Iffa, the 2nd grade Somali girl in Julia's classroom (described in the prologue) was paired up with another immigrant 4th grader for learning purposes! The shared culture and age difference encourage Iffa to strive and thrive in her new environment.

Howard Gardner (2000) talks about the different types of intelligence and how instruction should be adapted to tap into the different types of intelligences. An immigrant child might depict different types of intelligence due to his or her genetic makeup and other environmental factors related to where he or she grew up. It would therefore be necessary to figure out what kinds of intelligence the child possesses.

Bronfenbrenner's (1979) ecological model does not underestimate the power of the different systems or layers of the society as impacting the development of the child. He talks about 5 systems: microsystems, mesosytems, exosystems, macrosystems, and chronosystems. The family, school, peers, etc are microsytems. An immigrant child belongs to a family with a set of different values, beliefs and experiences which are often totally different from his or her classmates. The interaction between and among these primary systems bring out different outcomes which then become the second level; mesosystems. The exosystem—the third system—refers to such things as how a parent's employment or teacher's stress might influence the child. Immigrant parents have their share of a cultural adjustment and might have situations at work which exacerbate their stress. Their state of mind when they come home to their already stressed child can make the situation worse for the entire family. A teacher who might be dealing with family issues will have to work diligently and sensitively in order to meet the unique and demanding needs of the immigrant child. Policies, societal beliefs, and values influence how a child is viewed and treated. This is what is referred to as macrosystems.

The current view of the child as an individual has helped many educators focus on the needs of the many different groups of children. Policies about bilingualism come in this category. Also, the different events that have happened in the life of the child, referred to as chronosystems, affect the immigrant child. The moving to another country itself and dealing with the entire package affects the child tremendously.

It is also important to note that a young child has not experienced much to have a storehouse of strategies to use when faced with perplexing or frustrating situations that immigrating brings with it. Their levels of cognitive sophistication make them even more dependent on caring adults to help them adjust in their new environment.

# Challenges Immigrant Children Face in America

The journey of immigrant children in their new environs is followed by a complex path which is full of confusion, anxiety, stress, difficulty, struggle, and challenge (DebBurman, 2005; McCarthy & Willshire, 1988; Igoa, 1995, Souto-Manning, 2007). The nature of this complex path varies, but it also has some common features that accompany their transition to a different geographic and cultural context.

## *Cross-Cultural Conflicts*

The immigrant children bring a culture with them which is dramatically different than the culture of their country of residence. This cultural difference brings hardship and may result in traumatic experience while adjusting in the school system. Dipa, a four year old girl, came from India and Meem, a five year old girl, came from Jordan to the United States. Dipa is a vegetarian and Meem does not eat pork. In the school, their teacher did not show respect for their eating habits and religious observances. As a result, both of them were afraid to eat anything in the school. Families of Dipa and Meem viewed this as a cultural threat and caused emotional pressure and insecurity in them (Gay, 2004; Lal, 2004; Johnson, 2003 McCarthy & Willshire, 1988). This could eventually lead to defiance, or criminal behavior (Lal, 2004), and failure in school (Gay, 2004).

## *Language Barriers*

The teacher of Tom, a brilliant 8-year-old boy from Bangladesh with limited English proficiency, requested his parents to let him repeat third grade. Research suggests that many non-English speaking children go to school with well-developed skills in their first language (Yu-Lu, 2004), yet have to go through stressful and negative academic and personal experiences due to the language barrier. During the time they are learning the English language, reactions from peers often exacerbate stress.

## *Dual Cultural Identity*

Immigrant children have to play a dual role in their new land. In the home parents of immigrant children practice the norms, values, and traditions of their primary culture. But when the immigrant children go out they have to act based on the norm of the culture of a new land. This puts a child in a dilemma and gives him or her dual personality, which can be confusing and stressful for a child.

To illustrate, Albert, a five year old Chinese boy, does not want to practice his parents' culture. He does not like to introduce his parents in front of others because his parents do not speak English well. He requested that his parents rename him with an English name so that he could fit into his new culture, a phenomenon discussed by Souto-Manning (2007). Albert's father has made an appointment with his son's teacher to discuss an incident that the father finds very distressing. It seems that Albert has been seeking to get the approval of his peers by making them laugh. Recently, Albert decided to hang his sandals from his ears as a way of achieving this result. His father is very disapproving of such "foolishness" and suspects that the laughter is more ridicule than good humor. He tells the teacher to put a stop to this, even if it means punishing his son.

Research has found that this in-between cultural position may lead to behavior problems which can range from minor misbehavior to far more serious and illegal acts (Gay, 2004; Lal, 2004; Johnson, 2003; McCarthy & Willshire, 1988). DuBois (2004) explained the rationality behind this: "American born children of foreigners are much more likely to commit crimes than native born persons of native parentage, not because they are children of immigrants, but because they are Americans and are no longer controlled by the traditions and customs which keep their parents in the paths of rectitude" (DuBois as cited in Lal, 2004, p. 20)

## Loneliness and Isolation

After arriving in America, immigrant children may become lonely and isolated because they leave their friends and family members back at home (DebBurman, 2005; McCarthy & Willshire, 1988). Due to lack of English proficiency and cultural differences, immigrant children may take a longer time to make friends. They may want to play with someone who just looks like them, which might be impossible. Tommy, a four year old Chinese boy and son of graduate student parents, recently immigrated to a small rural community in the United States. There are no other Chinese children in his neighborhood and sometimes Tommy hits himself with a toy while saying loudly in Chinese, "mei you ren ai wo" which means "nobody loves me."

## Multiple Responsibilities

Immigrant parents who are less English proficient may rely on their very young children as interpreters. This gives the children undue responsibility, power, and pressure, which may have long-term consequences for overall development (McCarthy & Willshire, 1988). McCarthy and Willshire explained that this situation creates an emotional contradiction for young children. Also, a lot of immigrant children have to take responsibility for their sibling while their parents are at work. While a child is struggling with cultural shock, trauma and dramatic experience in the new land, the sibling responsibility adds more stress in his/her life.

## Supporting Immigrant Children in the Classroom

According to Bredekamp and Copple (2006), in order to implement a developmentally appropriate curriculum for young children a teacher must know child development, understand individual differences, and have insight into the social-cultural context of the child. These factors inform early childhood educators' practice with immigrant families.

The teacher should strive to help these children feel welcome in the classroom, adapt instruction/curriculum to take possible linguistic and cultural barriers into account, and develop a positive respectful atmosphere among all the students. Research has indicated that very often it is the attitude of the other children in the classroom that makes experiences of the immigrant children negative. Children as young as 4 years of age have been reported to show biases towards people who are different (MacNaughton, 2001). This might be explained by the egocentric nature of this age group as well as their tendency to classify. The younger the children are when they are given awareness and understanding about people who are different the better they become even as adults in their sensitivity and appreciation of those different from them. A positive cultural, national, and racial identity contributes to self-esteem and academic achievement (MacNaughton, 2001). Teachers of immigrant children need to help these children develop or maintain a positive identity.

### *Teacher Training*

Since the 1980s there has been an increasing emphasis on preparing teachers to meet the needs of diverse learners and many teacher education programs have integrated a multicultural focus in their programs. Unfortunately, there has been very minimal or no focus on the immigrant child (Goodwin, 2002), particularly in the field of early childhood education (Early & Winton, 2001). A national survey of administrators of higher education programs found that only 10% of bachelors programs and 8% of 2-year degree programs required pre-service teachers to take a course on working with multilingual children (Buysse, Castro, West, & Skinner, 2005; Wesley & Buysse, 2003). Part of the problem is lack of literature that focuses on the immigrant child, especially the strategies, skills, and content knowledge required to teach these children (Goodwin, 2002). Another issue is the existence of unlicensed, under-qualified teachers in the classrooms (Darling-Hammond, 2006).

Considering that immigrant children are often linguistically, experientially, and culturally diverse, any effective teacher preparation program should focus on:

- Understanding developmental theories that apply to teaching immigrant children. Examples of these theories include Vygotsky's socio-cultural theory, Piaget's cognitive-developmental theory, and Bronfenbrenner's ecological systems theory.
- Accurate information about general immigrant experiences. Such knowledge would help the teacher understand the students' plight and intervene with more empathy and an informed outlook. Goodwin (2002) suggests this content to include factors like previous schooling, cultural disorientation, language, and dislocation. It is critical to bear in mind that immigrants have different stories to tell, and that different children react differently to similar situations.
- Knowledge about second language learning (Buysse et al, 2005; Goodwin, 2002); specifically, teacher preparation should cover language acquisition theory, instructional strategies to support ELL students, etc. This knowledge could be used hand in hand with ELL experts, if available.
- Opportunities for preservice and inservice teachers to observe and reflect on personal/professional beliefs, attitudes, and practices (Exposito & Favela, 2003; Hepburn, 2004). Opportunities and support in developing a disposition to oppose inequity and be change agents (Achinstein, 2006).
- Experiences with creating or being a part of strong parent and community partnership (Buysse et al, 2005; Goodwin, 2002; Hepburn, 2004). The teacher will rely heavily on the parents to help bridge the home-school gap for the child. Continuing to help the child develop literacy in the first language and, if possible, transfer the skills to English learning, educating the teacher about the child's culture, etc, are some of the strengths of a good partnership.
- Instructional planning and teaching strategies that are responsive to a heterogeneous population. Beginning teachers should join the workforce with awareness of different forms of assessment, positive learning and behavior support plans. They also need to be aware of multiple ways to tap into immigrant children's knowledge rather than quickly labeling them as "at-risk students" This is so much the case with immigrant children who have varying experiences with school.
- Sufficient supervised field experience with children from diverse populations during field experiences (Darling-Hammond, 2006). Such experiences provide teachers the opportunities to try out their theoretical knowledge while under supervision.

On a positive note, the impact of the emphasis on cultural responsiveness in the classroom through pre-service education was demonstrated in Compton-Lily's (2006) study that found beginning teachers to be using more culturally sensitive strategies than experienced teachers. This indicates that in-service trainings on this issue would help. On the other hand, the emphasis on standards and accountability often compels some teachers to show less sensitivity to individual differences. Some teachers, however, have been able to work around these constraints successfully with the immigrant child (Compton-Lily, 2006).

## Practical Strategies for Working with Immigrant Children in the Classroom

Find out more about the family, what is valued by the child's culture and what their expectations from school are. A study done by Harding (2006) to find out what different groups expected for their children from Kindergarten found that the Euro-Americans valued getting along with peers. Latinos, irrespective of their immigration status, valued respect for adults, and African American mothers valued academic preparation. For minority immigrant families it is important to find out from the parents what they value and expect from the child's classroom. Going back to the case of Julia's classroom that began this chapter, Ming's parents, for instance, made it very clear that they valued science and math. Even if the teacher does not agree with all the family's views it helps to understand where they are and work from there.

When early childhood educators make an effort to learn and use the student's language (even if it is a few words), this can help the student feel a sense of belonging and can reduce behavior problems (Eubanks, 2002). It is commendable to at least learn to say "yes", "no", "please", "thank you" and "good" in the various languages spoken by children in the class.

Peer tutoring is another recommended strategy. Pair new students with another child from the same culture (Eubanks, 2002) even if the tutor is from a different classroom or grade level. If that is not possible teachers can assign buddies from within the child's classroom to help him or her to form new friendships. Cooperative learning projects give newcomers a chance to work in small groups and make connections with peer. Shy immigrant children may feel more comfortable participating in small groups rather than with the entire class.

Look for children's literature that supports the child's level of English proficiency, culture, and experiences (Dever & Burts, 2002). Work with the school or public librarian to identify books with pictures to support comprehension, and books in child's language or alongside translations. Also, use appropriate strategies to share the literature, such as oral story telling (Amour, 2003), puppetry, flannel boards and other visual cues, audiotapes, and gestures or drama to accompany oral reading as a way to support comprehension (Eubanks, 2002).

Make an effort to involve the family and find out if the parents can speak English. If not, seek translators in the community, if possible (Eubanks, 2002). Use the parent as a resource to find out more about every student and gauge how much parents are willing to be involved. Learn more about the family's experiences and other information pertinent to understanding every student.

Simplify tasks by breaking them down into steps. This helps to check comprehension and is less overwhelming for a student who is struggling with the language (Eubanks, 2002)

Use what Dyson (2003) calls "Bakhtinian hybrids" consists of using the official forms of language used at school to explore unofficial resources within the social context of the classroom (like film, television, music, etc). This method was successfully used by Compton-Lily (2006) with a first grade African American boy in Reading Recovery. After the teacher found that the boy loved characters like YU-GI-OH and Pokemon, she used these characters in her literacy intervention, and that caught the interest of the child. Motivate children to learn by connecting with their experiences and cultures.

## Julia's Classroom: An Epilogue

Julia took the same journey that this chapter has taken its readers: learning about the problems of immigrant children, especially aspects unique to her Chinese, Somali and Iranian students and seeking strategies that include them in the classroom community. She began by taking time to reflect on her own beliefs and attitudes about diversity and then worked very hard to implement an anti-bias, culturally responsive curriculum capable of meeting the needs of all her students. Six months into her quest to improve, Julia's classroom was undergoing a transformation. There was evidence of all kinds of literature that represented the culture of her students and their parents/families came in to help whenever they could, often sharing information and stories about their culture in the process. A typical class would have students in the classroom giving examples from their cultures, with the immigrant children feeling secure and accepted enough to talk about their experiences. The other children were very interested in what Iffa, Ahmed and Ming had to say. Ming asked the students to call him Ben or Ming and was very proud when his mother came and took part in activities. Some common words in the immigrant children's languages were posted on the wall for the other students to use. All children were equal partners in classroom learning community. Parents of the other children in class were amazed at the level of interest their children were suddenly showing in learning about other cultures. One parent shared her surprise when her daughter insisted on getting a world map for her birthday to put up in her room! Julia paired her second grade students with literacy buddies in fourth grade. She found same-culture students for her immigrant children, who turned out to be in different grade levels. It was not surprising that Ahmed, Iffa, and Ming not only liked their new school but were achieving academically as well. In addition, Julia's use of appropriate assessment strategies accurately assessed her students' performance and reported effectively on that progress to parents and families.

## Conclusion

In order for early childhood educators to effectively meet the needs of immigrant children in their classrooms they need to strive toward a level of cultural competence that will enable them to teach effectively across the many different backgrounds represented by their students. Part of the process involves teacher self-reflection and active professional seeking for information and ideas to help work with these children. Active seeking would reveal to the teacher that immigrant children are capable of more than they are able to portray because of multiple barriers like language and experiences different from those represented in the school curriculum. Some of the effective ways of working with these children in the classroom include involving their families, using differentiated instruction and assessment strategies, selecting and sharing children's literature appropriately, and learning some words in the children's language in order to communicate with them as well as enhance their self esteem. By putting all of these elements into place and putting forth a sincere and sufficient effort, teachers can see to it that newcomers to the culture and to their classrooms are treated fairly, taught in a developmentally appropriate way, welcomed by their peers, and given the opportunity to maximize their learning.

# References

Achinstein, B. (2006). New teacher and mentor political literacy: Reading, navigating and transforming induction contexts. *Teachers and Teaching: Theory and Practice, 12,* 123–138.

Amour, M. (2003). Connecting children's stories to children's literature: Meeting diversity needs. *Early Childhood Education Journal, 31*(1). 47–51.

Banks, J. A., & Banks, C. A. (2001). *Multicultural education: Issues and perspectives* (4th ed.). Boston: Allyn & Bacon.

Bronfenbrenner, U. (1979). *The ecology of human development.* Cambridge, MA: Harvard University Press.

Buysse, V., Castro, D. C., West, T., & Skinner, M. (2005). Addressing the needs of Latino children: A national survey of state administrators of early childhood programs. *Early Childhood Research Quarterly, 20*(2), 146–163.

Capps, R., Fix, M., Murray, J., Ost, J., Passel, J. S., & Hernandez, S. H. (2006). *The new demography of America's schools: Immigration and the No Child Left Behind Act.* Retrieved November 2, 2006, from http://www.urban.org/UploadedPDF/311230_new_demography.pdf

Compton, L. C. (2006). Identity, childhood culture, and literacy learning: A case study. *Journal of Early Childhood Literacy, 6,* 57–76.

Copple, C., & Bredekamp, S. (2006). *Basics of developmentally appropriate practice: An introduction for teachers of children 3 to 6.* Washington, DC: NAEYC.

Cross, T. L., Bazron, B. J., Dennis, K. W., & Isaacs, M. R. (1989). *Toward a culturally competent system of care.* Washington, DC: Georgetown University Development Center.

Couchenour, D., & Chrisman, K. (1999). *Families, schools & communities working together for children.* Florence, KY: Delmar/Thomson Learning.

Darling-Hammond, L. (2006). Constructing 21st-century teacher education. *Journal of Teacher Education, 57*(3), 300–314.

DebBurman N. (2005). *Immigrant education: Variations by generation, age-at- immigration, and country of origin.* New York: LFB Scholarly Publishing LLC.

Dever, M., & Burts, D. (2002). An evaluation of family *literacy* bags as a vehicle for parent involvement. *Early Child Development & Care, 172,* 359–370.

Diller, J. V., & Moule, J. (2005). *Cultural competence: A primer for educators.* Belmont, CA: Thomson Wadsworth.

Dyson, (2003). *The brothers and sisters learn to read: Popular literacy in childhood and school cultures.* New York: Teachers College Press.

Early, D.M., & Winton, P.J. (2001). Preparing the workforce: Early childhood teacher preparation at 2- and 4-year institutes of higher education. *Early Childhood Research Quarterly 16*, 285–306.

Eubanks, P. (2002). Students who don't speak English: How art specialists adapt curriculum for ESOL students. *Art Education, 55*(2), 40–45.

Exposito, S., & Favela, A. (2003). Reflective voices: Valuing immigrant students and teaching with ideological clarity. *Urban Review, 35*, 73–91.

Gardner, H. (2000). *Intelligence reframed: Multiple intelligences for the 21st century.* New York: Basic Books.

Gay, G. (2004). Beyond brown: Promoting equality through multicultural education. *Journal of Curriculum & Supervision, 19*, 193–117.

Goodwin, A. L. (2002). Teacher preparation and the education of immigrant children. *Education and Urban Society, 34*, 156–172.

Harding, N. (2006). Ethnic and social class similarities and differences in mothers' beliefs about kindergarten preparation. *Race, Ethnicity & Education, 9*, 223–237.

Hepburn, S. K. (2004). Building culturally and linguistically competent services to support young children, their families and school readiness. Retrieved April 6, 2007 from: http://eric.ed. gov/ERICDocs/data/ericdocs2/content_storage_01/0000000b/80/2f/2e/c5.pd

Igoa, C. (1995). *The inner world of the immigrant child.* Mahwah, NJ: Lawrence Erlbaum Associates.

Lal, S. (2004).1930 multiculturalism. *Radical Teacher, 69*, 18–23.

Landale, N. S., & Oropesa, R.S. (1995). Immigrant children and the children of immigrants: Inta- and intra-ethnic group differences in the United States. *Institute for Public Policy and Social Research,* East Lansing: Michigan State University.

Johnson, R. L. (2003). Multicultural policy as social activism: Redefining who 'counts' in multi-cultural education *Ethnicity & Education, 6*(2), 107–122.

MacNaughton, G. (2001). Silences and subtexts of immigrant and nonimmigrant children (Australia). *Childhood Education 78*(1), 30–36.

McCarthy, J., & Willshire, J. (1988). *New voices: Immigrant student in U.S. public schools.* Boston: The National Coalition of Advocates for Students.

Piaget, J. (1960). *The child's conception of the world.* Littlefield, NJ: Adams & Co.

Portes, P. R. (2000). *The role of language in the development of intelligence: Vygotsky revisited.* Paper presented at the annual conference of the American Educational Research Association, New Orleans, LA. (ERIC Document Reproduction Service N0. ED 253110).

Portes, A., & Rumbunt, R. (2001). *Legacies: The story of the immigrant second generation.* Berkeley, CA: University of California Press.

Reid, K. S. (2001). US census underscores diversity. *Education Week, 20*, 18–19.

Shorr, P. W. (2006). Teaching America's immigrants. *Instructor, 11*, 46–75.

Siegler, R. (1991). *Children's thinking.* Englewood Cliffs, NJ: Prentice-Hall.

Souto-Manning, M. (2007). Immigrant families and children (re)develop identities in a new context. *Early Childhood Education Journal, 34*(6), 399–405.

Takanishi, R. (2004). Leveling the playing field: Supporting immigrant children from birth to eight. *Children of Immigrant Families, 14*(2), 61–79.

United Stated Department of Education (2006). *Part I: Non-regulatory guidance on implementation of title III state formula grant program elementary and secondary education act, title III, part A as amended by the No Child Left Behind Act of 2001.* Retrieved April 3, 2007 from: http://www.ed.gov/programs/sfgp/nrgcomp.html#immg.

Wesley, P. W., & Buysse, V. (2003). Making meaning of school readiness in schools and communities. *Early Childhood Research Quarterly, 18*(3), 351–375.

**Jacqueline Onchwari, EdD,**
University of Minnesota, Duluth
120 MoH, Ordean Ct, University of Minnesota,
Duluth campus, Duluth, MN, 55812.
Email: jonchwar@d.umn.edu, Phone:1-218-726-6763
15 East Winona St, Duluth,
MN 55803. Phone: 1-218-722-9554

Jacqueline Onchwari is an Assistant professor of Early Childhood Education at the University of Minnesota, Duluth. She completed her doctorate In Curriculum & Instruction from Indiana University of Pennsylvania, PA. Her daughter came to America when she was 4, an experience that influenced the author's contribution to this chapter.

**Nurun N. Begum, EdD,**
East Stroudsburg University
209 Stroud Hall, 200 Prospect St.,
East Stroudsburg, PA 18301
3556 Vista Drive, Macungie,
PA 18062. Phone: 610-966-5658

Nurun Begum is an Assistant Professor of Early Childhood and Elementary Education at East Stroudsburg University, Pennsylvania. Her research interests include academic achievement of young children, and challenges of immigrant and minority children in the educational settings.

**Grace Onchwari, PhD,**
University of North Dakota
213 Centennial Drive, Stop 7189
Grand Forks, ND 58202
Email: grace.onchwari@und.nodak.edu,
Phone 701-777-3378
17833 82nd Ave. N. Maple Grove,
MN 55311.
Phone: 1-763-772-2083

Grace Onchwari is an Assistant professor of Early Childhood Education at the University of North Dakota. Her current interests include education of immigrant children, technology and teacher professional development.

# Chapter 12
# Young Children's Perceptions of School Administrators

## Fostering Positive Relationships

Sue A. Rieg

**Abstract** Relationship-building must be a top priority for administrators of young children. It is the principal's responsibility to get to know the children in order to build a lasting relationship of trust and support which, in turn, may raise test scores and diminish discipline problems. School leaders must understand the work of early childhood teachers, concerns of parents, and resources in the community in order to help young children develop intellectually, physically, emotionally, and socially.

**Keywords** children, principals, professional relationships, perceptions, elementary principals, headmaster, administrators, school leadership, kindergarten, National Association of Elementary School Principals (NAESP), Japan, Africa, China, Canada, Sweden

## Introduction

In a recent conversation with a small group of kindergarten children, I posed the question, "Do you have a school principal?" After a resounding "yes" I further probed by asking, "What does the principal do?" One blue-eyed, red-haired young lady told me "She comes and takes kids to the office when they are bad." So I asked, "Then what does she do?" Most innocently, the little one replied, "She calls the police!"

Reflecting on personal relationships I had with building administrators while in elementary school, I realized I do not remember meeting a school principal until I was in sixth grade. There probably were principals assigned

Indiana University of Pennsylvania

M.R. Jalongo (ed.), *Enduring Bonds.*
© Springer 2008

to the buildings I attended, but they did not make an impact on me nor did they leave a lasting impression. My sixth grade teacher was also "acting principal" of our K-6 elementary school building. His job appeared to be spanking students who were disruptive in class or who would not do their work. I remember sitting in his classroom holding my ears as he left the room with his paddle. The boom of the paddle resonated through the hallways and everyone in the building knew when a child had been punished. Often the students in our class would hear the cries from the young child who had just felt the pain of that wooden paddle, and we all felt it, too. At the time I vowed when I was an elementary school teacher I would never send a child to the principal's office. Little did I know one day I would be an elementary school principal, charged with the numerous responsibilities–including discipline–of running an elementary school.

Bodycott, Walker, and Lee Chi Kin (2001) conducted a study in Hong Kong of pre-service teachers' beliefs about principals based on the principals they remembered from when they were students. The pre-service teachers in the study preferred that principals use a humanistic approach to interpersonal language and leadership, believing the language and behavior of the principal influences the development of the students' constructs of self-esteem, interpersonal communication skills, and leadership. They highly valued the qualities of openness, empathy, support, and positive attitudes, and suggested principals display these qualities in the following ways:

- demonstrating ownership of feelings
- expressing empathy through facial expressions and body language
- portraying him/herself as someone with an open-minded attitude and a willingness to hear opposing views
- being willing to change one's position
- displaying positive regard for oneself and others in the school and community
- being prepared to acknowledge positive qualities in other people and their action research. (p. 26)

The researchers suggested that, since beliefs about the principalship are shaped from an early age, principals needed to view school operations more holistically and not break down professional interactions with the school community (including parents, students, and teachers). They also stated, "Primary school principals are the first role models of principalship" (Boycott, Walker, & Lee Chi Kin, 2001, p. 27). Thus, the early childhood principal has the responsibility of making positive impacts on students that could, and should, last a lifetime.

Throughout this chapter, I will use a personal and global perspective to define the various roles and responsibilities of the early childhood/ elementary principal. Also, I will discuss the relationships between principals and young children, teachers, and families and communities.

## School Principal as Defined in the Research

A principal is often defined as the person who is in a leading position in the school and possibly the most important member of the organization. He/she is the instructional leader of the school (Palaniuk, 1987) and an effective principal is thought to be a necessary precondition for an effective school (Marzano, Waters, & McNulty, 2005). A U.S. Senate Committee Report on Equal Education Opportunity (U.S. Congress, 1970) identified the principal as the most influential person in a school. The committee stated, "It is the leadership of the principal that sets the tone of the school, the climate for teaching, the level of professionalism and morale of the teachers, and the degree of concern for what students may or may not become... If a school is a vibrant, innovative, child-centered place, if it has a reputation for excellence in teaching, if students are performing to the best of their ability, one can almost always point to the principal's leadership as the key to success" (p. 56).

In the early 1980s, Jack Frymeir chaired a committee to conduct a *Good Schools Project*. Frymeir and his colleagues (1984) reported information from more than 28,000 students and 3,200 teachers who lived and worked in 106 "good schools" across America. They identified several characteristics as being persistent qualities or practices of effective schools. The first dimension was strong administrative leadership and their interview data supported the proposition that the principal was a significant factor contributing to school success. When the committee listed some "Earmarks of a Good School" one key indicator was "The school principal is a generally liked and respected leader who leads and collaborates effectively in school and community projects" (Frymeir et al., 1984, p. 221).

What makes principals effective leaders? Whitaker (2003) suggested that effective principals focus on people, not programs; focus on behaviors, then on beliefs; insist on loyalty to the students; base decisions on their best teachers; maximize the ability of their high achieving teachers; and establish expectations at the beginning of the school year. He stated, "When the principal sneezes, the whole school catches a cold... If we have great credibility and good relationships, people work to please us" (Whitaker, 2003, p. 30).

When asked by Chenfield (1988) just what is it that principals do, Kindergarten children gave various responses. A number of ideas were negative, including: "calling mom when you are bad," "taking bad kids to the office," and "going outside to see who is being bad" (p. 95). Other children apparently viewed the principal as more of an office manager as they responded the principal talks on the telephone, uses the computer, signs papers, and rings the bell. Other tasks of principals identified by children included using the loudspeaker to call buses, telling people when it is hot or cold, and "telling us everything he knows" (p. 95). Positive statements from the children included the principal says nice things to kids, comes to the room and asks the teacher how good the kids were, keeps the school in order, and is my friend. One young person, after thoughtful deliberation said, "A principal helps the secretary" (p. 95).

In Sweden the role of headmaster has recently changed from having formerly filled a mostly administrative function to the new primary change agent in schools.

Persson and colleagues (2004) attempted to answer the questions, what makes a headmaster successful and what does a successful headmaster do? Administrative directors suggested that headmasters should be loyal to decisions made at a higher level, manage scarce resources creatively, make decisions that are target and finance driven, and energetically implement the school administration's ideas regarding school development. Teachers who were interviewed believed headmasters should have experiential roots in the everyday life of the school, take part in school activities, support teachers, show respect for professional autonomy, be colleagues of equal merit, and have a vision. Students considered a good headmaster to be one who is visible in the school, a friend, and responsible for creating a good school environment. Parents responded that successful headmasters take responsibility for the working environment, are clear communicators, show sensitivity, understand the needs of students, demonstrate commitment to the district, and are competent. Interestingly, it appears that the students and parents were the only ones who shared a concern with the headmasters' relationships with, and an understanding of, children.

The National Association of Elementary School Principals (NAESP, 1998) recognized that elementary principals have an important role in shaping the social, emotional, and intellectual development of young children. The early years of children's education impact their futures as lifelong learners and contributing members to society. The NAESP stated, "Skillful principals, in partnership with faculty and community members, will plan for and provide the necessary information and resources to assure that their schools offer an enriching, joyful, and meaningful experience for the millions of young children whose education they lead" (p. 9). They believe the principal is responsible for the following:

- taking the lead in articulating the mission and beliefs of the early childhood program and the rationale behind them
- assuring the availability of appropriate curriculum and assessment materials and techniques
- assembling an appropriately trained and qualified staff
- stimulating parent involvement
- arranging collaboration with community agencies and programs that work with young children and their families (p. 23).

Once again, there is no mention of building quality relationships with the children. Do relationships not matter? How can a school experience be enriching and meaningful for young children if relationships are not established with the school leaders? Later in the chapter, I will explore the importance of, and ways for, principals to build relationships.

## The Principal as Disciplinarian

As early as 1963, authors Burr, Coffield, Jenson and Neagley recognized the negative impact of fear being used as a discipline approach:

Although for many years specialists in child development have been emphasizing the harmful effects of fear as a factor in maintaining discipline, there are still teachers and even entire schools where fear is the chief motivating force in maintaining discipline. It is, therefore, very important that the elementary school principal works with teachers, parents, and children to develop a modern philosophy of discipline for the school. (pp. 197–198)

The authors also encouraged principals to provide a school climate conducive to good discipline including providing a good physical environment, desirable human relationships, and a learning environment in which all children can realize their full potential. They mentioned that the "wise principal" attempts to ascertain the attitudes of parents toward discipline and should cooperate with all organizations and agencies in the community that are concerned with the welfare of children.

As a principal of young children, I often had the opportunity to work with parents and community agencies. Most parents were very accepting of my discipline approaches with their children. My main focus was to get children to understand why their behavior was not appropriate, and discuss ways to make better choices the next time. It was always my practice to put myself at eye level with students, which meant getting on my knees so I could have eye contact with them. It was not unusual to see me walking through the hallways holding the hand of a young child who was banned to the office for classroom misbehavior. When I contacted the parents, the child and I had typically resolved the matter; however, I always wanted the parents to be informed.

Agency meetings frequently included the social worker, teacher, parent(s), therapeutic staff support (TSS) person, occasionally the child, and me. We spent hours working with the parents and agencies to coordinate developmentally appropriate discipline approaches for the child that were consistent between home and school.

## The Principal's Understanding of Child Development

Prior to becoming a building principal, although I had no specific training in early childhood education, my first nine years of teaching were spent in K, 1, and 2 classrooms. That is where I developed my own philosophy of early childhood education. In China, Kindergarten educational reform emerged in the early 1980s. Respecting children, active learning, and play-based teaching and learning have been identified as key modern educational ideas that emerged in the field of kindergarten education in mainland China in the last two decades (Liu & Feng, 2005). Recently, I had the opportunity to question several educators from China who were serving as principals in their primary schools. Of the four principals surveyed, two had taught the "younger level" for two years, one had taught the "youngest, middle, and oldest grade each for one year," and the last had taught the "youngest level for three months, oldest level four months." In a study conducted by McBride-Chang and Treiman (2003), the researchers identified the three levels of kindergarten as the youngest having a mean age of 3.8, middle 5.0, and oldest 5.9. When I asked what training the principals had in the education of children ages three to eight, responses included kindergarten principal professional training, English training, teaching training of game-playing and literacy, Kaleidoscope Professional training of abacus teaching and mind-calculating training, and one person had a Bachelor's in Preschool Education from South China University. One other principal had a Bachelor of Education degree and the other two had three years of trade/technical school after sixth grade and are now pursuing associate degrees.

One of the questions posed to the principals was, "In your program or school, how are the curriculum and/or the instructional approaches used with young children distinctive from those used with older children?" One principal said for the younger students, the focus is on caring and nurturing and for the older ones the focus is on knowledge teaching. Two of the principals mentioned the shorter attention span of younger students, thus the sessions are shorter. One person stated younger children learn through play and older ones have more courses that require participation. Another respondent mentioned the curriculum is guided by standards and guidance, based on the characteristics of child development, taught from easy to difficult, and taught through a variety of teaching activities. The final principal said, "Basically there is no big difference. Different ways of treatment of different age groups are embodied in terms of student-teacher relationships and curriculum." A follow-up question was, "How does your curriculum respond to the diverse learning and developmental needs of young children?" Responses included expanding the breadth of the curriculum and allowing kids to develop individually in-depth; using integrative teaching materials and textbooks of English and literacy; offering courses such as dance, abacus teaching and mind calculating, and Chinese chess; keeping the balance between quiet learning and learning through movement; and, combining learning theory, game playing, and service learning activities. One principal suggested there is "always a gap between practice and theories, especially in kindergarten." This person stated first there is a social trend we must follow, second we have to satisfy the needs of parents and society in literacy and calculation, and third there is a limited teaching competence of kindergarten teachers. All these factors impact the decision of curriculum; and although our curriculum has been decided, it is not implanted "so we advocate that kids need more time to play and we purport to let kids have a wonderful childhood." With a small sample of only four principals, obviously this information cannot be generalized to all of China; however, the examples clearly relate to the reform efforts being made to Chinese Kindergarten education. Jalongo and her colleagues (2004) advocated that quality early childhood programs be administered, supervised, and monitored by leaders who understand child development and who advocate for excellence in curriculum and pedagogy.

The National Association of Elementary School Principals (1998) proclaimed that not only does curriculum define what the students are to learn and the skills they are to develop, but also to respond to the different learning and developmental needs of young children. They identified four principles that are fundamental for young children:

1. Curriculum should be presented in an integrated format and should reflect a conceptual organization that helps children make sense of their experiences.
2. Children should be engaged in active, rather than passive, learning activities.
3. Spontaneous play is a natural way for young children to learn to interact with one another and to understand their environment.
4. It is important that new learning be connected to something that is known and relevant to children with different knowledge, concepts, and experiences.

Curriculum expectations definitely shifted throughout my years in K-2 classrooms. When I taught kindergarten the academic curriculum was basically letter and number recognition with little to no focus on writing, and the remainder of the curriculum had a focus on social skills such as learning to share, taking turns, and getting along with others. Now, many early childhood programs have a stronger focus on academics in the kindergarten classroom. Children are leaving kindergarten with the ability to read and write. Is this developmentally appropriate for young children? The issue of the early push for academics still seems to be under debate. With the pressures of standardized testing, more and more schools are insisting upon a strong academic focus for very young children. Butterfield and Johnston (1995) stated that early childhood education is changing more rapidly than perhaps any other area of schooling in K-12 classrooms in the United States. They posed the question, "Are elementary principals behind the curve on current early childhood education practices?" (p. 5). School boards have been challenged to develop clearly stated policies affirming the districts' commitment to best practice of early childhood education in every school (Mitchell, 1991). As a result of a study in New York City, Mitchell (1991) discovered the schools that were working for young children had a clear sense of purpose in that they put children first, were committed to teamwork and shared decision making with administrators and parents, and put an emphasis on staff development.

In Japan, kindergartens vary from being very structured and learning-focused, to relatively unstructured with an emphasis on social interaction and play. The preschool curriculum is primarily non-academic; health, social life, nature, language, music, and crafts are emphasized (AsainInfo, n.d.). Many countries throughout the world, including but not limited to Australia, Germany, Turkey, United Kingdom, Japan, and the United States, are now participating in the International Baccalaureate Program (IBO). The Primary Years Program (PYP) is designed for children aged 3 through 12 years. It is a comprehensive approach to teaching and learning with an international curriculum model. Attention is given to the children's developmental needs including social, physical, emotional, aesthetic, cultural, and academic. Curriculum for the PYP has five essential elements: concepts, knowledge, skills, attitude, and action. The school principal, coordinator, and teachers all must undergo training (International Baccalaureate Organization, n.d.).

In parts of South Africa, many children do not have access to early childhood programs, or the programs lack adequate resources and trained staff. In August of 2004 several American educators, including principal Lydia Marie Zuidema, visited South African preschools to deliver educational supplies and hold seminars on child development and teaching strategies. Zuidema (2006) discussed what a joy it was to visit the schools and deliver much needed materials and resources. She said, "The children cheered, and the teachers wept" (p.49). In one school that the educators visited Zuidema noted, "The South African ladies were so proud to be at an educational seminar, even one that was held on a dirt floor!" (p. 49). Early intervention has been, and will continue to be, vital to the growth and development of young children all over the world.

## The Foundation for a Principal to Build Relationships

As a K-6 building principal, I spent what little free time I had in a kindergarten classroom. First of all, it was a refreshing change from the demands of the principalship to see those innocent, wide-eyed learners trying diligently to please their teacher. More importantly, I wanted the young children to know me by name and I wanted to know their names. They needed to know my role was not solely that of disciplinarian. I wanted them to identify me as a teacher, a helper, and in a professional way, a friend who cared about them and valued their learning. Palaniuk (1987) reminded us for a school to be truly effective the administrator needs to be aware of, and involved with, the school's vast array of activities, formal and informal. This means being in the classrooms as frequently as possible and knowing what is being taught to the students. This correlates with Abraham Lincoln's policy of stepping outside the office and interacting with people to establish human contact. By entering the workers' environment a sense of commitment, collaboration, and community are established (Phillips, 1992).

In a study in Alberta, Canada, a research team obtained information from elementary school principals concerning their job satisfaction (Johnson & Holdaway, 1994). The principals had the highest mean facet satisfaction scores for their working relationships with teachers, relationships with students, the teaching competence of their teachers, the satisfaction and morale of staff, and their sense of accomplishment. Dissatisfying facets included conflict, workload, capacity to innovate, budgetary constraints, and priorities of the school district. In a study conducted in Hong Kong, researchers discovered that principals experienced a moderate degree of stress in their work (Wong, Cheuk, & Rosen, 2000). Stressors included maintaining a sufficient number of students (kindergartens in Hong Kong are privately owned), obtaining a balanced or surplus budget, and convincing teachers of the importance of kindergarten education.

In order for a principal to build relationships with people and shape school culture, it is imperative for the leader to be visible in the school and community. That is easier said than done. Fullan (1997) said, "Principals are either overloaded with what they are doing or overloaded with all the things they think they should be doing" (p. ix). Perhaps now is the time to revisit the roles and responsibilities of the administrator and prioritize the responsibilities to make building relationships number one on the list. Witmer (2005) added relationships as the fourth R in education: "Reading, 'riting, 'rithmetic, and *relationships* are the foundations of effective education" (p. 224).

Administrators function as "ambassadors of the system" (Conors, 2000, p. 67). Conors stated that educators must like people to be successful as it is a people-focused partnership that requires human relations skills. She contended that the best administrators spend an intense amount of time developing, improving, and investing in relationships. Positive relationships are the heart of what makes a school extraordinary. The best leaders build environments of trust, respect, professionalism, caring, compassion, collaboration, teaming, advising, caring, and nurturing. Consistent with the old adage *Children don't care how much you know until they know how much you care* (author unknown), Connors (2000) stated, "An effective leader serves as the CARE police" (p. 14).

## Principals' Relationships with Students

As important as building relationships with early childhood students is, I assumed that I would find a plethora of research on those relationships; however, I was unable to find even one piece of research on the specific topic of principals or school leaders and relationships with young children. Thus, I thought about ways I tried to build relationships with young students and called on several colleagues for their advice on the topic.

One kindergarten teacher made it very clear she just wanted a principal to "come into the classroom often" to get to know the children. She mentioned that students did not even recognize one of their former principals because the school leader was basically invisible. The children thought the guidance counselor was the principal because the counselor was in the room more often than the building principal. However, she discussed another principal who came into her classroom regularly and invited the children to her office "just to see it." She said it was nice that the students all "piled into the office" and could sometimes joke with this principal and the principal joked back with them, appropriately of course, so as not to lose respect. This principal showed the kindergarten students she is a "real person" by sharing pictures of her family and telling the students a little about herself. The kindergarten teacher also said she has had principals who showed a true interest in the students and their learning by sitting at centers with the students, observing them, and talking with the children as they worked.

In my survey of principals of Chinese primary schools, I asked, "What do you do as a principal to build relationships with three to eight year old students?" Answers included visiting the classrooms and talking to kids, playing with kids and having one-on-one conversation with them, being their friend, respecting the kids and treating them equally, giving them care and nurturing, taking care of them like they are infants no matter how old they are, and knowing their psychological development and learning needs.

It is also important for a principal to learn the names of the children. One of my former principal colleagues knew the names of every student within the first week of school and the students responded positively to the recognition. Young children feel a sense of belonging when school personnel call them by name.

It was a positive experience for me to greet all students as they entered the building in the morning and wish them a good evening as they departed each night. Not only did that help with discipline in the hallways, but also the students left with someone smiling at them. Even if they had a bad day, they could still get a smile from the principal and end school on a positive note.

Knowing something about each child helps to build relationships. It is easy to find out what children like or dislike–just ask them. Then, remember those tidbits of information and ask the children a question that requires more than a yes or no response; this engages the children into extended conversations. Mark Twain once said we were given two ears and one mouth for a reason. It is amazing what we can learn from and about children just by listening to them. Unfortunately, some children do not have parents or caregivers at home who can listen to them when they need attention.

Another way I tried to build early and positive relationships with students was to acknowledge their academic and behavioral successes. As I walked through classrooms, I would compliment students on their efforts and achievements. If a child was sitting and working quietly during independent work time, I thanked him/her for it. When I saw groups of children excitedly working on a project in the classroom or hallway, I stopped to have the children tell me about the project then commented on their hard work. When students struggled with academic work, I helped and encouraged them. Several times a year, the Instructional Support Team assigned interventions to me to assist children who were at risk of failure. At report card time, I always wrote positive personal comments on report cards. Comments reflected strong academic achievement, improvements made in academic areas, and acknowledgements of good behavior. Not only did the students and parents enjoy the comments, but the teachers appreciated the support, as well.

A former first grade teacher shared how her principal built relationships with the students also through academics. He invited the first graders to come to his office and read to him or sing a song. Small groups of children would go to his office and enlighten him through prose or music. The teacher expressed how the children loved this as they got to know the principal as someone who valued education, rather than just a disciplinarian.

All children like to feel a sense of belonging and ownership to their school. One way to encourage this is to allow students to help develop the school rules. Each year, I had the teachers work with the students to develop their classroom rules then send a copy to me in the office. I took these rules and combined them to develop approximately five that would be our "All School Rules" then shared them at an assembly. I made the students aware that these were the rules they had helped to develop so they would want to follow the rules they created. Similarly Roberts (2006) identified a principal who came up with a solution for improving behavior and ensuring safety on the bus. This principal had teachers guide students to make observations on the bus then generated and discussed the rules. Students had a clear understanding of the purpose of the rules and behavior on the bus improved.

Building relationships with children extends outside the school walls. An advantage I had was I lived in the neighborhood with many of the students who attended my school. I could wave and smile as they walked, rode their bikes, and played ball. Several of them got to know my husband and dog, and it was especially "cool" that Dr. Rieg had a dog. Attending their sporting events, musical and drama performances, practices, and so on also helped to build relationships. The younger students were not in as many organized sports as the older children but many still participated in outside activities. After attending an evening or weekend event, children were excited to tell me they "saw me" the night before or over the weekend. There were other administrative duties that could have been done but watching the children involved in their activities was much more meaningful to the children, and yes, more enjoyable for me.

## Principals' Professional Relationships with Teachers

Some principals and directors of early childhood programs began their careers among the ranks of teachers. Zeng and Zeng (2005) conducted a study of U.S. principals and found that about 77% of principals never taught kindergarten and 25% have never taken any courses in early childhood education. However, as Sarason (1982) stated, being a classroom teacher by itself is not necessarily good preparation for being an effective school principal. In my case, after spending nine years in grades K, 1, and 2, I acquired a better understanding of young children and the needs of teachers who taught in the primary classrooms. Catron and Groves (1999) compared the similarities between good teaching and good leading. They noted that good teaching requires self-awareness, knowledge of developmentally appropriate practices, understanding of the multiple roles teachers play, and the ability to make wise decisions about classroom practices. Similarly, good leaders know one's own personal strengths and limitations, understand staff development and evaluation techniques, understand multiple roles directors play, and have the ability to make effective program decisions based on the needs of children, teachers, and families. The researchers continued their comparisons by stating that teachers and leaders are caring, model best practice in early childhood programming, value the uniqueness and diversity of young learners, and commit to excellence in all programs for young children.

How can principals support early childhood teachers? First, administrators must have an understanding of the unique characteristics of early childhood programs, the teachers' roles and daily experiences in an early childhood classroom, and be ready to provide moral and emotional support when necessary (Zeng & Zeng, 2005). The leader can utilize effective communication strategies to build a cohesive and committed team capable of setting common goals and implementing an effective early childhood program. The director can help teachers and staff keep the "big picture" in mind, involve them in setting goals and objectives, and encourage continued growth so the vision will be dynamic and evolving over time (Catron & Groves, 1999). Also, the principal can provide instructional materials that are appropriate for young children and facilitate ongoing curriculum evaluation that considers current trends and ideas in early childhood education (NAESP, 1998).

In a preliminary study of Nebraska's public school early childhood programs, Marvin and her colleagues (2003) discovered that most administrators advocate for quality early childhood programs and support teachers' unique budgetary requests and work-hour schedules. The teachers indicated that their administrators relied on them for knowledge about recommended practices for early childhood education. The authors gave the following suggestions to administrators of early childhood programs:

- Request and seek continuing education on early childhood issues.
- Petition higher education institutions to include coursework and/or practicum experiences in early childhood education in their administrator certification programs.
- Provide opportunities for administrators and early childhood teachers to network with community agencies regarding the needs of families and schools.
- Engage early childhood teachers in discussions concerning revisions of staff development opportunities, expectations, and performance evaluation forms and procedures.
- Promote coordination of staff development, space, and curricula between pre-kindergarten and kindergarten teachers (p. 226).

Along with the recommendations for principals, Marvin and her colleagues (2003) asked early childhood teachers to consider staying abreast of nationally recommended practices in early childhood programs by reading and attending conferences, recognizing expertise and keeping administrators and colleagues updated on best practices, advocating for quality programs for children and families, assisting principals and administrators in designing pertinent staff development activities for teachers, staff members, and colleagues, and assisting administrators in updating forms and procedures for evaluation of teachers in home-based or pre-school classrooms.

Positive relationships between principals and teachers do not happen naturally. Principals need to show their understanding of, support for, and commitment to quality early childhood programs. Teachers need to help their principals stay abreast of current best practices in the field of early childhood education and model those practices in their classrooms. Open communication is a key factor in any relationship; thus, teachers and principals must stay in constant communication with each other and the families and communities whom they serve.

## *Principals' Relationships with Families and the Community*

"Nothing motivates a child more than when learning is valued by school, family, and community working in partnership" (Fullan, 1997, p. 22). What can a school leader do to establish these partnerships? As with all other relationships, communication is vital. One principal reported that he opened his kindergarten orientation by stating, "We're starting a nine-year conversation together" (Lucas, 2000, p. 292). He noted that teachers build relationships with the children and their parents each year but it is the administrator's job to maintain those relationships. The NAESP (1998) recognized the importance of forming partnerships with parents when they stated that parent involvement is important to the success of all elementary programs; for an early childhood program, it is crucial and should be a high priority of the principal. The NAESP (1998) made the following recommendations:

- Parents share in the development of the school's educational program, and so understand and support it. The principal and staff can provide information through meetings, newsletters and conversations about the program and its goals.
- Parents are assisted to increase their effectiveness in working with their children, at home and in school.
- Parent concerns are addressed formally and informally.
- Parents are actively involved in the school's site council, helping to make decisions about the program.
- A reciprocal relationship is formed and nurtured. All parties try to make both school and home places where children feel secure and enjoy success (p. 28).

Unfortunately, there are barriers that hinder relationships between the parents/families and the school. First, some parents did not have positive experiences when they were students and are not comfortable in the school setting. Witmer (2005) encouraged administrators to make schools inviting to parents. Some schools have created lounges and other areas where parents can relax and meet other members of the school community. Other schools have active Parent-Teacher Associations who call parents of kindergarten children and personally invite them to participate in school activities. This makes it easier for principals and teachers to get to know the parents on a more informal level.

Secondly, parents/families receive forms and fliers that encourage them to "be involved" but some do not understand exactly how to become involved in the school. Deal and Peterson (1999) contended that parents are interested in their children's education but are unsure of what they are supposed to do, "but pretty sure they're not always wanted, welcomed, or listened to" (p. 133). At my former elementary school we involved parents in a wide variety of ways including volunteers to help tutor children in the classrooms, provide clerical support to teachers, chaperone fieldtrips, plan classroom parties, assist in planning assemblies and school-wide events, provide support with certain classroom projects when the teacher could use the extra hands, share careers, interests and/or hobbies, and so on. Parents were also invited by teachers, the principal, and the children to attend back-to-school nights, classroom visitation days, and parent-teacher conferences.

Language barriers may also keep parents from getting involved in the schools. We live in an increasingly multicultural society where English is often the second language. Teachers and administrators are often unprepared to help parents with language translation (Whitmer, 2005).

All of these barriers can be overcome and successful relationships can be established. Lam (2000) discussed the importance of actively listening to parents and stated principals are in a better position to understand children when they understand their families and backgrounds. Effective listening skills can help principals to gain trust and respect, two vital elements that foster cooperation between home and school.

Earlier in the chapter, I discussed one way that principals are involved with parents and community agencies–through attending interagency meetings to coordinate discipline methods that can be used at home and in school. There are many other ways that the school leader can, and should, be involved in the school community.

First of all, many children are involved in preschool settings prior to attending school. The NAESP (1998) recognized that effective transition is not a single event, but rather an ongoing process involving the child and family, as well as the sending and receiving programs. The principal is responsible for monitoring and sharing the developmental information about children as they transition from one program to the other, to ensure continuity of programming.

The NAESP (1998) also recommended the school principals collaborate with community agencies to support children's development, learning, and well-being; and, cooperate with local, state, and federal agencies in maintaining a directory of child-focused community agencies and services, and assist families who need those services. They also recognized that there are an increasing number of single-parent families or families with two working parents so before and after school programs are necessary. Suggestions for the principal included maintaining an assessment of the community's child care needs, reviewing the school's transportation plan to assure that child-care programs are accessible to those who need them, and initiating relationships with child-care providers and arranging for them to use school facilities.

Along with inviting parents to attend and participate in school events, it is also vital to invite community participation. Newspapers and other media often portray the "bad" things that happen in schools such as violence or decreasing test scores. There are more positive than bad activities happening in most schools and it is the school personnel's job to publicize the positive. Deal and Peterson (1999) identified schools as "producers of learning and purveyors of meaning" (p. 130). They stated that connections to the community seek both of those ends and gave examples of what school leaders should do:

- Market their schools by keeping the community updated on school successes.
- Build bonds with the community by bringing everyone together in a "meaningful ceremony."

- Tie the history of the school with the history of the community.
- Connect to all members of the community (p. 130).

Principals need to be advocates for their students and schools. In daily conversations and interactions with parents and community members, principals need to actively praise the children, teachers, and school personnel. They need to invite EVERYONE to come to school activities and when they do come, acknowledge them and welcome them.

# Conclusion

School leaders' attitudes, values, beliefs, and knowledge about early childhood education are crucial to the success of young children. Pre-school and kindergarten classrooms are where the basic foundation of learning is laid and will be built upon as the children grow. Instilling a love of learning is vital at these levels and must be maintained throughout a child's education.

Research has shown that the school leader can positively influence the culture and climate of the learning organization. Even though the principal must wear "many hats" and attend to a multitude of duties and responsibilities, relationship building must be a top priority. Obviously, if we did not have students we would not have schools; thus, student relationships must be number one. The students must see the school administrator not just as a disciplinarian but also as an instructional leader who is visible in the school and community, and truly cares about each one of them, their families and caregivers, and their learning. Secondly, the school leader must understand and support the teachers who teach in early childhood programs. The needs of teachers who work with young children are as diverse as the children they teach. Principals must encourage ongoing professional development for their teachers and participate themselves. And finally, school leaders must do all they can to develop and maintain relationships with families and communities. This means genuinely inviting people into the school as well as getting out of the office–perhaps even out of the school, to communicate with all stakeholders. Building relationships with the entire school community is vital to the success of all children and will dispel the notion that the principal is merely an enforcer of rules. It takes time, energy, persistence, and strong communication skills to effectively build the relationships necessary to foster the development of the whole child.

# References

AsainInfo (n.d.) *Japanese education and literacy.* Retrieved on August 15, 2006, from http://asianinfo.org/asianinfo/Japan/education_literacy.

Bodycott, P., Walker, A. & Lee Chi Kin, J. (2001). More heroes and villains: Pre-service teacher beliefs about principals. *Educational Research, 43*(1), 15–31.

Burr, J.B., Coffield, W., Jenson, T.J., & Neagley, R.L. (1963). *Elementary school administration.* Boston: Allyn and Bacon.

Butterfield, E.D. & Johnston, J.M. (1995). *The NAESP standards for quality programs for young children: Principals' beliefs and teachers' practices.* (ERIC Document Reproduction Service No. 392526).

Catron, C.E. & Groves, M.M. (1999). Teacher to director: A developmental journey. *Early Childhood Education Journal, 26*(3), 183–188.

Chenfield, M.B. (1988). Young children. *Educational Leadership, 46*(4), 95.

Connors, N.A. (2000). *If you don't feed the teachers they eat the students: Guide to success for administrators and teachers.* Nashville, TN: Incentive Publications.

Deal, T.E., & Peterson, K.D. (1999). *Shaping school culture: The heart of leadership.* San Francisco: Jossey-Bass.

Frymeir, J., Cornbleth, C., Donmoyer, R., Gansneder, B.M., Jeter, J.T., Klein, M.F., Schwab, M., & Alexander, W.M. (1984). *One hundred good schools.* West Lafayette, IN: Kappa Delta Pi.

Fullan, M. (1997). *What's worth fighting for in the principalship?* New York: Teachers College Press.

International Baccalaureate Program. (n.d.) *What is the primary years programme?* Retrieved on August 15, 2006, from http://wwwibo.org/ibo/index.cfm?ObjectID = FEF2E030-2466-4388-B189137759F790CF&language = EN.

Jalongo, M.R., Fennimore, B.S., Pattnaik, J., Laverick, D. M., Brewster, J., & Mutuku, M. (2004). Blended perspectives: A global vision for high-quality early childhood education. *Early Childhood Education Journal, 32*(3), 143–155.

Johnson, N.A. & Holdaway, E. A. (1994). Facet importance and the job satisfaction of school principals. *British Education Research Journal, 20*(1), 17–33.

Lam, Mei S. (2000). The gentle art of listening: Skills for developing family-administrator relationships in early childhood. *Early Childhood Education Journal, 27*(4), 267–273.

Liu, Y. & Feng, X. (2005). Kindergarten educational reform during the past two decades in mainland China: Achievements and problems. *International Journal of Early Years Education 13*(2), 93–99.

Lucas, T. (2000). The nine-year conversation. P. Senge (Ed.), *Schools that learn: A fifth discipline handbook for educators, parents, and everyone who cares about education* (pp. 289–303). New York: Doubleday.

Marvin, C., LaCost, B., Grady, M., & Mooney, P. (2003). Administrative support and challenges in Nebraska public school early childhood programs: Preliminary study. *Topics in Early Childhood Education 23*(4), 217–228.

Marzano, R.J., Waters, T., & McNulty, B.A. (2005). *School leadership that works: From results to research.* Alexandria, VA: Association for Supervision and Curriculum Development.

McBride-Chang, C. & Trieman, R. (2003). Hong Kong Chinese kindergartners learn to read English analytically. *Psychological Science, 14*(2), 138–143.

Mitchell, A.W. (1991). Schools that work for young children. *Education Digest, 56*(9), 43–46.

National Association of Elementary School Principals. (1998). *Early childhood education and the elementary school principal: Standards for quality programs for young children.* (ERIC Document Reproduction Service Number 450 466).

Palaniuk, S. (1987). Administrators in the classrooms: Where else? *Education, 107*(3), 272–275.

Persson, A., Andersson, G., & Lindstrom, N. (2004). Successful Swedish headmasters in tension fields and alliances. *International Journal of Leadership in Education, 8*(1), 53–72.

Phillips, D.T. (1992). *Lincoln on leadership: Executive strategies for tough times.* New York: Warner Books.

Roberts, P. (2005). The wheels on the bus. In Northeast Foundation for Children (Ed.). *Creating a safe and friendly school: Articles by elementary educators* (pp. 2–9). Turner Falls, MA: Northeast Foundation for Children.

Sarason, S. (1982). *The culture of the school and the problem of change.* Boston: Allyn & Bacon.

U.S. Congress, Senate Committee on Equal Educational Opportunity. (1970). *Toward equal educational opportunity*. Washington, DC: Government Printing Office.

Witmer, M.M. (2005). The fourth r in education: Relationships. *Clearing House, 78*(5), 224–228.

Whitaker, T. (2003). *What great principals do differently: Fifteen things that matter most.* Larchmont, NY: Eye on Education.

Wong, K.S., Cheuk, W.H., & Rosen, S. (2000). The influences of job stress and supervisor support on negative affects and job satisfaction in kindergarten principals. *Journal of Social Behavior & Personality, 15*(1), 85–98.

Zeng, G., & Zeng, L. (2005). Developmentally and culturally inappropriate practice in U.S. kindergarten programs: Prevalence, severity, and its relationship with teacher and administrator qualifications. *Education, 125*(4), 706–724.

Zuidema, Lydia M. (2006). South Africa early education project 2003. *The Delta Kappa Gamma Bulletin, 71*(2), 47–49.

**Sue A. Rieg, Ed.D.**
Associate Professor
323 Davis Hall
Indiana University of Pennsylvania
Indiana, PA 15705
724-357-2416
srieg@iup.edu
150 Robin Street
Indiana, PA 15701
724-349-8203

Dr. Sue Rieg is an associate professor in the Professional Studies in Education Department at Indiana University of Pennsylvania where she teaches undergraduate Pedagogy and graduate courses in Leadership and Curriculum Evaluation. She was a former elementary school teacher and principal. Research interests include students at risk, classroom assessment, curriculum, and teacher stress factors.

# Index

# EDUCATING THE YOUNG CHILD

Printed in the United States
95432LV00003B/232-270/A

9 780387 745244